Recent years have seen far-reaching changes in the way music theorists and analysts view the nature of their disciplines. Encounters with structuralist and post-structuralist critical theory, and with linguistics and the cognitive sciences, have brought music theory and analysis into the orbit of important developments in present-day intellectual history, challenging previous ideas of their place in musical studies. This book presents the work of a group of younger scholars who, without seeking to impose an explicit redefinition of either theory or analysis, explore the limits of both in this new context. Essays on the languages of analysis and theory, and on practical issues such as decidability, ambiguity and metaphor, combine with studies of works by Debussy, Schoenberg, Birtwistle and Boulez, together making a major contribution to an important debate in the growth of musicology.

Theory, analysis and meaning in music

Theory, analysis and meaning in music

Edited by

ANTHONY POPLE
Lancaster University

CAMBRIDGE
UNIVERSITY PRESS

Published by the Press Syndicate of the University of Cambridge
The Pitt Building, Trumpington Street, Cambridge CB2 1RP
40 West 20th Street, New York, NY 10011–4211, USA
10 Stamford Road, Oakleigh, Melbourne 3166, Australia

First published 1994

Printed in Great Britain at the University Press, Cambridge

A cataloguing in publication record for this book is available from the British Library

Library of Congress cataloguing in publication data applied for

ISBN 0 521 45236 8 hardback

AP

Contents

Contents

Preface

To tackle music theory, music analysis, and musical meaning at one and the same time may seem ambitious. The nature of musical meaning, and indeed the very possibility of its existence, have occupied philosophers for several centuries. Music theory has an even longer pedigree, having been established in classical antiquity, and has for at least a millennium served composition and musical pedagogy both in a utilitarian way and as a medium of reflective thought. Analysis, a relative newcomer, has often paid more heed to ends than to means, putting itself at the service of performers, listeners and historians rather than politely working within the boundaries of ramified theoretical systems. Yet theory and analysis in music have always been interlinked – at the very least by virtue of their common subject matter, and sometimes by far more – so that the relationship between them has come to be constantly redefined across changes in the currents of intellectual history.

Within the past decade or so the change has been quite dramatic. It seemed that theory and analysis had for some time been locked in a dualism deriving from the perceived methods of the natural sciences – rather along the lines of hypothesis and experiment – which was reflected both in the format of academic papers and in patterns of argument. Quite suddenly, under pressure from forces elsewhere in musicology, analysis was refocused during the mid-1980s as a critical discipline.[1] A comparison between, for example, Allen Forte's monograph on *The Rite of Spring*, which expounds an analysis in order to demonstrate a theory, and the essays collected in Lawrence Kramer's *Music as Cultural Practice*, suggests a paradigm shift of major proportions.[2] Certainly, the attendant contrasts and controversies have been clearly observable, and it must be

---

1 I refer, in particular, to Joseph Kerman's 'How We Got into Analysis, and How to Get Out', *Critical Inquiry*, 7 (1980), pp. 311–31, and *Musicology* (London: Fontana, 1985).
2 Allen Forte, *The Harmonic Organization of 'The Rite of Spring'* (New Haven: Yale University Press, 1978); Lawrence Kramer, *Music as Cultural Practice, 1800–1900* (Berkeley: University of California Press, 1990).

said that some recent examples of critical writing do little more than revert to the indulgence in personal idiosyncrasy on which scientistic theory and analysis had sought to improve. Yet, as has been recognised by a growing number of scholars, there is much about the practicalities of the new type of analytical writing that lies within the orbit of critical theory; and by projecting this awareness in their work – through an explicit concern with narratology, for example – these writers have demonstrated that a move away from certain kinds of music theory does not represent a retreat from theory *per se*. In this new context, analysis has come to be seen as one form of discourse or metadiscourse on music, raising the question of how music itself can be a text – sonic, written or remembered – and promoting analysis itself as a kind of theory through which a range of possible meanings can be described, prescribed or circumscribed. At the same time, and perhaps ironically, the interpenetration of analysis and theory – so evident in the explicitly scientific wave – has revealed theory, too, as a construction.

But it is not enough to characterise these developments as a reorientation of analysis achieved simply through a divorce from music theory followed by a honeymoon with narratology. Bringing analysis into the orbit of recent developments in intellectual history has not displaced its traditional concern with explanation and technical description; and any discourse that incorporates technical description seems bound to use the terminology of basic music theory – crotchets, quavers, pitches, dynamics[3] – even if the theoretical nature of such categories is not always acknowledged. Two concerns immediately flow from this: first, whether the use of such language is interpretive in the same sense as criticism is interpretive; second, whether the unhesitating use of such terminology, as if it were straightforwardly descriptive, reflects consistencies of musical cognition amenable to scientific enquiry. These are different sides of the same coin, of course, and the first is explored at length in this book's opening chapter by Naomi Cumming. With regard to the latter it is interesting to note, on the one hand, that a move in the direction of cognitive science was evident in theory/analysis circles just prior to the impact of Kerman's injunction to criticism;[4] on the other hand, it could be said that the failure of many of those most prominently committed to the theory/analysis dualism to embrace cognitive musicology as some-

---

3 This seems to me to be true even of Thomas Clifton's attempt to avoid it, in *Music as Heard: A Study in Applied Phenomenology* (New Haven: Yale University Press, 1983).
4 Notably in Fred Lerdahl and Ray Jackendoff's *A Generative Theory of Tonal Music* (Cambridge, Mass.: MIT Press, 1983) and the journal *Music Perception* (1983–).

thing that was genuinely scientific – or, at least, potentially so – confirms that the scientism of formalist analysis was illusory in epistemological terms, however decisive the impact of scientism on analytical language.

Choosing to examine theory and analysis in relation to musical meaning might appear to be a symptom of desperation – no more than an invocation of 'meaning' as a constant in a time of doubt. Certainly, very many analyses have been presented in the professed belief that they expound some kind of musical truth; certainly, there have been attempts to justify various kinds of musical theory on the grounds that they allow music artefacts to be discussed in relation to apparently objective knowledge of acoustic phenomena. But such strategies are no longer thought to be satisfactory – if indeed they ever were. If many of the essays in this volume do, admittedly, take meaning as a cipher for something opposed to vagueness, they do so in full recognition of the endless provisionality that comes when the question of what it means to 'mean' is addressed – a semiological Pandora's Box of differences, deflections and deferrals. But, if meaning is a journey rather than a destination, it is still a journey through terrain which can be mapped through an examination of linguistic usage, traversed sure-footedly through consideration of the pragmatics of the theory/analysis interface, and explored through the construction and evaluation of analogical narratives that are aware of their own status as text. The broad divisions of the book follow this outline.

Such relativism might appear to be decidedly at odds with the old analysis. Yet, as Jonathan Dunsby's chapter makes clear, an examination of the various modes of analysis can avoid historicism while confirming that old habits die hard. One may question whether the search for deeper meaning is anything other than constructively deflected by the recognition that a web of potential meanings may be construed within ever expanding boundaries of signification. That there are new difficulties need not and surely will not prevent the continuation of analysis as an activity, though it may redefine the parameters of the discipline. If one may easily, though perhaps misleadingly, read these in terms of an antithesis between theory and practice, then by this criterion the chapters of this book possess aspects of both in more or less equal measure. It is, however, the nature of that 'measure' that is arguably the most fundamental concern of the following pages.

Acknowledgements

The impetus for this book came when Jonathan Dunsby convened a group of four British-based authors to present papers under the heading 'Analysis and Meaning' at the 1990 meeting of the Society for Music Theory in Oakland, California. That we were not alone in our concern for this topic was confirmed by other contributions to that conference, and by papers given at the Music Analysis Conference at City University, London, in 1991. The collaboration that resulted has led to this book in some cases more or less directly from conference materials, in others not.

Among those who helped this book on its journey, I should like to thank Robert Pascall, Derrick Puffett and Alan Street for their help in the early stages; Arnold Whittall for his constructive criticism of the book's concept and layout; and my colleague Robert Samuels for providing a second opinion on numerous occasions. For Cambridge University Press, Helen Beach, Claire Brodmann, Karl Howe and above all Penny Souster have made my task far easier that it might otherwise have been. At home, Angela and Lucy sustained the conditions which enabled me to give long periods of time to the production of the book. The assistance of others may more formally but no less gratefully be acknowledged:

Music examples from *Répons* by Pierre Boulez, copyright Universal Edition, are reproduced by permission. All rights reserved. An extract from *Refrains and Choruses* by Harrison Birtwistle is reproduced by kind permission of Universal Edition (London) Ltd. Music examples from String Quartet No. 2 by Arnold Schoenberg are reproduced from Philharmonia score No. 229 by permission of Universal Edition. Five Orchestral Pieces, Op. 16, by Arnold Schoenberg. Copyright 1913 by C. F. Peters. Copyright renewed 1941 by C. F. Peters. Reproduced by kind permission of Peters Edition, London.

It goes without saying that a book of this kind is made by its contributors. By keeping to deadlines, by responding faithfully to enquiries and through their many fruitful suggestions, the authors whose work is gathered here have helped to make my self-appointed task a fulfilling and largely enjoyable one.

Contributors

KOFI AGAWU teaches in the Department of Music at Cornell University. He is the author of *Playing with Signs: A Semiotic Interpretation of Classic Music* (1991), and was awarded the Dent Medal of the Royal Musical Association for 1992.

CRAIG AYREY is Lecturer in Music (Theory and Analysis) at Goldsmiths' College, University of London. His recent publications include articles on Berg, Strauss's *Salome* and Mozart's *Idomeneo*, and he is currently working on studies of Debussy and Berg's *Der Wein*.

JONATHAN CROSS is Lecturer in Music in the School of Cultural and Community Studies at the University of Sussex. He is the author of many articles on contemporary music and Assistant Editor of *Music Analysis*.

NAOMI CUMMING is a Queen Elizabeth II Research Fellow of the Australian Research Council. She is currently undertaking research on the epistemology of twentieth-century music theories in the Music Department at the University of Melbourne, and has previously been supported by a Rothmans Foundation Post-Doctoral Fellowship (University of Adelaide, 1991–2) and a Fulbright Post-Doctoral Fellowship (Columbia University, 1992–3).

JONATHAN DUNSBY is Professor of Music at the University of Reading. Founding editor of *Music Analysis* and Chairman of the Society for Music Analysis, his books include *Structural Ambiguity in Brahms*, *Music Analysis in Theory and Practice* (with Arnold Whittall) and a study of Schoenberg's *Pierrot Lunaire*.

MARION A. GUCK is Associate Professor of Music Theory at Washington University in St Louis. Her work addresses the roles of figurative language in musical discourse, and recent articles include 'A Woman's (Theoretical) Work' and 'Two Types of Metaphoric Transfer'.

Contributors

ANTHONY POPLE is Senior Lecturer in Music at Lancaster University. He reviews regularly for *Music and Letters* and *The Musical Times*, and his books include *Skryabin and Stravinsky: 1908–1914* and a study of Berg's Violin Concerto.

ROBERT SAMUELS is Lecturer in Music at Lancaster University. He has translated *The Boulez–Cage Correspondence* for Cambridge University Press and is currently working on a study of Mahler's Sixth Symphony.

ROBERT SNARRENBERG is Assistant Professor of Music Theory at Washington University in St Louis. He received his PhD in music theory from the University of Michigan in 1991 and is currently writing a book about Schenker's conception of music's expressiveness.

ALAN STREET, Lecturer in Music at the University of Keele, has published articles and reviews in a number of major journals, including *Music Analysis*, the *Journal of Music Theory* and *Music and Letters*. Formerly a Research Fellow at Clare College, Cambridge, he was also a Visiting Fellow at Yale University during the autumn of 1992.

ALASTAIR WILLIAMS is Lecturer in Music at the University of Keele. He has published on cultural theory in relation to the music of Boulez, Cage and Ligeti, and is currently engaged on a book-length study entitled *New Music and the Claims of Modernity*.

Languages

1

Metaphor in Roger Scruton's aesthetics of music

NAOMI CUMMING

This article looks at the role of metaphor in Roger Scruton's aesthetic theory, specifically as it is applied to music. A preliminary exploration of musical understanding is found in *Art and Imagination*, but a more developed statement of Scruton's position on music is reserved for a later book entitled *The Aesthetic Understanding*.[1] Scruton's treatment of metaphor in this work poses questions, first, about the epistemological claims implicit in a musical analysis and, second, about the aesthetic relevance of structuralist approaches to music.

Hanslick's question of musical meaning

Scruton's concern with metaphor arises from his desire to provide an answer to the question posed by Eduard Hanslick, of how absolute music is capable of having an expressive content, given that emotions usually have an object, and music lacks reference to anything outside of itself which might serve to identify what is expressed. The problem is summed up in the question: 'If music has a content, how can that content be described?'[2] Scruton's strategy in exploring this question is to change the object of discussion from musical expression to musical understanding. Any content attributed to music must, he argues, be the object of a listener's understanding and, if this is accepted, a theory of musical expression should be susceptible to translation into a theory of musical understanding.[3] Scruton believes that access to the cognitive categories

I would like to acknowledge the support of the Rothmans Foundation, Australia, during the writing of this essay in 1991–2. I also wish to thank Professors Graham Nerlich (Philosophy, University of Adelaide) and Marion Guck (Music, Washington University) for helpful comments on earlier versions of the manuscript.

1 Roger Scruton, *Art and Imagination: A Study in the Philosophy of Mind* (London: Routledge & Kegan Paul, 1974); *The Aesthetic Understanding: Essays in the Philosophy of Art and Culture* (London: Methuen, 1983).
2 Scruton, *The Aesthetic Understanding*, p. 77.
3 Ibid., p. 77.

used by listeners is afforded by an analysis of the descriptive language used by them to characterise musical sounds. He attempts to find the most basic categories of musical understanding by distinguishing language that is appropriate for musical descriptions from that which is used in the scientific description of the acoustic or 'material' properties of sound. Certain basic categories used by listeners are, he claims, non-congruent with any physical property of sound, but are nonetheless essential to the understanding of music. His more general claim is that an 'aesthetic understanding' is quite distinct from a scientific one and that the use of language embodies this difference:

There is a kind of understanding which rests in appearance. I shall call this kind of understanding 'intentional'. A scientific understanding addresses the world as material object, and seeks out the causal connections which underlie and explain appearances. But scientific understanding does not eliminate appearance: it only dispenses with it. An intentional understanding considers the world as intentional object (or, to use the Husserlian idiom, as *Lebenswelt*): it therefore uses *the concepts through which we perceive the world*, and makes no connections or observations that are not in some way already implicit in them.[4]

Scruton sets out to show that musical content is embodied in the 'intentional' object. According to Hanslick's argument it is not attributable to the sounding medium itself (the 'material' object), since content has been defined as reference to an external object, a possibility denied to absolute music. The idea of an 'intentional object' is put forward as a path to solving this problem because it offers one way of describing how the understanding of a perceiver is implicated in the content ascribed to a percept. An intentional object is the object of a thought, belief or other cognitive attitude. While 'intentional objects' may include any objects of thought, whether purely imagined, conceptualised or perceived, Scruton is interested specifically in the object of *perceptions*, which are taken to embody thought and to be influenced by beliefs. Most important for his argument is the observation that the coincidence of an intentional object with a material object is not guaranteed, given that beliefs (and the perceptions founded upon them) may be false.[5] If he can show that the language used in our culture to describe the musical behaviour of sounds

---

4 Ibid., p. 78 (emphasis added).
5 A well-known example is given by Quine in his discussion of referential opacity. To paraphrase: Tom believes that Cicero denounced Cataline, but not that Tully did, even though (unbeknown to him) Tully *is* Cicero. The intentional object of Tom's thought is Cicero. In this case the intentional object of thought depends on a belief (and therefore, on a believed description) which is false. See W. V. Quine, *Word and Object* (Cambridge, Mass.: MIT Press, 1960), p. 145.

is inconsistent with what is known of their material attributes, he can also claim that the properties described belong to the intentional object and not to the material one. This argument serves the purpose of showing that musical content is an imposition on sound of the cognitive categories used in listening. Following this conviction through, Scruton is led to make an ontological claim, that 'music belongs uniquely to the intentional sphere, and not to the material realm'.[6]

Speculation of this kind might seem to be of dubious value, but its significance is found by keeping in mind the question of how music can have expressive content. Scruton takes melody, harmony and rhythm to be the most fundamental categories of music, and develops his case by looking at two properties which are attributed to them in various ways, namely space and motion. He argues that musical space and motion are attributes of the intentional object, not the material one, and then seeks to draw a parallel between the structural content which is described using these (or derivative) terms, and the expressive content which is described with affective language. Starting from an observation that the perceived motion of a pitch in musical space is different from, and lacks reference to, the motion of objects in physical space, he excludes the possibility that it might reflect any physical property of sound. He argues that pitch motion can only be understood by looking at those processes of understanding which create categories of 'space' and 'motion' applicable to music, *not* by examining music itself on the assumption that motion is present in the relationship of pitches. In his terms, 'A theory which tries to explain music in terms of musical movement is not a theory of music at all: it "explains" its subject only by blocking the path to explanation.'[7] By this argument, descriptions of musical motion in the analysis of specific structures are rendered intelligible not by reference to any objective state of affairs, but by reference to cognitive/perceptual proclivities. Scruton believes that the categories of space and motion are so basic to understanding that a description of music which substituted neutral acoustic terms ('change of pitch or frequency' for 'motion') would fail to capture the musical experience. Thus musical 'content', even when described purely in structural terms, is found to be in the intentional object of perception, and not to be an attribute of a material (acoustic) object.

Scruton concludes from his study of space and motion that 'any analysis of music must be an exercise in intentional rather than scientific

6 Scruton, *The Aesthetic Understanding*, p. 86
7 Ibid., p. 34.

understanding',[8] and on this conclusion builds the first part of his solution to the problem of musical expression. The aesthetic understanding displayed by a listener when expressive content is found in music has characteristics similar to those displayed when formal content is being identified. A description of musical form typically includes reference to the motion of pitches in musical space and this, no less than the use of emotive terms, reflects a cognitive attitude of the perceiver. Scruton believes that the content is, in both cases, in the intentional object. As a consequence, an acceptance of one kind of content as being 'in the music' should lead to an acceptance of the other. Like the 'motion' of a series of pitches, the 'sadness' of a motive derives its meaning from the imposition on music of a mental attribute, and its intelligibility from a common experience of such 'projection'. This does nothing to explain why we might commonly want to apply the epithet 'sad' or 'melancholy' to certain passages of Schubert, but it does attempt to legitimise expressive content as being no more nor less objective than other kinds of musical content.[9]

Metaphors and music as an intentional object

Scruton pursues a further discussion of how non-referential expressive content can be explained using the doctrine of *Einfühlung* as a more sophisticated substitute for the idea of 'projection', but his argument up to this point is already controversial and it is on this part that I propose to concentrate. It has been seen that Scruton suggests a commonality between the analysis of structural features in music and the analysis of its expressive content, but he does not convincingly reconcile technical analysis and aesthetic criticism without creating some confusion, particularly in the appraisal of how language is used in the two related disciplines. Most obviously problematic is the key word, 'metaphor' which is used, without explicit definition, to designate any term which refers to an attribute of music as an intentional object. The category 'metaphor' is thus taken to include both musical space and motion and terms referring to expressive content such as 'sadness'.

8 Ibid.
9 Ibid., p. 95:

> We project into the music the inner life that is ours, and that is *how* we hear it there. This is not the same as hearing resemblances between music and feeling, any more than hearing musical movement is hearing structural relations on which the movement depends. The experience of transfer is *sui generis*. The emotion that is heard belongs purely to the intentional and not to the material realm.

The argument can now be restated as Scruton typically expresses it, using the idea of metaphor. Stating his position that music is necessarily an intentional object, not a material one, he asserts that a capacity for 'metaphorical transfer' is essential to musical understanding, and that no substitution of literal terms could adequately convey what is perceived:

It seems that in our most basic apprehension of music there lies a complex system of metaphor, which is the true description of no material fact. And the metaphor cannot be eliminated from the description of music, because it is integral to the intentional object of musical experience. Take this metaphor away and you cease to describe the experience of music.[10]

It might appear from his discussion that intentional objects are always described metaphorically, but this is only because he does not deal with more mundane things as the objects of thought, things which might be described using literal (while possibly false) terms. Some clarification of the relationship between an intentional object and the use of metaphor is thus needed. An intentional object could be described using either literal or metaphorical terms: when I believe that Cicero – not Tully – denounced Cataline, Cicero is my intentional object, and I am thinking literally, even though I am partially mistaken. The use of metaphor in description is, however, taken by Scruton as an indicator that an intentional object is being described since the formation of metaphor involves a particular act of understanding where a word is transferred from one realm of experience to another, and is thus not used in its standard sense to designate the object 'in itself'. For the purposes of Scruton's discussion the intentional object (music) must be represented metaphorically.

The argument presented assumes the validity of two strong distinctions. First is the supposition that in all normal discourse a clear separation is possible between literal and metaphorical language. According to Mark Johnson, this position is that typically held in positivist and empiricist treatments of metaphor which, in distinguishing the 'cognitive' and 'emotive' functions of language, maintain an 'attendant belief that scientific knowledge could be reduced to a system of literal and verifiable sentences'.[11] As Johnson's comment suggests, the distinction between literal and metaphorical terms is necessary in a view of science which wants to protect the description of material things from the incursion of subjective or emotional attitudes. An appraisal of language is found to

10 Scruton, *The Aesthetic Understanding*, p. 85.
11 Mark Johnson, 'Introduction', in Mark Johnson (ed.), *Philosophical Perspectives on Metaphor* (Minneapolis: University of Minnesota Press, 1981), p. 17.

entail the assumption of an epistemological position, and it is this which makes the discussion of metaphor a non-trivial one. The second distinction made by Scruton accords with his empiricist position. Complementary to a separation of literal from metaphorical language is his distinction between a material object, which can ostensibly be described without contamination from the misleading categories of cognition, and an intentional object, which may or may not coincide with it, depending on the efficacy of the cognitive categories used (presumably reflecting the degree to which the thinker's experience is apposite to the situation in hand). Scruton is consistent in affirming the empirical view that when metaphorical language is used to describe something (e. g. 'an angry sore'), it can usually be replaced without loss of meaning by literal language (e. g. 'an inflamed and swollen infection of the skin').[12] The possibility of substitution is taken to confirm the material identity of the object described so that it is both the object of a propositional attitude and a material thing, independent in its attributes from any qualities imposed by an observer.

This assumption, that metaphors can be replaced by equivalent literal terms when a scientific understanding is conveyed, lies behind Scruton's claim about the ontological status of music. According to him, music belongs 'uniquely' to the intentional realm because such substitution is impossible. The terms which are used to describe the perceived structures of music (involving the motion of sounds in musical space) cannot, he suggests, be replaced by literal terms without sacrificing fidelity to what is perceived. Music is defined as distinct from noise by possessing attributes which cannot be reduced to any material property of sound. Scruton is apparently saying that although musical structures are genuinely perceived, they cannot be described as belonging to material reality. While 'there is a material base to the perception of these things, there is more to perceiving them than perceiving their material base'.[13]

What Scruton does not consider in espousing a traditional empiricist view of metaphor (without discussing it directly) is that all language is a product of human cognition and imposes order on the material world, often by transferring words between different realms of experience. Lakoff and Johnson's study of metaphor has shown that a clear delimita-

---

12 Ibid., p. 17:

> Typically, such treatments either ignored metaphor as wholly emotive or insisted that the truth claims of any nonliteral expression could be captured by a literal paraphrase without loss of cognitive content.

13 Scruton, *The Aesthetic Understanding*, p. 94.

tion of literal from metaphorical speech is by no means transparently obvious (is 'inflamed' really a literal word when applied to a sore?),[14] and if this distinction lacks clarity, it cannot be maintained as a fool-proof key to distinguishing material things (described in literal or 'objective' language) from 'things as the object of thought, belief, imagination or perception' (where metaphorical description acts as the possible marker of an intentional object lacking material reality). Even what we accept as objective descriptions of material things will always, and necessarily, make use of human cognitive categories, which may at times use metaphorical terms for their expression. The abundance of 'dead' metaphors in language warns against the belief that scientific descriptions can entirely exclude them, but the mere fact that an object is observed and described using available terms, with the belief-structures implied in them, does not necessitate a denial that the thing exists, even if more literal terms are substituted with the greatest difficulty. Saying that something is an 'intentional object' is entirely redundant in scientific description because it is taken for granted that something described is the object of perception (which is informed by experience and belief), and that the description coincides as far as possible with reality. When Scruton contrasts 'intentional understanding' with 'scientific understanding' he is interested in explicating those circumstances in which this assumption of congruence between perception and reality cannot be made. There would, however, need to be a convincing pay-off indeed (in the form of an answer to the problem of musical expression) to justify relegating musical structures, as well as musical expression, to the realm of material inexistence.

Forgetting for the time being that 'metaphor' has fuzzy boundaries, the sense in which musical space and motion are metaphors may be questioned according to Scruton's own idea that metaphor involves a transference of concepts from one sphere of experience to another. Taking an empirical stance, it is necessary to find out whether the use of these words in reference to music actually entails any such transfer, and an appraisal of language which accepts a limited standard definition of terms proves to be a handicap here. Following from this discussion it can be asked whether the fundamental terminology of musical description really justifies giving music a unique status as an 'intentional object', distinct from other things. Finally, the impact of Scruton's argument on the problem of musical expression can be assessed. (Is there a genuine

---

14 George Lakoff and Mark Johnson, *Metaphors We Live By* (Chicago: University of Chicago Press, 1980).

connection between words for space and motion, and words denoting affective content?) I will look in some detail at Scruton's discussion of musical space and motion before proceeding to look at his views on affective language in aesthetic description, in order to establish whether any connection between them can be substantiated.

Musical space and motion: are they metaphors?

The simplest case of perceived motion is found in melody:

Tones, unlike sounds, seem to contain movement. This movement is exemplified in melodies, and can be traced through a 'musical space' which we describe in terms of 'high' and 'low'.[15]

The apparent movement of tones in an auditory space is, Scruton claims, unlike the movement of an object in a physical space because 'it does not involve an act of re-identification: it does not require the perception of the same thing at different places, and the consequent inference of a movement from one place to the other'.[16] In addition to this apparent disanalogy between motion in musical and physical space he finds another disjunction, between a chord in musical space and an object in physical space. He asks how a chord might display spatial orientation and reaches the conclusion that 'there is only genuine orientation in the musical space if a chord can be considered as a single musical object, spread over the "area" which it "occupies"'.[17] Any such perceived unity is, he believes, attributable to an act of the understanding, not to an objective property of the combined pitch frequencies.

Scruton takes these examples to demonstrate that qualities of space and motion are heard by listeners only because a (presumably innate) conception of space guides hearing. He assumes that there is a standard understanding of space which serves to limit the ways in which the word 'space' can be used literally (his discussion being founded on that given by Kant). It is implied that space is a concrete thing even though it is non-physical, because constant factors can be found in the way that objects occupy or move through space.[18] When space is perceived in a context (such as music) where these constants are violated, the space

15 Ibid., p. 80.
16 Ibid., p. 84.
17 Ibid., p. 83.
18 This point is illustrated in a discussion of dimension (Scruton, *The Aesthetic Understanding*, pp. 81–2):

perceived is deemed to be part of an intentional object which does not coincide with any material thing. Putting a name to the perception, and calling it 'space' (or pitch motion up and down, implying space) thus entails using the term in a sense which is literally false according to the premises of this argument. It is nonetheless true of the intentional object – which is what we experience – and, given that the perception itself would not be possible if the concept of space did not already exist in the mind, Scruton is led to believe that a 'capacity for metaphorical transfer' is essential to musical perception.

I would like to take issue, first, with the limited definition of what might be the literal properties of space. In mathematics 'measure spaces' are not physical things, but the mere fact that space is used to conceptualise abstract measurement does not make it a metaphor.[19] Such non-metaphorical spaces lack many, indeed most, of the features Kant used to characterise physical space, and they provide an alternative model for understanding the simplest characteristics of space perceived in music. That sounds may form a two-dimensional 'measure space' quite literally, providing that each has a definite pitch, is attested by the convention of arranging pitches in formalised 'scales'. The absence of metaphor at this level of description is further supported by the lack of any genuine conceptual 'transfer' in the act of perceiving these pitch relationships. When I hear 'motion through space' in a series of proximate pitches (i. e. a scale) the perception is a direct auditory one and does not require mediation from visual channels. Giving words to this experience, which is founded on the cognitive measurement of pitch distances through time, does seem to require spatial words whose most standard usage occurs in relation to visual objects. The use of 'space' to express measurement in a non-visual perception does not, however, suggest that the act of understanding involves a transfer of this category from the visual realm of experience to the auditory one.[20] The 'metaphorical transfer' is not expe-

A dimension stands in a specific relation to the things that it contains. For example, an object is located *in* space; it *occupies* a certain position which might have been occupied by something else; it is also oriented in space. . . . Orientation is present whenever there is 'incongruity', of the kind displayed between an object and its mirror image.

19 See, for example, R. B. Reisel, *Elementary Theory of Measure Spaces* (New York: Springer Verlag, 1982) or Irving Kaplansky, *Set Theory and Metric Spaces* (Boston: Allyn and Bacon, 1972). I am grateful to Professor Graham Nerlich for pointing this out to me.

20 On musical measurement see Eugene Narmour, *The Analysis and Cognition of Basic Melodic Structures* (Chicago: University of Chicago Press, 1990), part III.

riential, but purely semantic (and that only to the extent that a limited definition of space is accepted). The most basic material foundation for musical 'space' is an actual differentiation between pitches. 'Motion', on the other hand, is an indicator of change occurring through time as one pitch is succeeded by another. These words, applied to music, are not literally false, but trivially true.

Once it has been established that there is an empirical basis for using the terms 'space' and 'motion' in relation to music, the idea that music is an intentional object in any extraordinary sense (based on the use of these terms) loses its point. It has been shown that the pitch relationships demonstrated in a scale may be regarded as literal properties, their foundation lying both in a physical difference between frequencies, and in a cognitive/perceptual capacity to discriminate these differences. Metaphor does not play a cognitive role in any strong sense here. Musical understanding at this level is better investigated using the methods of cognitive psychology than by analysing individual elements of language, which have here given the misleading impression that visually-derived metaphors shape auditory cognition. If the words 'space' and 'motion' express a perceptual attitude it is one which is entirely involuntary, being determined by cognitive mechanisms which are not susceptible to conscious control. Perceptual constructions of this kind bear no useful relation to the judgements of affective content which are made at a higher cognitive level, where metaphors are genuinely used in acts of conscious discrimination.

Scruton's argument is weakened by his reliance upon the abstract idea of pitch motion in space, when his real interest lies in the quality of musical motion heard in specific contexts which require interpretation. When they remain at an abstract level, his observations do not successfully identify the qualities which distinguish music from a collection of sounds, since a discrimination of pitches in relation to one another is required even in the description of bird-song or train signals, and the vocabulary used for these sounds might also refer to 'motion' in an implied auditory space (e. g. a train signal is motion *down* a minor third; a lark has an *undulating* warble). There is no justification for distinguishing the simple musical relationships found in a scale as belonging uniquely to an 'intentional sphere', if the language used indicates that a similar level of perceptual construction is involved in the perception of other sounds.[21] Both a train signal and a scale could be an intentional object in a trivial

---

21 Scruton, *The Aesthetic Understanding*, p. 86.

sense, accepting that they are both material (acoustic) objects in the world and that perceiving them does nothing to alter their objective reality. Scruton's attempt to give music a unique ontology thus cannot be founded on an account of space and motion as ways of describing simple sound relationships. The endeavour to solve the problem of musical expression by saying that *any* description of musical relationships must entail the use of metaphor, and hence the imposition on sound of qualities created in the act of perception, is not successful.

The kind of language which Scruton really wants to get at in his discussion is, however, at quite another level, where the qualities described clearly do *not* belong to the material object in a literal sense. He suggests that 'the intentional object of experience must be described using a concept that is known not to apply to the material object of perception. This transfer is not unlike that which occurs in metaphor.'[22] Here the idea that metaphor has a role in the deliberate construction of an intentional object begins to be more interesting. Scruton says, for example, that 'in hearing rhythm we hear the music as *active*; it seems to be doing something (namely, dancing) which no sounds can do', but 'at the same time, we do not believe that any such thing is happening in the realm of sound: in a crucial sense, we are aware of the movement as *ours*'.[23] The experience which he wishes to elucidate is one in which the listener is actively involved, using what he calls 'imaginative perception'. Voluntary and conscious activity are essential to his conception of this way of perceiving:

To be 'active' a perception must exhibit that kind of conscious participation that is involved in the perception of an aspect [e. g. seeing a face in a cloud, p. 87]: it must involve an engagement of attention, an interest in surface, a transference of concepts from sphere to sphere (as in metaphor); in the limiting case it may itself be a voluntary act.[24]

A much higher level of interpretive activity is clearly attributed to the perceiver in this description than that which is implied in the mere identification of pitch motion. What is not explained within the article is that a whole theory of imaginative perception underlies this reference to 'aspects', and it is to this that I shall now briefly turn.

22 Ibid., p. 87.
23 Ibid., p. 90.
24 Ibid., p. 88.

Scruton's theory of imaginative perception

In *Art and Imagination*, Scruton elaborates the kind of cognitive activity which he believes to be involved in aesthetic descriptions which employ metaphor or other forms of non-literal language. His apparent concern is to justify the use of metaphor to an empiricist audience who might be inclined to reject it as inferior to literal speech, and the text consequently reads as a dialogue with his own intellectual background. Acknowledging the traditional position that 'the philosopher's task in analysing language is to give an account of meaning and truth conditions for literal cognitive utterances',[25] he aims to expand the range of discussion to include other forms of discourse. As guiding questions he asks 'What is it to assert a sentence?' and 'What are the conditions for its acceptance?' In order to answer these questions he has recourse to a consideration of the speaker's state of mind, her attitude both to the object being described and to the act of communication itself. Statements using non-literal language are found to express a different relationship of the speaker to an object than those using literal terms, and also to reflect a different communicative intent. A statement 'X is Y' normally indicates that the speaker *believes* X to possess a certain characteristic, Y. The condition for its acceptance is a sharing of that belief. When a metaphor (or other non-literal descriptor) is used, as in 'he is a beast', it is, however, possible to say that X is Y without believing this to be literally true (that is, to make a statement without 'asserting' it),[26] and since the speaker does not imply a belief in the empirical grounding of her descriptive terms, neither does she ask the hearer to adopt such a belief in order to make sense of the statement. The normal 'acceptance conditions' are waived when metaphor is used in this way, to make observations without asserting beliefs.

In order to unravel how such non-literal statements become meaning-ful Scruton explores the state of mind which is substituted for belief when they are made. He is concerned primarily with the cognitive atti-tude embodied in acts of perceiving a work of art, and he describes it rather ingenuously as a 'non-cognitive state of mind' before developing a more sophisticated concept of the 'imagination'.[27] This term, 'imagina-tion', is used in order to convey the idea that understanding art is a

25 See Johnson, 'Introduction', p. 17.
26 In this case the literal truth is clearly not the point of the description.
27 Scruton, *Art and Imagination*, p. 49:

> Aesthetic descriptions are related to certain non-cognitive states of mind in the same intimate fashion that genuine descriptions are related to beliefs.

Figure 1.1   The duck/rabbit figure

distinctive kind of mental activity encompassing aspects of both thought and perception in a single experience.[28] Scruton finds that a study of mental imagery discloses two key features of what is involved in imaginative perceiving: first, that the experience is subject to the will,[29] and, second, that it has a specific duration and intensity.[30] In illustrating this point he uses an ambiguous figure previously discussed by Ludwig Wittgenstein (Fig. 1.1).[31] Both the duck and the rabbit are aspects of the figure, though neither is a literal property, and perception shifts from one to another at specific intervals with some control of the will. Wittgenstein describes it as a case of seeing X as Y ('seeing as'). Scruton suggests that 'the element of thought involved in "seeing as" lies clearly in the field of the imagination: it is thought that goes beyond what is believed or inwardly asserted, and beyond what is strictly given in perception'.[32] When a person seeks to communicate a perception of the shifting aspects of the figure, she does not assert that either aspect is literally present, but rather seeks to facilitate another in sharing the perceptual experience, engaging in an act of instructive persuasion. The criterion for accepting the description is, then, not a sharing of a belief, but the actual ability to see the two aspects.

The experience of 'aspect perception' is taken by Scruton as a model for the perception of music, where an active imaginative engagement with the work will allow the perceiver to hear qualities which, he believes, go beyond the material attributes of sound. He argues that 'seeing as' in the visual field has its equivalent in the auditory realm, where it is

28 Ibid., p. 89.
29 Ibid., pp. 94–7.
30 Ibid., pp. 101–2.
31 Ludwig Wittgenstein, *Philosophical Investigations*, trans. G. E. M. Anscombe (New York: Macmillan, 1953), p. 194.
32 Scruton, *Art and Imagination*, p. 112.

15

Example 1.1   Brahms, *Variations on a Theme by Robert Schumann*, var. 8

designated 'hearing as'.[33] As an example, he points out that in a passage taken from Brahms' *Variations on a Theme by Robert Schumann* we may hear the bass notes *as* forming a melody, or possibly fail to so connect them (Ex. 1.1). His comment is that 'the difference between hearing this sequence as a melody and hearing it as a jumble of disconnected notes is a difference in the experience, and not in its (material) object'.[34] Two further qualities are also found to connect the perception of a melody with that of aspect perception. 'Not only does hearing something as a melody have a precise beginning in time: it also has a precise duration', and 'it is to some extent within voluntary control'.[35] This last attribution is essential in clarifying the kind of experience intended by Scruton when he describes 'the sensory "embodiment" of a thought' in imaginative perceiving.[36] It is tautologous to say that perceiving involves thought, if all perception is a cognitive activity,[37] but the kind of hearing which he wants to describe is a particular one, one in which the listener can exercise choice about how she hears a given passage, and where she is therefore susceptible to persuasion that she might hear it another way. Listening of this kind is an interpretive activity, exemplified in the possibility of exercising choice about how one hears the grouping of notes. A listener

33   Ibid., pp. 174–83.
34   Ibid., p. 175.
35   Ibid., pp. 177, 178.
36   Ibid., p. 180.
37   A contentious point. See Jerry A. Fodor, 'Observation Reconsidered', in *A Theory of Content and Other Essays* (Cambridge, Mass.: MIT Press, 1990), pp. 231–51.

might, for example, hear trochaic or iambic patterns in a duple metre, her choice reflecting some degree of control over what she perceives within the limits imposed by the given context. This act of grouping could be designated a form of thought whose content cannot be specified 'independently of the "perception" in which it is embodied'.[38]

It is not, however, clear that all of the cases chosen by Scruton as exemplars of 'hearing as' belong to the same class of thought. In *The Aesthetic Understanding* he mentions that we hear notes *as* moving,[39] rhythm *as* dancing,[40] collections of notes *as* forming chords, which may be analysed under varying descriptions[41] and the separate musical movements of counterpoint *as* harmonising.[42] That classifying these activities together is quite problematic can be seen simply by testing them against his own criteria for 'aspect perception' or 'hearing as'. It has already been seen that the act of identifying pitch motion in a simple musical context (such as a scale) does not entail or even permit choice.[43] In asserting the inescapability of space and motion terms when describing any music as it is perceived (as 'intentional object'), Scruton has in fact ruled out the possibility of choice and hence of active interpretation on the part of the listener who hears a scale in this way, excluding the most obvious examples of hearing pitch motion from the criterion of being subject to voluntary control. To demonstrate the influence of choice on perception, a specified musical context is required (such as that cited from Brahms) in which the listener can be demonstrated to (actively) interpret pitch motion during the act of listening, hearing as a melody a passage which might appear disconnected.[44] There is, however, no possibility of making a clear distinction between cases of imaginative 'hearing as' and cases where involuntary perceptual mechanisms impose order on pitch successions, given that an extensive variation in the degree of conscious control over perception must be assumed. Judgements of how susceptible a listener's perceptions are to such control cannot be made simply on the

38 Ibid. Examples of note grouping are discussed by Scruton in *Art and Imagination*, p. 179 and *The Aesthetic Understanding*, p. 89.
39 Scruton, *The Aesthetic Understanding*, pp. 80, 84.
40 Ibid., p. 90.
41 Ibid., pp. 91–4.
42 Ibid., p. 91.
43 Nicholas Cook likens it to the Phi phenomenon, saying that 'to regard the perception of a musical scale or the Phi phenomenon as instances of imaginative perception is, in effect, to render the term coextensive with what psychologists refer to as "perceptual construction"' (*Music, Imagination, and Culture* (Oxford: Clarendon Press, 1990), p. 25).
44 Scruton, *Art and Imagination*, p. 175.

basis of the language used to describe a musical passage, and further investigations into this question require the methods of experimental psychology rather than those of analytical philosophy.

The difficulty in determining when imaginative or volitional activity directs perception is further confirmed by Scruton's references to rhythm, harmony and counterpoint. Hearing rhythmic motion as a dance certainly suggests an imaginative activity directed by the listener, but hearing a collection of notes as a chord, or recognising that a given chord is dissonant and implies resolution within the dictates of its style are two quite distinct perceptual capacities in which innate perceptual proclivities and learning are dominant to differing degrees. If cognitive control is exercised by a listener who hears a chord in its appropriate stylistic context there is no reason to suppose that the choice made in so placing it should enter consciousness, since perception in real time must limit the possibility of monitoring such basic choices. Scruton's criterion for aspect perception, that it is subject to the will, can only be attributed to these differing cases in the loosest sense. The idea of 'hearing as' does not link them in any strong way.

Scruton's analysis of auditory perception is founded on the vocabulary used by listeners to describe musical structure, rather than on a study of perception itself, and the posited link between 'seeing as' and 'hearing as' rests in part upon an assumed commonality in the kinds of statements which people make about perceptions in the two media. If '"hearing as" shares with "seeing as" a formal relation to the concept of (unasserted) thought'[45] it must give rise to statements which are not asserted as being literally true. When someone describes an 'aspect' in a visual image they do not believe in or assert its literal presence, but simply entertain the idea 'X is Y' ('the cloud is a face' or 'the ambiguous figure is a rabbit'). The terms of description ('face' and 'rabbit') are viewed by Scruton as metaphorical, since they are transferred from a standard application, where their literal sense is defined empirically, to a non-standard application, where the point of using them can only be grasped by someone who shares the immediate perception.[46] To carry through the intended comparison between descriptions of visual aspects and descriptions of perceived musical content, Scruton needs to show that a similar imaginative engagement typifies statements about the two media. He must maintain

45 Scruton, *The Aesthetic Understanding*, p. 178.
46 Scruton is influenced by the speech-act theories of Austin and Grice in looking at the whole context of communication in order to give meaning to the utterance, rather than simply at the relationship of the word to the object (*Art and Imagination*, pp. 58–9).

that an attenuation of belief in the literal truth of any description is manifest in an avoidance of making asserted statements about music (rather than suggested interpretations). The comparison is predictably successful only in those cases where all of the criteria for 'aspect perception' are present, including the requirement that a perception be subject to voluntary control. A musician would not believe or assert that 'the notes are dancing', although he might entertain this as an apt description of how he hears them. Statements that 'in this context the chord is dissonant and requires resolution', or that 'the notes *move* toward resolution on the tonic' are, however, asserted as literal truths within the domain of music theory, where the application of the terms 'motion' and 'resolution' is quite standard.

Scruton does not accept standard usage in music theory as being any indicator of a word's meaning. Building further from his analysis of hearing notes as a chord, or dissonances as requiring resolution, he is led to assert that the language of harmonic description, like that of pitch motion, involves a metaphorical transfer which precludes it from being literally true:

Just as melody involves the metaphorical transference of ideas of 'movement', 'space', 'height' and 'depth', so does harmony involve the metaphorical transfer of ideas of 'tension', 'relaxation', 'conflict' and 'resolution'. Although there is a material base to the perception of these things, there is more to perceiving them than perceiving their material base.[47]

His basis for denying that a harmonic description can be asserted as true rests on the assumption, seen earlier, that words have a standard meaning which reflects an empirical truth. Metaphors are negatively defined as terms given a non-standard application, not applying to their objects in any empirical sense (just as a face is not in a cloud), and not asserted but entertained by an imaginative perceiver (who holds an attitude like that appropriate to cloud gazing). Applying this position, it might be asked what makes the typical statements used to describe musical structure more metaphorical than statements about mundane products. If I say that 'I hear these notes as a melody' or that 'I hear this dissonant French sixth as producing a harmonic tension which is resolved by motion to the dominant' is my statement more metaphorical than when I inform you (boringly) that 'I see this piece of forged metal as a fire poker'? I certainly would assert my analysis of the music as being true, giving no unusual

47 Scruton, *The Aesthetic Understanding*, p. 94.

meaning to my functional harmonic terms. It is, however, suggested by Scruton that the imposition of human cognitive categories on a material thing is greater when I hear 'tension and resolution' in sound, than when I categorise a piece of metal by its human function.

Scruton's distinction between metaphor and literal language requires further clarification. One of his apparent criteria for recognising a metaphor is that it should be a term which does not describe the material properties of an observed thing, but goes beyond them by imposing qualities derived from perception, thus indicating that an intentional object (rather than a material one) is being described. This is inadequate. Calling a piece of forged metal 'a fire poker' goes beyond the material properties of the thing by imposing a functional category on it, but the terms of description are accepted as literal when they fit the human design, and are not an imaginative imposition on any arbitrary piece of scrap metal. Many ordinary names for functional objects are not applied simply to their physical properties, and in music it is similarly the case that descriptive terms describe functions according to the categories accepted by the musical community.[48] No-one can deny that dissonance and resolution are not simply derived from the material properties of the overtone series, but neither is the perception of, say, a minor ninth or a French sixth typically greeted with scepticism, a doubt in what is perceived leading to the attenuation of all belief in the possibility of asserting a true description of the harmony. The terms 'dissonance' and 'resolution' have a musical meaning as legitimate as that found in their other applications, and, this being the case, Scruton's second criterion for recognising metaphor, that it involves a transference of concepts between spheres, does not apply. It certainly cannot be assumed that using such harmonic terms entails a significant transference of meaning from other contexts, and within the musical community they are accepted as literal.

Scruton believes that through his analysis of melody, harmony and rhythm he has uncovered in music 'a realm of intentional understanding which is both active in the manner of imaginative experience, and also essentially dependent upon metaphor'.[49] What he convincingly uncovers

48 Mark DeBellis distinguishes 'strong' ascriptions of a harmonic label to a chord, as those in which a *function* is ascribed, from alternative 'weak' ascriptions, where simultaneities are recognised without reference to their function. In either case he believes that structural descriptions are 'truth valued' because they 'enter into all the usual truth-functional contexts' ('Conceptions of Musical Structure', *Midwest Studies in Philosophy*, 16 (1991), pp. 381–2).

49 Scruton, *The Aesthetic Understanding*, p. 94.

is something more limited, that is, the imaginative attitude underlying descriptions of affective qualities or particular kinds of movement in music (such as the impression of notes dancing). This attitude is modelled on that of aspect perception, where belief is attenuated, thought becomes inseparable from perceptual experience (with respect to timescale, intensity, and subjection to volitional control), and statements are not asserted as being literally true. A psychological attitude which might indeed underlie some uses of metaphor cannot, however, be transferred without confusion to all of the cases identified by Scruton as 'metaphorical'. This is particularly so, considering that Scruton does not accord a linguistic community (such as that of music theorists) the power to define its own literal terms, but instead looks for a stronger empirical foundation for literal meaning. To be consistent with his argument, the idea that melodic motion and harmonic dissonance are metaphors should entail a belief that theorists make their statements unasserted. But the attitude of music analysts to their own assertions has not been adequately explored. An interchange between Jonathan Bernard and Marion Guck provides an interesting example of two differing attitudes to analytical assertion, where Bernard strongly asserts his analysis as literal and incontrovertible, while Guck offers a reading which gives greater recognition to her own perceptual response to the work.[50] Even while affirming her own active role in interpretation, Guck is able to assert her analysis of the music as equally related to the pitches concerned. She is not claiming that the intentional object of her experience is any more idiosyncratic than that offered by Bernard, but is instead questioning the strength of his epistemological position by showing that even literal terms can disclose an individual perceiver's position in relation to the work. The next section will explore a little further how literal and metaphorical language might function within the theoretical community.

Systemic metaphors in music theory

I have so far discussed Scruton's treatment of musical discourse at two different levels: the first level includes references to musical 'space and motion', terms expressing the capacities to measure differences in pitch and to hear ordered change between pitches, while the second level is

---

50 Marion Guck, 'The "Endless Round"', *Perspectives of New Music*, 31/i (1993), pp. 306–14. This followed an interchange in *Perspectives of New Music*, 30/ii (1992), pp. 244–89, in which Guck reviewed Jonathan Bernard's *The Music of Edgard Varèse* (New Haven: Yale University Press, 1987) and Bernard replied.

that of conventional theoretical discourse, naming harmonic, rhythmic or melodic functions. I question Scruton's designation of terms at both levels as being necessarily metaphorical, because I concur with Eva Kittay's view that it is necessary to maintain a distinction between literal and metaphorical language if the cognitive function of metaphor is to be understood.[51] This distinction is maintained by Scruton when he deals with non-aesthetic discourse, but is found by him not to hold in aesthetic descriptions. His designation of musical terms as metaphors arises largely because he limits literal language to a certain class of sentences which satisfy the 'truth condition' of direct empirical verification:

The empiricist argues that we can understand a language only if at least some of its sentences are given truth conditions in a stronger sense: conditions which show how a sentence should be verified. We must ascribe meaning to certain sentences directly, without the mediation of others that 'give their truth conditions' in a purely formal manner.[52]

The literal cannot, however, be limited to the giving of names to objects whose qualities can be empirically verified, since it must embrace abstract conceptualisation, and neither can it be limited to narrow definitions which make one application of a term prescriptive, as has already been demonstrated for the term 'space'.

A relativist position, which allows terms to assume a variety of meanings, is suggested by Kittay, who believes that the literal/metaphorical distinction can only be made 'relative to a given synchronic moment in a given language community',[53] so that the users of a language in effect determine what is understood as being literal at any given time, this including terms which might formerly have been metaphors or which have metaphorical potential. A metaphor is accordingly defined by her as 'any unit of discourse in which some conceptual or conversational incongruity emerges',[54] with the proviso that 'there is nothing in the context to persuade us that the conventions of our discourse have been altered in specifiable ways (for example, to include technical language)'.[55] The incongruities in musical discourse identified by Scruton are not ones commonly recognised by the habitual users of its specialised language, since they are created by the provision of an external context (for example, an

---

51 Eva Kittay, *Metaphor: Its Cognitive Force and Linguistic Structure* (Oxford: Clarendon Press, 1987), pp. 19–22.
52 Scruton, *Art and Imagination*, p. 6.
53 Kittay, *Metaphor*, p. 22.
54 Ibid., p. 24.
55 Ibid., p. 91.

understanding of non-musical space), while a tension of a word with its given context only makes it a *current* metaphor if the context is that understood by current practitioners of the language.[56]

It is well understood that contextual incongruity may come from the transference of concepts between spheres. Max Black's work of 1954–5 suggested that in employing metaphor 'we use one entire *system* of commonplaces to "filter" or organise our conception of some other *system*'[57] and Kittay describes the same phenomenon when she says that 'metaphor is the linguistic realisation of a leap of thought from one domain to another – in which the springboard is a structure-preserving mapping'.[58] One way of gaining a new perspective on current theoretical discourse is to retrieve the metaphorical origins of words which are accepted within a specialised system (such as that of Schenkerian theory) as being literal, and thus to gain access to conceptual frameworks which have influenced the building of the theory.

Space and motion terms in music, designated by Scruton as examples of metaphor, have been shown to possess a literal musical meaning, but they may indeed acquire a metaphorical status, for reasons other than those proposed by Scruton, when the theorist takes a conception of non-musical space and (whether consciously or not) allows it to shape his or her idea of how sounds are connected in time. Kevin Korsyn has shown how 'Schenker alludes to the Kantian doctrine that space and time are the *a priori* forms of intuition':

Only the genius is blessed with the feeling for tone-space. It is his *a priori* exactly as each man, from his feeling for his own body, is already born with the concepts of space (as extension of his body) and time (as the growth and becoming of his body) *a priori*.[59]

Contrasting to the Kantian influence on Schenker is the reception by Leonard Meyer and Eugene Narmour of Gestaltist notions of linear continuity and visual Gestalt formation as models for dealing with pitch connection. The consequence of assuming an alternative system for interpreting the abstract notion of 'space' is a pronounced difference in the actual analyses made by these theorists of tonal connection. The analyses

---

56 See also Johnson, *Philosophical Perspectives on Metaphor*, p. 23.
57 Ibid., p. 28; Max Black, 'Metaphor', *Proceedings of the Artistotelian Society, N. S.*, 55 (1954–5), pp. 273–94.
58 Kittay, *Metaphor,* p. 90.
59 Kevin Korsyn, 'Schenker and Kantian Epistemology', *Theoria*, 3 (1988), p. 8, quoting Heinrich Schenker, *Das Meisterwerk in der Musik*, 2 (1926), p. 204 (Korsyn's translation).

by Schenker and Meyer of the opening of Beethoven's Piano Sonata, *Les Adieux*, represent two different ways of hearing the passage, one emphasising the continuities which are discernible below the surface and the other drawing attention to ambiguity and the thwarting of expectation.[60] Each analysis is asserted by its author as being literally true of the music, showing that the assimilated conceptual scheme forms part of a theoretical belief system and does not lead to musical descriptions which are merely entertained as possible ways of perceiving (as one might entertain the perception of a cloud as a face). The metaphorical transference of ideas is not consciously recognised by either theorist. In Schenker's case the displacement of Kantian concepts to music is not made explicit by him because it forms part of his unchallenged intellectual framework. In Meyer's case, the transference of Gestalt ideas is assumed to be empirically founded, no incongruity between the visual conception of space and the new musical context being recognised.

Recognising that analytical judgements reflect a system of belief does not, however, discount them from including a component of aesthetic interpretation. Given that its aim is to persuade the reader to perceive in a certain way, not simply to think about the music in abstraction, the analytic notation does represent a 'perceptually embodied thought' and not simply a conceptualisation. 'Imaginative perception' and 'belief' are compatible with one another in music analysis, since both are involved in constructing a representation of the music as an intentional object. At their most persuasive, the theoretical beliefs embodied in an analysis act to influence the reader's perception, so that they become an inseparable part of an act of listening. Deconstruction of the metaphoric content of a particular belief system (such as Schenker's or Meyer's) may enrich the analyst's (or reader's) experience by allowing her to approach each system with a degree of scepticism, as one possible way of thinking and perceiving, allowing tolerance for alternatives. She can take the attitude that 'I might hear this passage *as* continuous or *as* disconnected depending on which conceptual scheme I choose', and possibly experiment with hearing it in different ways. Under these circumstances, Scruton's interpretation of hearing *as* becomes plausible. Like any other perception, one that is theoretically-informed must have a definite duration and intensity, and where alternatives are considered the perception is also more obviously subject to conscious control, satisfying Scruton's third criterion for as-

60 Schenker, *Free Composition*, trans. and ed. E. Oster (New York: Longman, 1979), vol. 2, Fig. 124.4; Leonard B. Meyer, *Explaining Music: Essays and Explorations* (Berkeley: University of California Press, 1973), p. 250, Ex. 141.

pect perception. When the metaphoric content of a theory being employed is recognised by the analyst, any particular analysis may be asserted as provisionally true, rather than as the one true representation of its object.

This appraisal of analysis presents it as a form of music criticism involving, in Scruton's terms, 'the deliberate construction of an intentional object',[61] but in it I have begged the question of whether all the structures amenable to analysis can actually be perceived. Scruton believes not, and is strongly sceptical about the value of music theory. In an article entitled 'Analytical Philosophy and the Meaning of Music' (1987) he attacks what he calls the 'false sciences and cabbalisms of musicology' as being

of no significance; not because they are badly argued, nor because they misrepresent what they describe, but because they describe the wrong thing. They offer to explain how the notes are *in themselves*, and not how they are *in the ear of the listener*.[62]

In this article, Scruton condemns the disparity between the terms of music analysis and those of aesthetic description in the strongest possible way, but he can do so only by departing from his earlier position on the intrinsic metaphoricity of musical terms. The negative judgement quoted above applies to discourse which must include the melodic, rhythmic and harmonic terms described in *The Aesthetic Understanding* as 'metaphors'. While it was there understood that metaphors referred necessarily to the 'intentional object' of a particular attitude (namely 'imaginative perception'), and thus could not avoid describing notes as they were 'in the ear of the listener', it is now found that the technical language of music theory – although it does not conform with Scruton's criteria for literal reference – fails to satisfy his earlier expectations of metaphorical utterance, and instead addresses the notes 'in themselves', with no apparent reference to the perceiver. If the terms explain notes 'in themselves' they are, for practical purposes, literal terms, but it is not Scruton's purpose here to pursue the subject of literal and metaphorical reference, so no explicit revision of his views is given. His lack of sympathy for music theory arises from an incomplete grasp of the theories themselves.[63] Implicit in his dismissal of the discipline is a false polarisation of the attitude

61 Scruton, *The Aesthetic Understanding*, p. 88.
62 Scruton, 'Analytical Philosophy and the Meaning of Music', *Journal of Aesthetics and Art Criticism*, 46 (1987), p. 171.
63 Evidence for Scruton's unfamiliarity with the details of Schenkerian theory is found in his summary of the *Ursatz*, which is incorrect (ibid., p. 171).

of *belief*, which gives rise to asserted analytical judgements, against that of 'imaginative perception', which he thinks should engender the use of descriptive metaphors (like notes 'dancing'). Scruton fails to appreciate the perceptual input and interpretive value of approaches like Schenker's, because he is looking for an explicit use of terms which might currently be recognised as metaphors – perhaps in the style characteristic of Donald Tovey – as evidence of a critical interpretation.[64]

A reappraisal of Scruton's musical aesthetics

Scruton's claim that 'music belongs uniquely to the intentional sphere and not to the material realm'[65] has been judged inadequate as a foundation for addressing the problem of musical expression because it rests on an account of metaphor which is insufficiently developed. A number of points stand out. First, straightforward empirical reasons for referring to musical space and motion can be found, even if their application deviates from the standard one used in other spheres, and there is reason neither to designate these terms as metaphors, nor to sever music from material reality on grounds of their use. Second, the attitude of imaginative perception, explained by Scruton in his discussion of visual aspects, does not have a simple relationship to the utterance of metaphor, because insufficient limits are placed on the circumstances in which it might be said to hold. Any perception must have a definite duration and intensity, as Scruton observes, but the degree to which perceptions are subject to volitional control is highly variable. Words describing such things as musical 'drama' might suggest a way of hearing music which is subject to the control of the perceiver, who expresses his imaginative involvement with an obvious metaphor. It is nonetheless difficult to classify terms neatly by asking 'How much is the perception described by this term subject to the perceiver's volition?' The psychological attitude of 'imaginative perception' might accompany some metaphorical utterances, but the criteria defining aspect perception (on which it is founded) are not, in themselves, strong enough to identify when metaphor is being used.

64 This being said, it is fair to recognise that structures beyond the lower levels of the middleground in a Schenkerian analysis might be imperceptible to those who are not experienced proponents of the theory, and that no perceptual immediacy is claimed for the background level, the kernel from which middleground structures grow. Despite the interface with music criticism, this form of analysis has a degree of autonomy, and not all of its theoretical maxims are accessible to the needs of critical interpretation conceived more broadly.

65 Scruton, *The Aesthetic Understanding*, p. 86.

Scruton implies that metaphor may also be identified as a deviation from the standard reference of a word, or as a description which does not have any single material basis (like 'dissonance', which varies with context). It cannot, however, be assumed that the attitude of 'imaginative perception' exists simply because these conditions are met. The perception of something (like dissonance) may be entirely involuntary, the label given to it being accepted as literal, and asserted as true, even if it does not conform to the empirical standard of truth set down by Scruton.

A third central point is that several levels of discourse need to be recognised in the discussion of metaphor. One of the defining criteria used by Scruton is that metaphor involves a transference of concepts between fields. Such transference may occur in the construction of music theories, so that the metaphor exists in the conceptual scheme itself (as in Schenker's organicism and the use of Kantian notions of space) rather than in any individual term taken alone. In this case the attitude appropriate to overtly recognised metaphors need not necessarily hold. Belief in the efficacy of a theory may lead analysts to make statements which are 'asserted' as true of a passage, and not simply entertained (in the manner of more ephemeral aspect perceptions). Once conceptual metaphor is recognised it might, however, suggest an attenuated certainty in the finality of any analytical judgement. It should also be recognised that a lack of obvious metaphors does not exclude perceptual content from analyses, which are made in order to persuade the reader of a way of hearing the music.

Despite difficulties in applying Scruton's ideas to music theory, his attempt to compare the grounding of judgements about structural content (through the analysis of 'harmony, melody and rhythm') with the grounding of judgements about expressive content is an interesting one. His explanation of what makes a metaphor may be inadequate, but his intuition about its significance for gaining a new orientation on questions of musical content is quite compelling. The discovery that theoretical systems have hidden metaphorical content in their most conventional (and pragmatically literal) terms, acquired in some cases through the transference of non-musical conceptions of space and motion to the application of these terms in music, must lead the theorist/analyst to eschew holding any dogmatic stance about the intrinsic objectivity of these theories. If Joseph Kerman is correct in his assessment of why systematic theories became popular in the post-war era, recognising metaphor could entail a radical shift in attitudes toward them, a shift which is already evident in current research on organic and other metaphors in Schenker's work.[66] Kerman writes that 'the appeal of systematic analysis was that it provided for a positivistic approach to art, for a criticism that could draw on precisely defined, seemingly objective operations and shun subjective criteria (and that would not even call itself criticism).'[67] Once it is recognised that even a systematic theory such as Schenker's may be grounded on conceptual metaphors which are not directly articulated due to their cultural pervasiveness at his time, there is no reason to assume that this system (or any other) has a unique and unassailable hold on musical reality, nor to condemn attempts at explaining the expressive content of a work as being intrinsically 'subjective'.

Recognising the partial dependence of an absolutist theory of music upon non-musical ideas should warn against that epistemological totalitarianism which refuses to look at any informal explanations connecting music to its historical and cultural milieu as a means of explaining its expressive content. This is the underlying point of Scruton's treatment of metaphor. If explanations of music commonly make it an 'intentional object' by treating it as the object of understanding, not as a thing which can be described 'in itself' (his sceptical comments about musicology notwithstanding), then references to qualities which derive from our own cognitive mechanisms rather than from any acoustic property of the music are bound to appear. The reference may be explicit, as when Schenker says that 'we perceive our own life-impulse in the motion of the fundamental line, a full analogy to our inner life',[68] or merely implicit in the theory's conceptual metaphors. The recognition that metaphor discloses a hidden mental reference at whatever level of discourse it occurs (by showing that the music is being treated as an intentional object) does, however, necessitate a further admission, that allusions to the expressive content of music do not belong in an entirely separate class of explanation, since they, too, demonstrate a projection onto sound of aspects of our own mentality.

66 See Robert Snarrenberg, this volume, pp. 29–56 [Ed.]
67 Joseph Kerman, *Musicology* (London: Fontana, 1985), p. 73.
68 Schenker, *Free Composition*, p. 4.

2

Competing myths: the American abandonment of Schenker's organicism

ROBERT SNARRENBERG

As is by now well known, descriptions, translations, and presentations of Schenker's texts have been marked by attempts to subdue various distasteful aspects of Schenker's world view, in particular his egotism and his disparaging attitude toward everything non-German. Even the most faithful translation, Rothgeb and Thym's translation of *Kontrapunkt*, is accompanied by a warning from Rothgeb:

We urge the reader to recognize that however much Schenker may have regarded his musical precepts as an integral part of a unified world-view, they are, in fact, not at all logically dependent on any of his extramusical speculations. Indeed, no broader philosophical context is necessary – or even relevant – to their understanding.[1]

Rothgeb continues a tradition of thinking whose most notorious manifestation is without doubt the mangled translation of *Der freie Satz*. The work was started by Oswald Jonas, who, for the second German edition (1956), cut nearly one fifth of the foreword and first chapter and rearranged what was left.[2] Ernst Oster's translation, which began life in a draft by Allen Forte,[3] left nearly all of Jonas's emendations in place. The editors of *Free Composition* eventually furnished translations of most, though by no means all, of the deleted material, without, however, mentioning Jonas's reordering of paragraphs and sentences. In his 'Introduction to the English Edition', Forte colluded with Jonas and Oster by counselling readers to ignore Schenker's 'polemical and quasi-philosophical material' because it lacked 'substantive relation' to Schenker's theory of musical structure.[4]

---

1 Heinrich Schenker, *Counterpoint*, trans. J. Rothgeb and J. Thym, ed. J. Rothgeb (New York: Schirmer, 1987) [1: *Cantus Firmus and Two-Voice Counterpoint*; 2: *Counterpoint in Three and More Voices, Bridges to Free Composition*], p. xiv.
2 Schenker, *Der freie Satz* [*Neue musikalische Theorien und Phantasien*, 3], ed. and rev. O. Jonas (Vienna: Universal Edition, 1956).
3 See Allen Forte, 'Ernst Oster (1908–1977) In Memoriam', *Journal of Music Theory*, 21/ii (1977), p. 341.
4 Schenker, *Free Composition*, trans. and ed. E. Oster (New York: Longman, 1979),

While such attention was being lavished on Schenker's polemical excesses, there was another, less well known attempt underway to subdue Schenker's rhetoric. This assault on Schenker's writing was not carried out with as much fanfare, but it has had a much more lasting and radical effect on the practice of Schenkerian theory. This was the effort made by Forte and other writers to change the aesthetic commitments of Schenkerian discourse. William Rothstein, in a perceptive essay on Schenker's American reception, narrates the sociological history that led American writers to shun the 'poetic flights so characteristic of Schenker, Jonas, and Oster' in favour of the cool, rational, scientific dialect of the American academy.[5] In order to be accepted into the academy, music theorists had to demonstrate their acceptance of its creeds. The anti-dogma rule, for one, writes Rothstein, compelled Schenkerians to moderate their rhetoric, to cease and desist from making the impassioned claim that Schenker's is the only one true approach to tonal music. Acceptance of such rules affected the rhetorical tone of Schenkerian discourse in ways which Rothstein brings into focus by using a series of verbal oppositions (see Table 2.1).[6] To Rothstein's analysis I would add that the rhetoric which replaced Schenker's was no less figurative for its being scientific.

In this essay I shall demonstrate that the reaction of the Schenkerians was not an outright dismissal of figurative speech, but rather a dismissal of figures considered discordant with the prevailing myths of the academy, and, as a result, a partial abandonment of Schenker's aesthetic. Schenkerian writers are seldom as explicit as Schenker about their aesthetic commitments, and so I have had to use a more circuitous means for demonstrating this claim. What I found, as I read Schenker in German

p. xviii. More and more one finds expressions of discomfort with the editorial handling of Schenker's texts: see, for example, William Drabkin, 'The New Erläuterungs-ausgabe', *Perspectives of New Music*, 12 (1973–4), pp. 319–30; Joseph Dubiel, 'A Schenker Analysis and Some of Schenker's Theories', paper delivered at the Society for Music Theory, Philadelphia, 1984; and Nicholas Cook, 'Schenker's Theory of Music as Ethics', *Journal of Musicology*, 7/iv (1989), pp. 415–39. The point of Cook's essay is to establish that 'if we want to understand Schenker's thinking about music in his own terms, rather than simply ours, then we should not . . . discount the polemical and quasi-philosophical nature of his writings' (p. 416).

5 William Rothstein, 'The Americanization of Heinrich Schenker', *In Theory Only*, 9/i (1986), pp. 5–17; repr. in Hedi Siegel (ed.), *Schenker Studies* (Cambridge: Cambridge University Press, 1990), pp. 193–203.

6 Rothstein cites the younger scholars Charles Burkhart and Carl Schachter as examples of a second phase of Schenkerism in America that he sees as a 'synthesis of fairly orthodox Schenkerian thought with a more relaxed rhetoric' (ibid., p. 13). Marion Guck's analysis of Schachter's writing supports this assessment ('Analytical Fictions', paper delivered at the Society for Music Theory, Oakland, 1990).

Table 2.1   Verbal oppositions used by Rothstein to depict a shift in
Schenkerian rhetoric

Viennese	*American*
poetic	sober
poet	scientist
fire	dispassionate
flowery	dryness
dogmatic	objective
claim to truth	scholarly
philosophical	rationalism
prophet	cool taxonomist

and Schenkerian literature in English, was that aesthetic differences were obliquely manifested in the metaphorical weave of the texts. I begin, then, by examining one of Schenker's favourite rhetorical figures – the metaphor of human procreation. After tracing some of the ways in which this metaphor threads through his writings, I examine the transformation and eventual replacement of this metaphor during the period when a Schenkerian discursive practice emerged in America, from the early 1930s through to the publication of *Free Composition* in 1979. Finally, I reflect on the rhetorical role of such metaphors as a kind of myth. My aim in singling out this particular metaphorical shift in Schenkerian rhetoric is not so much to claim that inattention to the metaphoric weave of Schenker's texts, deliberate or not, has given rise to misunderstandings of his ideas, though that is undoubtedly the case, but more to exemplify a point that is pressing for the future of theoretical discourse, which is that the central metaphors by means of which authors shape their musical conceptions inescapably affect the kinds of activities and aesthetic attitudes that readers find themselves invited to adopt.[7]

Schenker's metaphors of procreation

Schenker uses the figure of procreation to articulate one of the primary tenets of his first major speculative essay, 'Der Geist der musikalischen Technik': namely, that the true nature of music consists in the free play

7 My analyses of Schenker's rhetoric and that of Forte and other Schenkerian writers is deeply indebted to recent work by Marion Guck, in particular her paper 'Analytical Fictions', which was first presented, along with an earlier version of the present essay, at the Society for Music Theory, Oakland, 1990. I am also indebted to the many stimulating conversations we have had about these matters. Both papers are discussed in Henry Kingsbury, 'Sociological Factors in Musicological Poetics', *Ethnomusicology*, 35/ii (1991), pp. 195–219.

of the composer's imagination giving birth (*hervorbringen*) to melodic content.[8] He prepares his discussion of the fertile free play of the composer's imagination by making a distinction between improper and proper uses of the term *organisch*. The term is often used, he says, to induce false beliefs about aspects of music that are really a matter of compositional artifice: 'They put a veil and make-up on her [i. e. artifice]' in order that the artificially produced whole would seem to appear 'naturally born'. People had come to believe that 'there rests in the artificial formation precisely such a necessity as rests in a natural organism'. Consequently, 'the highest praise paid today to a musical artwork is to say that the work is "organically" built'.[9] The crux of Schenker's objection, as William Pastille points out, is that without a true 'causal nexus' there can be no legitimate talk of something organic in music.[10] No law of cause and effect governs the succession of melodies or moods in a musical work, and we cannot assume that one follows organically after another merely because they are in that order.[11] The only connection between melodies or moods that we can infer, says Schenker, is that the composer

---

8 Schenker, 'Der Geist der musikalischen Technik', *Musikalisches Wochenblatt* (Leipzig), 26/xix (1895), pp. 245–6; 26/xx, pp. 257–9; 26/xxi, pp. 273–4; 26/xxii, pp. 285–6; 26/xxiii, pp. 297–8; 26/xxiv–xxv, pp. 309–10; 26/xxvi, pp. 325–6; repr. in Hellmut Federhofer, *Heinrich Schenker: Nach Tagebüchern und Briefen in der Oswald Jonas Memorial Collection, University of California, Riverside* (Hildesheim, Georg Olms, 1985), pp. 135–54. For discussion of Schenker's views in this and other early essays, see Allan Keiler, 'The Origins of Schenker's Thought: How Man is Musical', *Journal of Music Theory*, 33/ii (1989), pp. 273–98.

9 Schenker, 'Der Geist', pp. 297–8. This is an ironic caricature of what his contemporaries thought high praise; Schenker, who will seldom borrow words from the language of architecture (English translations notwithstanding), here juxtaposes the organic with the built, mocking his contemporaries with the oxymoron.

10 William A. Pastille, 'Heinrich Schenker, Anti-Organicist', *Nineteenth-Century Music*, 8/i (1984), pp. 29–36. Pastille recognises Schenker's critique of the term's misuse but ignores Schenker's effort to recuperate the term *organisch* in 'Der Geist' and, more importantly, the broader biological metaphor. Pastille tells us that Schenker 'firmly denies that music can be organic', quoting him as saying 'In reality, musical content is never organic' (p. 31) – Schenker: 'In der That ist kein musikalischer Inhalt organisch' ('Der Geist', p. 309) – but he fails to indicate that Schenker argues in the end for a proper use of *organisch*. Pastille's title, 'Heinrich Schenker: Anti-Organicist', therefore seems more hyperbolic than descriptive (the same criticism of Pastille's essay is made in Keiler, 'The Origins of Schenker's Thought'). Furthermore, although Pastille concludes in the end that Schenker's later acceptance of organicist ideas is predicated on his notion of genius as one whose compositional acts are beyond consciousness, he fails to acknowledge that this theme is explicitly expressed in 'Der Geist' – indeed, in the very passage that concludes the translated excerpt in the appendix to his article.

11 For discussion of causality in Schenker's writings, see Kevin Korsyn, 'Schenker and Kantian Epistemology', *Theoria*, 3 (1988), pp. 44–50.

exercised his will and chose their ordering – he produced order through artifice. One of the main tasks of *Harmonielehre* will be to sort out more precisely what contributions are made by artifice and Nature in the creation of the musical art. Here Schenker announces that his contemporaries are mistaken about where to draw the line between Nature and artifice.

Insofar, then, as it assumes a law of cause and effect, the natural-scientific notion of the organic has no application to the internal chronology of the musical artwork; we would be deluded to think that the artifices of harmony and counterpoint are anything more than simulations of causality.[12] Later in 'Der Geist', however, he claims to know something about music that does, in fact, fit the scientific concept of 'organic':

The imagination (*Phantasie*), after it has given birth to a specific entity (*Gebilde*), is practically besieged by many such entities of a similar nature, and the power of these similar entities over the composer is often so irresistible that he includes them in the content to be built without their similarities ever having reached his consciousness.[13] Often – and one can only guess this through very devoted observation of the artwork – the composer would have preferred to conjure up a completely dissimilar entity, and behold, the imagination does not depart from her first-found type and simply forces upon him a similar one. Cannot the principle 'Omnis natura vult esse conservatrix sui' now be justly applied to this?

This organic phenomenon, however, is naturally only organic so long as it is not sullied by consciousness. In the instant when the composer has commended to his imagination the path and the hunt for similarities, what to us could easily seem otherwise organic sinks to the merely '*thematic*', that is, *what is willed as similar*. What is organic on this account is something that is only to be dealt with hypothetically and cautiously: it is assumed that every similarity the composer has *not willed* actually arose *organically* in the imagination.[14]

12 Earlier in the essay Schenker writes that harmony 'helps music to deceive itself and the listener about the problem of a logic and a causal nexus' ('Der Geist', p. 274). In *Harmonielehre*, as well as in later writings, he will use the image of logical consequentiality to depict the inexorable pull of a harmonic progression.

13 One wonders whether Schenker knew of Brahms's response to Schubring's analysis of thematic relations in the German Requiem. Brahms writes, 'I disagree that in the third movement the themes of the different sections have something in common. . . . If it is nevertheless so – I deliberately [*absichtlich*] call back nothing from my memory – I want no praise for it, but do confess that when I am working, my thoughts do not fly far enough away, and thus unintentionally come back, often with the same idea.' The translation here is by Walter Frisch (*Brahms and the Principle of Developing Variation* (Berkeley and Los Angeles: University of California Press, 1984), p. 31), who has many interesting things to say about the passage and about Schoenberg's attitude toward the unconscious in composition.

14 Schenker, 'Der Geist', p. 310. The same view of imagination, without the biological metaphor, is articulated some years later in Schenker's *Ein Beitrag zur Ornamentik* (Vienna: Universal Edition, rev. 1908), when, speaking of C. P. E. Bach's imagination,

The composer's imagination is portrayed in this passage as a feminine figure who propagates a species of melody. So long as the composer's will (a masculine figure?) does not intrude on this natural process, her compositional process is organic, and the melodious composition is legitimate. In later writings, Schenker will be more precise in his description of the composer's unconscious imagination. One might even go so far as to say that the purpose of his theory is to explicate the compositional habits of the master composers: how the laws of figured bass, harmony, and counterpoint, instilled through thorough practice, created a psychological disposition whence spontaneous, improvisatory composition could arise.[15] The composer's consciousness is, in fact, so far removed from the organic process that Schenker in some places uses the image of melodic birth without giving roles to either the composer or his imagination, instead personifying music: 'Repetition, this original invention of music, might now best demonstrate that music has already for centuries *borne in its own womb a secure formative principle of its own.*'[16]

In the essay's concluding paragraph, Schenker turns the image of procreation against a promiscuous formalist conception of music:

To me, however, the superficial cataloguing of [musical] ideas [i. e. themes], as I portrayed it above, proves most surely how strong, even today, is the musical instinct that seems to say: *the actual nature of music is creating melodies*, which, like folk songs, live together freely and independently, family-like and conciliatory, and which, like the first humans in Paradise, can bustle about naked and unclothed in the paradise of music. Indeed, since music put on fig leaves and became Art, one began to reckon how many entities could actually be welded together; one melody, so to speak, established a hearth, and [then] families came, and [then] a dense population, for which there is unfortunately no Malthusian law![17]

he writes, 'When the first idea is done with, in the same moment there is already a second one – unbidden, unintended, unwilled. One may in this sense call his imagination a completely unintentional and unforced imagination.' (p. 11) This view is also expressed in the well-known 'sleepwalker' passage in *Harmonielehre* [*Neue musikalische Theorien und Phantasien*, 1] (Stuttgart: J. G. Cotta, 1906), pp. 76–7, §29.

15 Schenker's earliest discussion of the importance of compositional habit and its connection with what listeners do is found in 'Das Hören in der Musik', *Neue Revue*, 5/xxxii (1894), pp. 15–21 (repr. in Hellmut Federhofer (ed.), *Heinrich Schenker als Essayist und Kritiker: Gesammelte Aufsätze, Rezensionen und kleinere Berichte aus den Jahren 1891–1901* (Hildesheim, Georg Olms, 1990), pp. 96–103). His concluding paragraph is quite interesting with respect to his later writings, for in it he speaks of the hope that the ear might find a lofty place from which it could survey the entire content of a musical work: 'Whoever finds this pinnacle – from which the composer, too, must unfurl his work – may safely say he has "heard" the work.' (p. 103)

16 Schenker, 'Der Geist', p. 297.

17 Ibid., p. 326.

Schenker here sets out his belief that the creation of melody must take place in a proper, legally sanctioned setting. In later writings he will depict this creation as the product of a monogamous union: melody born of one triad and one passing.

Schenker returns to music's biological dimension eleven years later in *Harmonielehre*.[18] On the second page of his foreword he draws special attention to this facet of his 'new musical theories and fantasies':

Particular value I thought should be laid in general on the biological moments in the life of tones. If we would only just become friends with the thought that the tones have an actual life of their own, a life which in its animality seems more independent of the artist than one would venture to assume! (p. vi)

In the first chapter it becomes clear that this biological life is key to music's artfulness. The first theme of the chapter is how music became an art with the discovery of repetition, and, as in 'Der Geist', Schenker presents repetition as a procreative principle:

One eventually gets in the habit of seeing tones as creatures; one gets in the habit of assuming biological drives are inherent in them as they are in the living being. Are we not faced, then, with an equation:

In Nature: procreative drive → repetition → individual kind.

And in the world of tone, just this: procreative drive → repetition → individual motive. (p. 6, §4)[19]

Despite his earlier apprehension about using organic language to describe compositional artifice, Schenker seems to have decided that the benefits of that habit of speaking outweigh the problems that flow from mistakenly attributing causality to music. Since Schenker recognises that his use of organic language is figurative, an acquired linguistic habit, in contrast to the literal-minded uses he earlier thought improper, we will need to ask, at a later point, what purpose is served in using such imagery.

Schenker also uses a procreation metaphor in *Harmonielehre* to model his concept of the harmonic system. The basic material of music, supplied by Nature, is endowed with its own procreative impulses: a fundamental gives birth to its first overtone, which in turn gives birth to the second, and so forth; this family line comprises the major triad, Schenker's *Naturklang* (pp. 40–42, §13). Each overtone, too, has a desire

---

18 Passages quoted in the following discussion are translated by the author from the German edition (1906, see n. 14). [Ed.]
19 Cf. 'Even the *Urlinie* hearkens to the law of procreation, that is, the law of repetition' (Schenker, 'Die Urlinie (Eine Vorbemerkung)', *Der Tonwille*, 1 (1921), p. 22).

to become a parent in its own right, to be the head, as it were, of its own family line. This desire is what he calls the natural egoism of the tones, each seeking to be the root of a *Stufe*. (In later writings this idea takes on added significance by providing for the generation of voice-leading layers, as each passing tone within an *Urlinie* seeks the comfort of its own immediate consonant family.) The initial generation of the fundamental thus spreads like a genealogical tree (p. 36, §10).[20] Schenker uses generational proximity (parent–child) to underscore the systematic importance of the fifth relation (pp. 42–3, §14) and from this devises a series of the fundamental's 'descendants', the naturally ascending (!) series of perfect fifths.[21] It is this series that models relations and movements among and between scale degrees. The artist enters the picture at this point with a limiting device: where Nature had only offered unending procreation and development, the artist, by inverting the direction of motion through fifths (i. e. descending through the series), invented a means for ending Nature's proliferation and producing closure through a return to Nature's origin (p. 44, §16).[22]

The procreative play of tones, however, is only the origin of life in the tonal system. The conduct of that life requires a consideration of social relations among the tones. Here the artist again enters the picture, now making a more active contribution:

The artist now stood before the ultimately difficult task in his art of uniting in one system all these [procreative] urges of the individual tones – their fundamental quality, as it were – and also the relations of tones to one another. . . .

For on one hand stood the egoism of the tones, the right to retain their own fifth and major third as a fundamental, in short, the right to their own generation, while on the other hand the interests of universality, that is, of the community that will be produced through more intimate intercourse, demanded a sacrifice from the generations. (pp. 43–4, §15)[23]

20 See also p. 42, §13. Schenker's analogy – the genealogical tree of Christoph Bach – suggests that the tone is masculine, since the tree is patrilineal. The insistence on the role of nature (*die Natur*), however, feminises the tonal procreation.
21 Schenker has to finagle at this point, for the fifth, in terms of the metaphor, is twice removed from the fundamental and not its first descendant, as he claims in §12 (p. 39). One might reason, however, that the octave is but a repetition, whereas the fifth is the first reproduction.
22 One of the marks of *Künstlichkeit* in *Harmonielehre* and in later writings is the artist's use of a limiting device. In addition to cutting short the progressive cycle of fifths, he abbreviates the number of motivic repetitions (§6) by eliminating ones that do not further clarify the character of the motive, and he abbreviates the space in which the tones of the *Naturklang* are presented (§13; cf. *Der freie Satz* [*Neue musikalische Theorien und Phantasien*, 3] (Vienna: Universal Edition, 1935), §1).
23 See also pp. 54–5, §18. The figure of tonal intercourse is repeated on p. 197 (§82):

Schenker thus pictures music as a kind of natural system with which the artist has to contend as an outsider, a system whose laws and practices are set forth in *Harmonielehre* and in the two volumes of *Kontrapunkt*.[24] But the artist is not master of the system:

I all the more urgently invite every music lover not to lose sight of what remarkable forces of Nature and what artistic drives are kept hidden behind [the major system].

. . . a considerable part of the system is the completely original property of the artist . . . so the system as a whole is to be comprehended only as a compromise between Nature and Art, a mixture of the natural and the artistic, though, to be sure, with the power of Nature overwhelming, which of course had been the point of departure.[25]

In this fuller statement on the role of the artist vis-à-vis the tonal system and, as in the explanation of the organic compositional process in 'Der Geist', Schenker leaves the reins of power clearly in the hands of a feminine figure, Nature.

Schenker has been telling stories in which a paternal figure is distinctly absent and in which (pro)creative agency is attributed primarily to feminine figures: Mother Nature and her surrogate, the composer's imagination. Having introduced the metaphor of procreation, however, Schenker is bound to find a paternal agent, for the presence of such a mother figure tends to bring with it the trappings associated with it in normal usage and Schenker is not one to miss the obvious potential of his rhetorical figures. Not only is such an agent necessary to complete the image of human conception, but such a thoroughgoing feminisation of genius would be unconscionable to a man who, in the foreword to his first book on counterpoint, writes the following:

Even today one no longer understands the simplest things. Everything in the world surely has a connection and is necessary, but for this reason alone, however, i. e. merely because of this necessity, each and all do not alike have the same

'Hence, [the scale degrees], speaking metaphorically, have intercourse only among themselves.'

24 Schenker recounts and expands upon these various fragments of the tones' biological life in 'Biological Arguments of the Principle of Mixture', (*Harmonielehre*, pp. 106–7, §38). He tells us in *Kontrapunkt* that 'tones . . . are as living beings with their own social laws' (*Kontrapunkt: Cantus Firmus und Zweistimmiger Satz* [*Neue musikalische Theorien und Phantasien*, 2/i] (Stuttgart and Berlin: J. G. Cotta, 1910), p. 24) and that there are 'social relations among tones' (*Kontrapunkt: Drei- und Mehrstimmiger Satz, Übergänge zum freien Satz* [*Neue musikalische Theorien und Phantasien*, 2/ii] (Vienna: Universal Edition, 1922), p. xiv).

25 Schenker, *Harmonielehre*, pp. 55, 59, §19.

value. The husband (*der Mann*) – mind you, with a necessity that in other respects remains the same – nevertheless has greater value than the wife (*die Frau*), the producer more than the merchant or the labourer. . . . The genius means more than the people.[26]

As if to rectify the imbalance resulting from the prominent roles assigned to feminine elements in his discussions of music's birth, Schenker eventually creates a role for a significant and more valuable masculine figure.

The theoretical groundwork for a more complete image of procreation is laid in the middle of *Harmonielehre*, where, in a lengthy note appended to an explanation of the 'Physiognomy of Free Composition', Schenker defends a claim that the horizontal dimension of music has more value than the vertical:

From the fact that the principal element in music, even after the addition of the vertical dimension, nevertheless ever remains the horizontal line, thus melody itself, and that in this sense the vertical direction is a secondary element . . . , it follows finally and incontrovertibly how then in general the spirit of harmony is perhaps at bottom only called upon to make broad melodic plans arise systematically and at the same time to organise them.[27]

It would have been quite easy to have mapped the male–female distinction onto the opposition of vertical and horizontal elements, say by identifying the horizontal with Nature's triad and the vertical with some artistic device of man. Such a straightforward mapping, however, would allow no role for the triad in the horizontal dimension, which is surely undesirable if one is going to make the traversal of consonant intervals (the *Zug*) the hallmark of the horizontal. So while the femininity of the vertical triad may be clear, it is not so clear how Schenker will gender the horizontal. At any rate, Schenker makes it clear in §88 that the horizontal element manifests itself unmistakably in the dissonant passing tone, his model for all musical motion. It is interesting to note that, although Schenker does not yet explicitly identify the passing tone in the formation of the seventh chord (§99), he portrays the dissonant seventh as manifesting an agency which lies outside the realm of Nature. The passing effect of that agency is wrought in the temporal-horizontal dimension; the effectual agent is the masculine composer.

the seventh-chord steps beyond Nature's directions and therefore must be regarded purely as a product of Art. . . . Obviously, the artist was charmed [by the prospect of] muddying the purely natural effect of the triad in passing

26 Schenker, *Kontrapunkt*, vol. 1, p. xi.
27 Schenker *Harmonielehre*, p. 214, §88 (note).

Example 2.1

(*vorübergehend*), in order to engender a certain tension and the expected return of the pure triad, [and] by that, to turn it all the more effectively, as it were, into a higher affirmation of Nature as the familiar godmother of the triad.[28]

The passing effect, says Schenker, results from the artist's assumption of an active role in relation to Nature's passive triad.

The passing dissonance, as one would expect, is treated more carefully in *Kontrapunkt*, particularly in the discussion of second species in three parts.[29] The passing dissonance (see Ex. 2.1) does not erase the original consonance; on the contrary, it extends the influence of that consonance, an idea which Schenker represents by the semibreve in parentheses (Ex. 2.1b).

It is precisely the dissonant passing tone that confirms the harmony of the downbeat more reliably and emphatically than the consonant upbeat. . . . The implications of this effect are highly significant: we recognise in the dissonant passing tone the most reliable, indeed the sole, bearer of melodic content.[30]

It is only a small step from here to the *Ursatz* as a quasi–second species representation of tonal music: a representation of the chord of Nature, its extension in time, and the filling of one of its spaces with a descending passing motion.[31]

This second-species model of tonality is quite often presented in *Der Tonwille* and *Das Meisterwerk in der Musik* in terms of the metaphor of procreation. The masculine element begins to assume a more definite form in these metaphorical pictures. In the first issue of *Der Tonwille*, Schenker writes that 'the *Urlinie* harbours in itself the seed of all the

---

28 Ibid., p. 242, §99. The first explicit connection between sevenths and passing tones is stated in the 'Vorwort' to the first volume of *Kontrapunkt* (p. xxxiii), where Schenker summarises the concept of *Stufe* presented in *Harmonielehre*. Schenker says he had already made the connection in *Harmonielehre*, contrary to what Jonas claims in his footnote to §99 of the English translation (Schenker, *Harmony*, ed. O. Jonas, trans. E. M. Borgese (Chicago: University of Chicago Press, 1954), p. 188). In the same passage of *Kontrapunkt*, Schenker applies the procreative metaphor to the scale degree, there identifying it as a mother of content (*Inhaltserzeugerin*).

29 Schenker, *Kontrapunkt*, vol. 2, pp. 56–70.

30 Ibid., p. 59.

31 This definition of tonal music is adumbrated at least as early as §88 of *Harmonielehre*,

powers that shape tonal life'.[32] He tells us a bit more about the seed of life in the second yearbook of *Das Meisterwerk*: 'As humans, animals, and plants are figurations of the tiniest seed . . . so also are the compositions of the genius figurations of only a few intervals.'[33] On the following page he introduces a feminine element to complement the masculine seed: 'Only because of its emergence from the *Urlinie*'s motherly womb is an inner unity even possible for diminution; this unity becomes the figure of the whole and alone is the organic element in music.'[34] Schenker thus portrays the *Urlinie* with both feminine and masculine features: seed and womb. The scale degree is a triad, a feminine figure, who, when fertilised with passing tones, gives birth to content (linear progressions, thence melody). In the first yearbook of *Das Meisterwerk*, he identifies the parents:

Music is a living motion of tones in a naturally-given space, a composing out, a melodicising and horizontalising of the chord given in Nature. The law of all life – motion – which as a procreation transcends the limits of individual existence, is borne by man into the chord which Nature has prescribed in advance in his ear. Everything in music depends on this motion, on this procreation.[35]

The masculine element has gained considerably in these pictures, for the activity of music is cast in terms of the composer's activity and its musical manifestation, the passing tone.[36]

where the following figure (omitted in the translation) illustrates his remarks on the connection between strict and free composition:

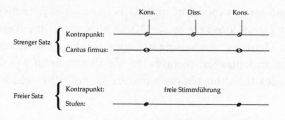

32 Schenker, 'Die Urlinie (Eine Vorbemerkung)', p. 22.
33 Schenker, 'Fortsetzung der Urlinie-Betrachtungen', *Das Meisterwerk in der Musik*, 2 (1926), p. 40.
34 Ibid., p. 41.
35 Schenker, 'Die Kunst der Improvisation', *Das Meisterwerk in der Musik*, 1 (1925), p.12.
36 Schenker is not thoroughly consistent in his gendering of *Stufe* and *Durchgang*. Although in most cases the *Stufe* and the vertical are gendered feminine in the manner I have just described, the following passage casts the horizontal element in a feminine role: 'The temporal-horizontal element of musical motion, *no matter how one wishes to*

It is this active component that Schenker has in mind when he writes in *Der freie Satz* that the *Urlinie* signifies motion, as does its counterpart, the bass arpeggiation,[37] for he is speaking here of the motion of *Auskomponierung*, a motion rooted in the passing tone of the *Urlinie* and its reproduction in diminution. The effectual agent of *Auskomponierung* is, of course, the composer. Nature's triad, because it is a static simultaneity, is incapable of giving the effect of movement. Only when the composer acts upon that triad, turning the simultaneous into the successive and creating unmistakable movement in passing tones, does a tonal life begin to take shape.[38] To search for any other form of music, he writes in *Der freie Satz*, is as fruitless as the alchemist's search for a homunculus.[39] Only music conceived of the *Ursatz* is fully human. And, more importantly, man's contribution to the conception of music – in particular his hallmark, the passing tone – receives the higher value (though the triad is, of course, necessary and there is a mutual dependence). Schenker thereby restores the order that he sorely missed in the world around him: at least man's rightful place in the world of tone is assured: the husband is rightly valued more than the wife.

Schenker, well aware of the usefulness of rhetorical figures, does not let the rhetorical potential of his birth metaphor lie fallow. Just as he eventually supplied a father figure in order to complete the procreative act, so too does he give us a child who grows to maturity. In the last yearbook of *Das Meisterwerk* he spells out his familiar theory of levels in terms of this very metaphor:

But the depth-connection from background to foreground is also the breadth-connection in the horizontal of the foreground: such a connection, even taken biologically, constitutes the actual organic [aspect], the synthesis of a tonal piece, its living breath. Just as man, as a living being, passes from his first existence in his mother's womb, from his first cry at the moment of birth, through all the years of childhood and maturity up into old age, living through a development of body and mind as from a background out to a foreground, so too in the fantasy of the genius, who sees clairvoyantly into the depths and breadths, does a living art-thing develop from a background to a foreground.[40]

explain its laws, is therefore that which alone gives birth [*hervorbringt*] to musical content and secures its organic coherence.' (Schenker, 'Rameau oder Beethoven? Erstarrung oder geistiges Leben in der Musik?', *Das Meisterwerk in der Musik*, 3 (1930), p. 12)
37 Schenker, *Der freie Satz* (1935), pp. 16–17.
38 Cf. ibid., p. 30, §1.
39 Ibid., p. 27.
40 Schenker, 'Rameau oder Beethoven?', p. 20.

Schenker's reasons for using a personifying figure to present his model of free composition are encapsulated in the first issue of *Der Tonwille*, in a passage that rails against the excesses of 'certain muscle-men of expression' and 'certain hermeneutic babblers of affect'.[41] After using the concept of the *Urlinie* to extricate the artistic evolution of instrumental music from the traditional explanation that it is rooted in dance music, Schenker uses the concept to chastise those who would define music's artistic quality in terms of a 'poetic idea'. He concludes that 'music remains a world unto itself'. But just here, where one would expect him to draw the line between the extra-musical and the truly musical more sharply than ever, Schenker surprises us, for although the expression mongers and affect babblers too often sweep analogies of human life over into music, their fault lies more in the direction of analogical superfluity than in the mere use of such analogies: 'How', asks Schenker, 'should a humanly conceived art *not* contain the human?'

Schenker's surprising turn is rooted in his belief that a human artefact which so deeply engages the most ingenious members of society cannot fail to reflect the humanity of its creators. This is the source of Schenker's humanising of music, and the language of procreation is but one manifestation. A paragraph from early in *Der freie Satz* draws out this connection by echoing one of the procreation stories found in *Harmonielehre*:

Music is not an object of theoretical observation alone; it is a subject just as we ourselves are subjects. Indeed, the octave, fifth, and third of the overtone series are an organic function of the tone as subject just as man's drives are organic.[42]

Commenting on this passage, Kevin Korsyn writes:

Music is subject because its unity parallels that of a cognitive subject. It is this analogy to the structure of our minds that enables us . . . to have, in Buber's terms, an I-Thou relationship with music. Schenker's theory explains why music matters so intensely to us.[43]

41 Schenker, 'Die Urlinie (Eine Vorbemerkung)', pp. 22–3.
42 Schenker, *Der freie Satz* (1935), p. 27.
43 Korsyn, 'Schenker and Kantian Epistemology', p. 39. There is a paper to be written here on the possibility that what Schenker has in mind is more Hegelian than Kantian. Hegel writes, 'What [music] claims as its own is the depth of a person's inner life as such; it is the art of the soul and is directly addressed to the soul. . . . Its content is what is subjective in itself, and its expression likewise does not produce an object persisting in space but shows through its free unstable soaring that it is a communication which, instead of having stability on its own account, is carried by the inner subjective life, and is to exist for that life alone.' (G. W. F. Hegel, *Aesthetics: Lectures on Fine Art*, trans. T. M. Knox, 2 vols. (Oxford: Clarendon Press, 1975), pp. 891–2).

Achieving this explanatory effect is precisely what I believe to be Schenker's motivation for using procreation metaphors.

Jamie Kassler, in an essay that argues a convincing alternative to the typically botanical construal of Schenker's organicism, also suggests that Schenker's primary model for music is human consciousness:

For Schenker, evolutionary processes cannot be reduced to natural selection, to dialectics or to any other mechanistic principle. To describe creative evolution, Schenker employs a psychophysical parallelism, for he treats music as the image of human consciousness. . . . Schenker holds that mind is an epiphenomenon of the physical world: ideas create our world; and music, as an image of consciousness, also creates, since the causes of its unfolding are immanent within the system of tonality itself.[44]

Korsyn arrives at the same conclusion, that 'an organic composition is alive in much the same sense that a mind is alive',[45] but he connects this imaginary life to the imagination of those who create or otherwise experience the music:

When Schenker charges, for example, 'that Rameau's theoretical following has arrived at a dead point', his accusation is not merely a polemical thrust. The single instant that is not apprehended through time-consciousness is dead, since consciousness, which is alive, requires manifoldness grasped in unity.[46]

The grasping of a manifold, which for both Kant and Schenker is a matter of making mental connections, is cast by Schenker in terms of procreation:

If a person's tonal sense is not mature enough to be able to bind tones into traversals (*Zügen*) and to lead off [more] traversals from [the first] traversals, that person is obviously lacking in musical far-sightedness and in procreative love: only living love composes and leads to traversals and coherence.[47]

---

44 Jamie C. Kassler, 'Heinrich Schenker's Epistemology and Philosophy of Music: An Essay on the Relations between Evolutionary Theory and Music Theory', in David Oldroyd and Ian Langham (eds.), *The Wider Domain of Evolutionary Thought* (Dordrecht: Reidel, 1983), p. 247. The literature on Schenker's so-called organicism does not distinguish his decided preference for distinctively human images from his occasional uses of botanical or zoological figures. See Pastille, 'Heinrich Schenker, Anti-Organicist'; Ruth A. Solie, 'The Living Work: Organicism and Musical Analysis', *Nineteenth-Century Music*, 4 (1980), pp. 147–56; Gary W. Don, 'Goethe and Schenker', *In Theory Only*, 10/viii (1988), pp. 1–14; and Nadine M. Hubbs, 'Musical Organicism and Its Alternatives' (PhD dissertation, University of Michigan, 1990).
45 Korsyn, 'Schenker and Kantian Epistemology', pp. 24–5.
46 Ibid., p. 32.
47 Schenker, *Der freie Satz* (1935), p. 20.

To bind tones together mentally into traversals of consonant spaces is to bind individuals together into a group, a family as it were, which has more significance than a mere sum.

Procreation, then, is one among several rhetorical means whereby Schenker prepares readers to accept the idea that music is infused with subjectivity, that it is capable, as Korsyn puts it, of sustaining an I-Thou relationship. The idea is equally evident in the way he speaks of 'tonal will' and the dramatic roles of motives. Even the cantus firmus in strict counterpoint, writes Schenker, even 'the little organism, artificially produced with the observation of so many prohibitions, nevertheless has its own soul!'[48] Schenker, in short, interprets the musical work as a fully human image, using a wide range of personifying imagery to describe musical meanings, imagery ranging from procreation and physical gesture to mental states. An example of the latter appears in his discussion of the prohibition against diminished fourths in the cantus firmus:

The tortuously beautiful and overpowering diminished fourths in the development of the last movement of Mozart's G-Minor Symphony [bars 191–202] result from the following: Mozart, having thus far shaped the motive currently in use from one single triad or seventh-chord [as in bars 1–2 and 5–6], now for the first time, and indeed within the space of a single bar, bends it to fit two different harmonies. He thus creates the impression of an enormously vehement tearing asunder of the former whole, as though in the most frenzied mental state [*Stimmung*], so that the counterpoint in each case is forced to follow the two different harmonies and, in so doing, to produce the diminished fourth (and also the augmented fifth in the bass).[49]

Because its notes belong unmistakably to different triads, the diminished fourth gives the impression of disunity, hence mental disequilibrium (the justification for prohibiting such intervals lies in the desire always to maintain equilibrium in the cantus firmus). One might say that the qualities of the *Stimmung* supervene on the triadic effects of the diminished fourth.[50]

---

48 'Der kleine, mit Beobachtung so vieler Verbote künstlich hergestellte Organismus hat dennoch auch seine Seele!' (*Kontrapunkt*, vol. 1, p. 134). Rothgeb and Thym translate the end of the statement as 'has its own animation', thereby depersonalising the figure (Schenker, *Counterpoint*, vol. 1, p. 95).

49 Schenker, *Counterpoint*, vol. 1, pp. 69–70. The original passage is in *Kontrapunkt*, vol. 1, pp. 98–9.

50 On Schenker's concept of *Wirkung*, see Dubiel, '"When You are a Beethoven": Kinds of Rules in Schenker's Counterpoint', *Journal of Music Theory*, 34/ii (1990), pp. 291–340.

The American abandonment

Despite its pervasiveness in Schenker's writings, biological imagery figures only briefly, and the metaphor of human procreation hardly at all, in the development of rhetorical style among Schenker's American exponents. The following chronicle demonstrates that the transformation and eventual abandonment of Schenker's organic imagery makes manifest a shift in aesthetic ideology.[51]

The very first essays in English dealing with Schenker already show a reduction in the intensity and richness of biological and other anthropomorphic imagery. A number of articles which appeared in the 1930s – by Hans Weisse, Adele Katz and Israel Citkowitz, for example[52] – adhere closely to Schenker's language about the biological life of musical tones, strongly emphasising the dynamic aspects of Schenker's conceptions. Roger Sessions, even though he found himself unable to accept it as an apt metaphor for the *Ursatz*, nevertheless explicitly acknowledges Schenker's procreation figure: 'the formula of the *Ursatz* . . . is so attenuated, so inflexible, and so devoid of any dynamic quality that it is quite impossible to regard it as the kind of musical spermatozoon which Schenker conceives it to be'.[53] Other authors, however, radically altered Schenker's procreation rhetoric. Some reduced the organic figure to a botanical analogy and changed the musical work into a scientific object. Other authors replaced Schenker's organic image with an altogether different one, that of architecture.

All of these alterations are juxtaposed in one of the early essays, co-authored by Arthur Waldeck and Nathan Broder.[54] In one sentence they even mix biological and architectural figures of speech, asking how a

---

51 With the notable exception of Rothstein's 'The Americanization of Heinrich Schenker', little is written on Schenker's American reception. My discussion is variously indebted to Rothstein's chronicle of the general shift in Schenkerian rhetoric.

52 Hans Weisse, 'The Music Teacher's Dilemma', *Proceedings of the Music Teachers National Association* (1935), pp. 122–37; repr. in *Theory and Practice*, 10/i–ii (1985), pp. 29–48; Adele T. Katz, 'Heinrich Schenker's Method of Analysis', *Musical Quarterly*, 21/iii (1935), pp. 311–29; repr. in *Theory and Practice*, 10/i–ii (1985), pp. 77–95; Israel Citkowitz, 'The Role of Heinrich Schenker', *Modern Music*, 11/i (1933), pp. 18–23; repr. in *Theory and Practice*, 10/i–ii (1985), pp. 17–22.

53 Roger Sessions, 'Escape by Theory', in *Roger Sessions on Music: Collected Essays*, ed. Edward T. Cone (Princeton: Princeton University Press, 1979), p. 257. Originally published in *Modern Music*, 15/iii (1938), pp. 192–7.

54 Arthur Waldeck and Nathan Broder, 'Musical Synthesis as Expounded by Heinrich Schenker', *Musical Mercury*, 11/iv (1935), pp. 56–64; repr. in *Theory and Practice*, 10/i–ii (1985), pp. 65–73.

composer can '*evolve* his elaborate structures from so simple a *foundation*' (p. 59, emphasis added). When they summarise Schenker's theories, the language of architecture is clearly foremost: 'The ties that really bind the parts of a great composition are not so obvious; they are *imbedded* in a *sub-stratum* of the work. . . . [Musical laws] guide the genius, and help him *to erect structures* that cohere.' (p. 57, emphasis added) And yet they stand in awe of how Schenker portrays the old familiar masterpieces as 'radiant with new life'. Such praise, however, rings hollow when they tellingly prefigure the fate of Schenker's musical conception in a most gruesome, forensic description of his achievements:

Schenker's pen cuts deeply into the living tissue of a musical masterwork; it exposes the vital organs, directs the attention to the flow of life-bearing blood from the heart to the furthest extremities; it demonstrates the function of every nerve and sinew in the wonderfully wrought synthesis that is a great composition. (p. 56)

The exploratory surgery that promised access to the secrets of musical life would become, in the hands of American practitioners, a dissection that spelled the death of Schenker's conception.

Adele Katz and Felix Salzer, who wrote the first books using Schenker's ideas, avoid the procreation metaphor, preferring instead to speak only vaguely of 'organic' coherence or 'organic' structure. And as the metaphor disappeared, so did Schenker's emphasis on dynamic qualities. The abandonment of Schenker's procreative, personifying rhetoric also made room for new figures of speech to be used in articulating a different aesthetic attitude.

Katz's text[55] is the first of the Schenkerian texts to relinquish Schenker's dramatic and procreation metaphors, retreating into what Marion Guck has called 'music-literal' language.[56] Schenker's analytical writing tends to particularise the theoretical language by introducing vivid modifiers, often accompanied by the word *gleichsam*, in order to pinpoint the significance of an event or passage. Katz's writing, by contrast, is for the most part a colourless application of general terms. The tenor of her prose is typified by statements like the following: 'the harmonic principle provides the structural framework', and 'motion within a single chord [can be] widened through the use of prolongations' (p. 15). Motions are characterised only in the most general of terms, such as 'space-

55 Katz, *Challenge to Musical Tradition: A New Concept of Tonality* (New York: Knopf, 1945).
56 Guck, 'Two Types of Metaphoric Transfer', in Jamie C. Kassler (ed.), *Metaphor: A Musical Dimension* (Paddington, NSW: Currency Press, 1991), pp. 1–12.

outlining', 'space-filling', 'delaying', and 'ascending' or 'descending', while Schenker's term *Ursatz* is translated as 'basic structure' or 'primordial structure'. In the few passages to retain any flavour of a biological metaphor, all that remains is an allusion to very early steps in the chain of evolution:

The single all-embracing structural outline is the *primordial structure*, the protoplasm out of which all structural and prolonging motions evolve. As the fundamental source from which all further melodic and harmonic activity springs, it is the synthesis of all other motions that are offshoots of it. (p. 23)

Or, writing of Beethoven's compositional technique, she says that he 'selects a fragmentary phrase as the germ plasm from which every melodic impulse springs' (p. 155).

Salzer, who studied with Schenker in the early 1930s, maintains a balance between biological and architectural images and retains an emphasis on motion.[57] Like Katz, however, the range of metaphors he uses to describe such motion is severely limited.[58] Schenker's biological conception remains implicit in the buzzword 'organic', but throughout his text Salzer freely combines the terms 'organic' and 'structure' in a way reminiscent of Schenker's disavowal in 'Der Geist' of his contemporaries' loose praise of musical works. For Salzer, structure and growth are intertwined in the essence of the tonal organism. 'Understanding of tonal organisms', he writes, 'is a problem of hearing; the ear has to be systematically trained to hear not only the succession of tones, melodic lines and chord progressions but also their structural significance' (p. xvi). Salzer's structure becomes explicitly architectural on the following page: 'It seems to me that Schenker's concepts provide . . . for an intimate understanding of musical architecture of the past centuries' (p. xvii). And in discussing a musical example early in the book, Schenker's term *Ursatz* is translated by Salzer as 'structural framework or fundamental structure' (p. 12).[59] By focusing on the static terms of an architectural figure, Salzer's influential presentation of Schenker's theories displaced the lifeblood of

57 Felix Salzer, *Structural Hearing: Tonal Coherence in Music*, 2 vols. (New York: Charles Boni, 1952).

58 Motion, itself, is of course metaphorical as a musical description. (See Naomi Cumming, this volume, pp. 10–13. [Ed.])

59 When translated into German in 1977, the passage was rendered as 'und stellt ihre *strukturelle Fortschreitung*, ihr *strukturelles Gerüst* oder, kurz, ihre *Struktur* dar' (Salzer, *Strukturelles Hören: Der tonale Zusammenhang in der Musik*, 2 vols. [Taschenbücher zur Musikwissenschaft, 10] (Wilhelmshaven: Heinrichshofens Verlag, 1977), p. 11; emphasis original). It is surprising that Schenker's own terminology is not even mentioned.

those theories, namely, Schenker's dynamic, personifying metaphors by which he expressed his belief in a connection between the events of musical masterworks and the events of our own lives. There is, in other words, a profound difference in their conception of music: Salzer speaks as if music were a thing whose parts and spaces were all observable at one time; Schenker speaks as if music were something which undergoes changes in the process of coming to be.

In the two decades following Schenker's death there emerged a number of voices speaking to varying degrees in Schenker's name, and since Schenker's texts remained inaccessible to most English-speaking readers, many Americans assumed these exponents accurately represented Schenker's teaching. Paul Henry Lang, for example, wrote an editorial which, although ostensibly reviewing Katz's book and Tovey's *Beethoven* (both published in 1945), nevertheless ends up, as David Beach puts it, 'as an irrational and emotional attack against Schenker' that condemns his 'coldness and dogmatism'.[60] Lang writes that 'Schenker – and his fervent disciples even more – attack all those who find beauties that cannot be proved by logic or be reduced to their constituent atoms'.[61] Lang, like many others, appears to have trusted Katz and Salzer as faithful proponents of Schenker's perspective. Wilfred Mellers, who even speaks of a hybrid author 'Schenker-Salzer' in his review of Salzer's book, shares Lang's error, as does Norman Lloyd, whose review faces against Jonas's review, ideologically as well as literally on the page.[62]

Some writers, however, did discern a difference between Salzer and Schenker: most notably Jonas[63] – no doubt because he had been a long-time student of Schenker – but also Milton Babbitt and Leonard B. Meyer.[64] Meyer's insights are particularly relevant to my concerns here, for he distinguishes between Schenker's dynamic conception of music, which characterises music in terms of growth and process, and the more static views of certain disciples, who characterise music in terms of architectonic structure (p. 52). In short, he contrasts the biological with

60 David Beach, 'A Schenker Bibliography', *Journal of Music Theory*, 13/i (1969), p. 19.
61 Paul Henry Lang, 'Editorial' [Tovey versus Beethoven], *Musical Quarterly*, 32/ii (1946), p. 300.
62 Wilfred Mellers, review of Salzer, *Structural Hearing*, in *Music and Letters*, 34/iv (1953), pp. 329–32; Norman Lloyd, review of Salzer, *Structural Hearing*, in *Notes*, 10/iii (1953), p. 438.
63 Oswald Jonas, review of Salzer, *Structural Hearing*, in *Notes*, 10/iii (1953), p. 439.
64 Leonard B. Meyer, *Emotion and Meaning in Music* (Chicago: University of Chicago Press, 1956).

the architectural. Meyer singles out Salzer in particular for criticism, writing that 'only when the piece of music is complete, when it is timeless in memory, does Salzer's picture of music exist' (p. 53). To back up his interpretation of Salzer, he points to figurative aspects of Salzer's discourse: his criticisms, he writes, 'are directed merely against those aspects of [Salzer's] theory that tend to treat a musical composition as a thing instead of as a process which gives rise to a dynamic experience' (p. 54). Meyer makes the important point that the terms of discourse – thing or process – have consequences for musical experience.

Salzer's transformation of Schenker's rhetoric in his own writings even insinuated its way into the translation of *Der freie Satz*. Oster credits both Salzer and Forte with providing 'English equivalents' for Schenker's key terms.[65] These so-called equivalents, however, bear distinctive traces of the rhetorical transformations which Salzer and Forte were effecting in their own writings, so much so that an emphasis on structure encroaches on Schenker's more dynamic language in *Free Composition*: *Satz* (composition or contrapuntal setting) becomes 'structure', *Ursatz* (basic compositional setting) becomes 'fundamental structure', *Schicht* (layer) becomes 'structural level', *Zusammenhang* (coherence) becomes 'structural coherence', and *Auswirkungen* (consequences) becomes 'structural consequences'. The transformation that Meyer points to is equally evident in the fact that Schenker's graphs came to be read as spatial things and not temporal processes, a transformation effected· in part by substituting the opposition of *higher* and *lower* levels for Schenker's opposition of *earlier* and *later* layers.[66] The temporal connotation of the prefix *Ur-* is also erased in the standard translation of *Ursatz* as 'fundamental structure'.

Other events of the 1950s suggest that Schenker's American reception was in the process of entering a third and decisive stage, a stage marked by Milton Babbitt's review of Salzer's book[67] and the publication of Allen Forte's first sustained theoretical texts.

In order to make the distinction between Salzer and Schenker clear, Babbitt focuses on Schenker's ideas in the first half of his review. Babbitt concludes his second paragraph by stating in précis what Schenker was working up to:

---

65 Writing in Schenker, *Free Composition*, p. xiii.
66 See, for example, Charles Burkhart, 'Schenker's "Motivic Parallelisms"', *Journal of Music Theory*, 22/ii (1978), pp. 145–75.
67 Milton Babbitt, review of Salzer, *Structural Hearing*, in *Journal of the American Musicological Society*, 5/iii (1952), pp. 260–5.

The gradual evolution of his thought . . . reveals the constant growth, from the most tentative adumbrations, of the awareness of the basic continuity of the musical organism in terms of the correlation and interaction of the linear realization of a triadic span with the specific triadic harmonic articulations. (p. 260)

One striking feature of Babbitt's nutshell description, as striking as his retention of Schenker's 'organism', is the preponderance of Latinate nominalisations: 'evolution', 'adumbrations', 'correlation', 'interaction', 'realisation', 'articulation' – all frozen verbs. Also striking is the presence of the two standard musical terms, 'triadic' and 'harmonic' – Schenker's musical substantive – and the absence of terms such as the 'passing' tone, Schenker's musical verb. Other passages from the review provide a picture of how Babbitt recasts Schenker's ideas. Though he would not fall under Meyer's criticism, Babbitt's language nonetheless indicates an attitude toward theoretical rhetoric which differs markedly from Schenker's own:

The *Urlinie* . . . is . . . completely acceptable as an axiomatic statement (not necessarily *the* axiomatic statement) of the dynamic nature of structural tonality. Stated in such terms, it becomes the assertion that the triadic principle must be realized linearly as well as vertically; that the points of structural origin and eventuation must be stabilized by a form of, or a representation of, the sole element of both structural and functional stability: the tonic triad. (p. 260)

The *Ursatz* is the projection in time of a single triad by means of synthesized linear and harmonic prolongations of this triad. (p. 261)

Schenker's essential concern is with the means whereby the inceptually static triad is activated in time in accord with the principles of structural polyphony, which makes possible the unfolding through various levels of the total temporal-spatial unity which is the musical composition. (p. 262)

In characterising Schenker's theory, Babbitt draws on rhetorical sources more closely identified with the natural sciences than with descriptions of experiences such as birth or travelling (*Weg, Gang, Zug*), or mental equilibrium. The words 'axiomatic', 'assertion', 'principle', 'structural', 'functional' and 'element' are more at home in descriptions of formal systems, while such terms as 'points of structural origin' and 'projection' are likely as not to evoke memories of sophomore geometry. In short, Babbitt's rhetoric, though his discussion is brief, insinuates a new model for musical description, one drawn from the sciences. And in his 1965 essay, 'The Structure and Function of Musical Theory', Babbitt makes an explicit plea for scientific language and scientific method.[68] Forte and

---

68 Babbitt, 'The Structure and Function of Musical Theory', *College Music Symposium*,

other writers heeded the first part of Babbitt's exhortation by turning to scientific imagery as the source for their theoretical and analytical fictions.[69]

The scientistic transformation of Schenker is evident right at the outset of Forte's 1959 essay on Schenker:[70]

From the viewpoint of the present-day music theorist, [Schenker's achievement] may be likened to a particular kind of high-level achievement in science: the discovery or development of a fundamental principle which then opens the way for the disclosure of further new relationships, new meanings. (p. 3)

Forte begins with the drawing of a comparison, and then, as the following examples illustrate, he proceeds to re-inscribe Schenker's ideas in the language of the comparison:[71]

I wish to emphasize at this point that the bases of Schenker's concept of structural levels, upon which his theory of music rests, are not to be found in abstruse speculation, or in acoustical or metaphysical formulations (although Schenker was not averse to these), but in the organization of the music itself. Schenker *consistently derived* his *theoretical formulations* from aural experiences with actual musical compositions, and *verified* them at the same source. Furthermore, his *analytic techniques*, as well as his *analytic concepts*, are directly related to performance and compositional practices which stand at the very center of the development of tonal music. (p. 4, emphasis added)

The important deficiencies in his system arise from his failure *to define with sufficient rigor the conditions under which particular structural events occur.* (p. 16, emphasis added)

A *technical* history of triadic tonality has yet to be written. When it is, it will have to *demonstrate* historical continuity in other than poetic [sic!] terms. (p. 21, emphasis added)

---

5 (1965), pp. 49–60, repr. in Benjamin Boretz and Edward T. Cone (eds.), *Perspectives on Contemporary Music Theory* (New York: Norton, 1972), pp. 10–21.

69 On the notion of analytical fictions, see Guck, 'Analytical Fictions'. Babbitt's call for the employment of scientific method, particularly the kind of empirical phenomenology that he describes in the Salzer review, was not widely adopted by music theorists (see Guck's essay in this volume, pp. 57–73).

70 Forte, 'Schenker's Conception of Musical Structure', *Journal of Music Theory*, 3/i (1959), pp. 1–30. For a fascinating account of Forte's rhetoric that complements and expands upon the ideas presented here, as well as compares Forte's figurative language with that of other writers, see Guck, 'Analytical Fictions'. I am indebted to Marion Guck for drawing my attention to the roles of nominalisation and scientific imagery in Forte's rhetoric.

71 Forte also draws a comparison with the work of Freud, but his reading of Freud seems more coloured by his reading of Schenker than vice versa. Unlike his comparison with scientific achievements, the comparison with Freud has no rhetorical consequences in the essay.

We all recognize that the serious student of music today is faced with an enormous task. . . . In order to relieve this situation we would do well to *emulate science education*. (p. 25, emphasis added)

Forte concludes the article by stating his hope that 'the image of Schenker as a visionary will be replaced by one of a unique, original and highly gifted person' (p. 30), a hope that, in the context, amounts to replacing Schenker the artist with Schenker the scientist.

Competing myths

The continuing influence of Forte's scientification of Schenkerian rhetoric is attested by William Pastille in his essay on Schenker's concept of the background:

We have become quite content to think of [the *Ursatz*] as a 'theoretical construct', or as a 'hypothetical substructure', or as an 'axiom'. In other words, we speak of the *Ursatz* in terms that sound scientific, perhaps because the atmosphere of science has a reassuring bouquet of scholarly rationality about it, or, at any rate, because we breathe it more easily than the atmosphere of organicism, life forces, and the will of the tones.[72]

Pastille's examples of science-like descriptions are strikingly similar to those of Babbitt and Forte. By using first person plural, he indicates that the scientific way of speaking is widespread enough that he can trust his readers not only to be aware of it but, by implication, to be participants in it. Finally, Pastille speculates that the motivation for the rhetorical shift away from Schenker is a matter of comfort, which bespeaks a change in beliefs about the practice of music theory and, conjointly, about music.

These differences in beliefs are given expression in the contrasting images of procreation and natural science. Each image is more than just an isolated analytical fiction, more, that is, than a story created to represent one's interaction with a particular composition. Rather, each image is a source that funds a repertory of analytical fictions. And they can do so because authors find in them something which accords with their beliefs about what analysis does and what music is. Such images have a cultural function akin to myth. A myth is a repertory of rhetorical imagery that can be used to describe coherently the actions and roles of various members of a society – in our case, the musical society of listen-

---

72 Pastille, 'The Development of the *Ursatz* in Schenker's Published Works', in A. Cadwallader (ed.), *Trends in Schenkerian Research* (New York: Schirmer, 1990), p. 71.

ers, composers, performers, analysts and readers. The representation of relations among cultural actors is what might be called the internal social dimension of myth.

The procreation metaphor, for example, focuses on the musical work but at the same time creates roles for other musical actors. The central character is the living musical work, on whose behalf Schenker's synthesist labours as a dedicated biographer, revealing and chronicling the life histories of the masters' works in order that we might marvel at them and learn from them how to live out the tensions of our own lives.[73] This myth also gives an explicit and active role to composers, who are intimately involved in the birth and cultivation (*Bildung*) of the musical personage and who thereby body forth an image of themselves.[74] Just as importantly, the procreation myth allows readers to adopt any of a number of different roles. Readers can take up the role of the analyst and read themselves as biographers of tones. Or, since the musical work has been personified, they are also given the option of identifying with the composition: Schenker writes in *Der freie Satz* that 'it is our own life-drive that we carry into the movement of the *Urlinie*'s traversal', meaning that we can experience as our own the striving and completion that the legitimately conceived work experiences, either in our imaginations as listeners or in deed as performers.

In Forte's myth of the natural scientist, the composer is a marginal figure and the musical work is relatively passive. One's attention is drawn instead to the activity of the analyst. In all of the seven pages, for instance, in which Forte discusses the second song from Schumann's *Dichterliebe*, he only once mentions Schumann by name (right at the outset to identify what the object of study is) and thereafter only rarely even implies that Schumann has anything to do with the matter at hand.[75] As Guck points out, there is a strong tendency in Forte's texts to mask the actions of the composer behind passive verbs, suppressing an explicit statement of agency.[76] By way of vivid contrast, Schenker's name, first person pronouns – and their surrogates, ideas and sketches – figure prominently as grammatical agents throughout Forte's essay. Occasionally the song itself or an element of it is said to do something or other, but its agency is always subsumed by an act on the part of Schenker or Forte. This rhetorical move – a strong self-depiction of the analyst at the

73 Schenker, *Der freie Satz* (1935), p. 9.
74 Ibid., p. 18.
75 Forte, 'Schenker's Conception of Musical Structure', pp. 7–13.
76 Guck, 'Analytical Fictions'.

expense of composition, composer, and performer – invites the reader to contemplate the actions of a master analyst.[77] The most obvious readerly role would seem to be as a student on whose behalf the scientist examines and demonstrates; on this interpretation the reader appears in a subordinate position vis-à-vis the analyst, which is consistent with the internal social hierarchy of the myth. If a reader is relatively self-confident, he or she might consider the possibility of identifying with the text's first person, the natural scientist who plays the analyst; on this interpretation the reader is invited to act the part of the masterful analyst: examining, regarding, demonstrating, indicating.

Using the imagery of a myth expresses aesthetic and ethical commitments and in turn shapes the behaviour of those who participate in the myth's culture. This is what might be called the external social dimension of myth. Myths are stories we tell among ourselves, repeatedly and in a wide variety of contexts, in order to preserve ourselves as a community of like-minded music-makers. Myths are shared publicly at conferences and symposia, and privately in our classrooms and studios, those intimate gatherings where the myths are repeated and interpreted for the younger members of our communities. As Pastille's remark suggests, myths constitute an atmosphere within which we live, move, and have our being as musicians. A theoretical myth is thus a sort of communal mind-set that allows members of the culture to get on with their work without having constantly to ask what their job is. Myths are the parts of discourse to which we pay little attention: characterising all discourse within the culture, they remain more or less invisible to those within the culture.

One reason the procreation myth appealed to Schenker was that it supplemented the second-species model of tonality with a chronology from background to foreground. It is not coincidental, I think, that after the disappearance of the procreation figure from Schenkerian rhetoric there follows a new conception of chronology. This new conception is one that recasts the analytical enterprise in terms of 'reduction'. Forte describes reduction in *Contemporary Tone-Structures* in a passage that resonates with Waldeck and Broder's dissection of Schenker's organism:

The reduction procedure is, in fact, best understood in terms of the three levels of structure, for it also has three levels, or stages, which correspond to the

---

77 This analysis of Forte's self-depiction of himself as an active, masterly analyst was first made by Fred Everett Maus ('Self-Depiction in Writing about Music', paper delivered at the Society for Music Theory, Oakland, 1990).

foreground, middleground, and background of the structure being examined. Each successive sketch includes fewer and fewer details until only the skeletal structure (background) remains.[78]

Forte indirectly portrays himself in this passage as a scientist, standing before an examining table, wielding a reductive pencil which he uses to pare the work down from foreground to background. In his 1959 essay, he even attributes this notion of reduction to Schenker.[79] Forte must thus be reading Schenker's sketches as beginning with the highly detailed foreground and moving toward the schematic background, eliminating or reducing the amount of information as he reads from one level to the next. The one-who-reduces is unmistakably – appropriate to Forte's chosen rhetorical strategy – the analyst. Schenker, however, wrote his sketches in the same manner in which he wrote prose, namely, left to right and down the page, and spoke of the more detailed layers as *later* than the less detailed ones. Thus the proper way of reading the sketches, as Schenker makes abundantly clear, is from top to bottom, from background to foreground, resulting in elaborative rather than reductive pictures of musical works.[80] (The agent of Schenker's elaboration is not as unequivocal as that of Forte's reduction.) Unfortunately, Schenker's term *zurückführen* is usually translated as 'reduce', despite the clear expression that when one is led back (*zurück-*) from foreground to background one is moving against the conceptual grain, from later layers back to earlier ones. To be fair, there are places in which Schenker talks of reading or making sketches from foreground to background, but he is nearly always explicit about the concession he is making to those who cannot readily comprehend the background and the way it reaches out toward the foreground.[81] Lest anyone get the wrong idea, Schenker used

---

78 Forte, *Contemporary Tone-Structures* (New York: Bureau of Publications, Teachers College, Columbia University, 1955), p. 20.
79 Forte, 'Schenker's Conception of Musical Structure', p. 8.
80 One occasionally finds instances in Schenker (see, for example, 'Fortsetzung der Urlinie-Betrachtungen') where the most detailed level is placed above the simpler levels, but Schenker is always careful to alphabetise the graphs beginning with the simplest. Schenkerians who have adopted this layout, by contrast, tend to reverse Schenker's order (see, for example, Allen Cadwallader, 'Motivic Unity and Integration of Structural Levels in Brahms's B Minor Intermezzo, Op. 119, No. 1', *Theory and Practice*, 8/ii (1983), pp. 5–24). For further discussion of the differences between Schenker's approach and the idea of reduction, see Gregory Proctor and Herbert Lee Riggins, 'Levels and the Reordering of Chapters in Schenker's *Free Composition*', *Music Theory Spectrum*, 10 (1988), pp. 102–26.
81 See Schenker, *Der freie Satz* (1935), pp. 50–1, §49.

the familiar chronology of human life to set the direction and focus of his analyses: as a deepened understanding of unique individuals.

Schenker's myth, in addition, says something of the kind of interpretive interest he takes in musical works. Comparison with the more narrowly biological myth that survived in Katz and Salzer brings this out. As a plant organism, the musical work became something to ponder dispassionately, a change amply reflected in Katz's dispassionate prose. One would hardly be morally or viscerally squeamish about dissecting a bit of primordial protoplasm, but a living, breathing person is surely another matter altogether. A person deserves consideration. As Stanley Cavell puts it, 'objects of art not merely interest and absorb, they move us; we are not merely involved with them, but concerned with them, and care about them; we treat them in special ways, invest them with a value which normal people otherwise reserve only for other people'.[82] Schenker cared deeply about individual musical works, and so he saw it fitting to find language in which to express that feeling. His personification thus places music in a rhetorical position that accords with the value music obviously had in his life.

82 Stanley Cavell, *Must We Mean What We Say?* (Cambridge: Cambridge University Press, 1976), pp. 197–8.

3

Rehabilitating the incorrigible

Marion A. Guck

In three early methodological papers, Milton Babbitt found discourse about musical works intellectually indefensible, rife with unverified and unverifiable claims.[1] The worst excesses of irresponsibility were exemplified by 'that language in which the incorrigible personal statement is granted the grammatical form of an attributive proposition, and in which negation – therefore – does not produce a contradiction'.[2] He thought that musical discourse could be improved through adherence to standards of clarity and rigour associated with what he termed '"scientific" language and "scientific" method'. Whatever the shortcomings of the remedy he proposed, this endorsement has been enormously influential.

Babbitt's statements address three aspects of analytical and theoretical language. *Formal* aspects concern whether a statement is well-formed and capable of validation; *empirical* aspects concern questions of evidential support for a statement; and *pragmatic* aspects concern the outcome or results of a statement's use. He is best known for his endorsement of stringent formal requirements – '"scientific" language' – but I shall argue

A version of this paper was presented at the 1987 meetings of the New York State Theory Society in New York City. I am grateful to Joseph Dubiel and Fred Everett Maus for conversations that helped me to clarify the conceptual elaboration of this paper and for their thoughtful, critical readings of previous drafts.

1 The three papers are 'Past and Present Concepts of the Nature and Limits of Music', *Congress Report of the International Musicological Society* (1961), pp. 398–403, repr. in Benjamin Boretz and Edward T. Cone (eds.), *Perspectives on Contemporary Music Theory* (New York: Norton, 1972), pp. 3–9; 'The Structure and Function of Musical Theory', *College Music Symposium*, 5 (1965), pp. 49–60, repr. in ibid., pp. 10–21; and 'Contemporary Music Composition and Music Theory as Contemporary Intellectual History', in Barry S. Brook, Edward O. D. Downes, and Sherman Van Solkema (eds.), *Perspectives in Musicology* (New York: Norton, 1971), pp. 151–84.

2 'Structure and Function', p. 11. 'Incorrigible' statements are unsupported opinions or personal interpretations. See also 'Past and Present Concepts', p. 4, where he speaks of

> an incorrigible statement of attitude grammatically disguised as a simple attributive assertion. If it is taken at its grammatical face value, then it creates inevitably a domain of discourse in which negation does not produce contradiction, and in which a pair of such assertions entails, in turn, any statement and its negation.

that, when Babbitt is faced with the particularities of a musical work, empirical requirements – '"scientific" method' – and pragmatic claims take precedence.

This interpretation suggests that the discursive clarity Babbitt required of musical discourse can be achieved with a wider range of linguistic resources than he could have foreseen. In particular, 'incorrigible statements' can be rehabilitated using a method outlined in Babbitt's statements about the evaluation of musical discourse. The musical analyses that result create the individuating accounts of music that he advocated, in part by opening analysis up to questions of expression.

Babbitt discusses two types of 'incorrigible personal statement' in the passage cited: 'evaluatives'[3] and what I will call interpretives. Perhaps the more reprehensible are 'evaluatives': 'non-explanations that invoke terms such as "taste", "emotional cogency", or even "beauty"' and assertions like 'X is a masterpiece'.[4] Such statements, Babbitt asserts, are means of passing judgement on pieces without being required either to admit that they are only opinions or to have reasons for such opinions.[5]

Interpretives are statements that pass for analytical observations, like Hans David's 'apparently factual scholarly statement that the c-flat of measure 53 of the second movement of the Mozart G Minor Symphony (K. 550) is "an unexpected c-flat"'. (pp. 11–12) The transgressor in David's statement is, of course, the qualifier 'unexpected'. Its syntactical attachment to the observable (that is, evident in the score or sounds to anyone with the relevant training) C♭ seems to grant it, too, factual status. In reality, though, it is an interpretation of how C♭ can be heard, and the source of that interpretation is neither presented in the paper nor evident through its connection with some theory held by the community.

Both types of 'incorrigible' assertion masquerade as verifiable statements about some observable – that is, public – property of a musical work, when, in fact, they report the speaker's 'personal disposition'[6] – an

3 'Nor can the performer . . . be permitted his easy evaluatives which determine in turn what music is permitted to be heard, on the plea of ignorance of the requirements of responsible normative discourse.' ('Structure and Function', p. 11) Babbitt, always more a composer than a theorist, would like performers and others to be required to make a case if they wish to dismiss any (especially contemporary) piece.
4 'Contemporary Composition and Theory', p. 182. See also Benjamin Boretz, 'Meta-Variations: Studies in the Foundations of Musical Thought (I)', *Perspectives of New Music*, 8/i (1969), pp. 11–12 and 21–3.
5 In an interview in July 1988 with Fred Everett Maus and Marion Guck, Babbitt maintained that he is not 'allergic' to claims about beauty, for example, but that the evidence for the claim must be given.
6 'Contemporary Composition and Theory', pp. 182–3.

opinion that cannot be either true or false and cannot, therefore, be corrected. Babbitt insists on the possibility of determining whether statements are well-formed in order, then, to determine whether they make sense or are 'grossly "meaningless"'.[7] This is the motivation for his assertion that:

There is but one kind of language, one kind of method for the verbal formulation of 'concepts' and the verbal analysis of such formulations: 'scientific' language and 'scientific' method. . . . Our concern is not whether music has been, is, can be, will be, or should be a 'science', whatever that may be assumed to mean, but simply that statements about music must conform to those verbal and methodological requirements which attend the possibility of meaningful discourse in any domain.[8]

Babbitt seems sometimes to apply this standard to musical discourse generally, sometimes to music theory in particular.[9] However, musical theory must be distinguished from at least musical analyses, which describe how an individual can hear or otherwise 'rationally reconstruct' a piece or passage, and practical discourse, which characterises a piece or passage in a particular way in order to effect a behavioural change, say, in the course of coaching a performer. Their different ends may very well require different means of expression, and the failure to distinguish between different kinds of discourse can cloud the issues, as the case of 'incorrigible statements' shows.

7 For a consideration of a formalist approach to theory construction, see John Rahn, 'Aspects of Musical Explanation', *Perspectives of New Music*, 17/ii (1979), pp. 204–24. Rahn contrasts Babbitt's approach, designated 'digital . . . discourse' in Nelson Goodman's *Languages of Art* sense (Indianapolis: Bobbs-Merrill, 1968), with 'analog modes of discourse' such as J. K. Randall's 'Compose Yourself: A Manual for the Young', *Perspectives of New Music*, 10/ii (1972), pp. 1–12.

8 'Past and Present Concepts', p. 3. A second statement is in 'Structure and Function', p. 13, where Babbitt says that:

> musical discourse or – more precisely – the theory of music . . . is . . . subject to the methodological criteria of scientific method and the attendant scientific language . . . not because of the nature of musical theory, but because of the nature and scope of scientific method and language, whose domain of application is such that if it is not extensible to musical theory, then musical theory is not a theory in any sense in which the term ever has been employed.

9 In 'Past and Present Concepts', p. 4, Babbitt elaborates an ideal of music theory:

> Progressing from the concept to the law (synthetic generality) we arrive at the deductively interrelated system of laws that is a theory, statable as a connected set of axioms, definitions, and theorems, the proofs of which are derived by means of an appropriate logic. A musical theory reduces, or should reduce, to such a formal theory when uninterpreted predicates and operations are substituted for the terms and operations designating musical observables.

Rather than dismissing such statements outright, Babbitt proposes a formal remedy. He proposes that they become subject to normal methods of evaluation if they are first 'translated into a logically tenable form with a two-place (relational) predicate'.[10] Such formulation would presumably make explicit the relation between the speaker and the ascription: for example, Hans David might have recast his statement as something like 'C♭ is unexpected for me'.

The additional phrase clarifies the fact that the statement is a personal opinion rather than a public truth and makes it verifiable: yes, indeed, C♭ is unexpected for Hans David. It also points out the route to a wider validation, which is subscription, individual by individual, to the statement, 'C♭ is unexpected for me (too)'. Thus it seems that the form of 'incorrigible statements' can be corrected quite easily.

The really serious issue is akin to that of providing empirical support for scientific statements. The grounds for making a statement must be made available for scrutiny and evaluation by the community to whom it is made. Babbitt finds it indefensible if no reasons are – or can be – given for an attribution.[11] This fear is warranted, and must be addressed if analytical and critical discourse is not to risk slipping back into the morass of verbal carelessness and self-indulgence that Babbitt's papers first brought to our attention.

Babbitt's treatment of David's claim encapsulates the problem and points to a solution. After dismissing a first example of 'the incorrigible personal statement' that he clearly considers ludicrous, he introduces the 'unexpected C♭' as another example. In full, what he says about David is:

And what of the more apparently factual scholarly statement that the c-flat of measure 53 of the second movement of the Mozart G Minor Symphony (K. 550) is 'an unexpected c-flat'; overlooking for the moment the dubious status of such expressive descriptives, what can the term 'unexpected' be inferred to designate when applied to the succession b-flat, c-flat, which had been stated in the movement in question at the outset in measure 2?[12]

His initial intention seems to be to dismiss this second incorrigible statement, too. However, faced with an observation about a piece of music, he puts aside its 'dubious status' in order to point out events in the piece that he believes make the C♭ in bar 53 not unexpected (though not expected, either).

This change of course in mid-sentence locates the crux of my argu-

10 'Past and Present Concepts', p. 4.
11 'Contemporary Composition and Theory', p. 182.
12 'Structure and Function', pp. 11–12.

ment: Babbitt offers an example of incorrigibility that he intends to reject on formal grounds, but it presents him with an account of a musical passage that overlooks particular relations evident in the movement. He sets aside the formal impropriety in order to present the evidence that contradicts the musical claim, thereby refuting it on empirical grounds. Faced with a musical question, '"scientific" language' makes way for '"scientific" method'.

Granting priority to empirical issues seems consistent with concerns Babbitt expresses in both earlier and later essays. In 1950, he asks, 'What of the significance of the event at precisely its own moment of occurrence, at its own tonal level, and in its relation to other such events and to the work as a whole?'[13] More recently, in *Words About Music*, his consistent concern for 'purely contextual contingencies and dependencies'[14] has been persuasively demonstrated in analyses that trace networks of subtle parallelisms between events that contribute to the individual character of a work.[15] It should not be surprising that an individual so acutely aware that the subtle details of musical events create the contextual identity which *is* the musical work abhors language that serves only as a blanket and a sedative – the musically soporific language of pat explanations and thoughtless labels.

To return to the main point, Babbitt indicates how personal statements might be rehabilitated when he refutes David's statement by producing evidence.[16] A notion of what evidence will be useful can be derived from positivist ideas that Babbitt endorses, requiring linkage between theoretical and observation statements.[17]

As I understand the linkage, David's statement invokes a personal theory about pieces according to which he interprets a complex of more

13 Babbitt, review of René Leibowitz, *Schoenberg et son école* and *Qu'est ce que la musique de douze sons?*, in *Journal of the American Musicological Society*, 3/i (1950), p. 57.

14 Babbitt, *Words About Music* (Madison: University of Wisconsin Press, 1987), p. 150. Babbitt did not – and may not have been willing to – speak so informally of these questions at the time when he wrote the methodological papers, but I think it unlikely that he had held different views during this middle period.

15 Ibid., chap. 5, pp. 121–62, includes several exemplary analyses of passages and short pieces.

16 If Babbitt's formal strictures seem like the invocation of a gag rule – 'say it right or don't say it' – requiring the evidence seems like an invitation to a conversation. Certainly, increasing the body of detailed information about pieces seems a desirable end in itself.

17 Babbitt remarks on the distinction between theoretical and observational language in 'Contemporary Composition and Theory', pp. 177–80. Though this distinction is not as clear as Babbitt and his sources thought, it is useful for characterising the kind of analytical evidence desired.

directly observable features in terms of an equally personal theoretical term. Babbitt would say that David's statement must be linked explicitly with statements that use only observation language and/or theoretical language that is closer to the observable features of the music. This is especially important for personal terms since their relation to other theoretical terms and to observation statements is not stipulated. Ultimately, the covertly theoretical language must be linked to specifically musical descriptions of individual events and relations between those events so that David's (thought) experiment can be duplicated.[18] This is the means for rehabilitating 'incorrigible statements'.

Before taking up pragmatic issues, I must digress in order to consider the 'incorrigibility' of the subjective process of hearing: we each have our own hearing and only our own hearing, and we cannot know anyone else's. Verbal descriptions like 'C♭ is unexpected' are reports of an aural experience. Where verbal explanations are offered for claims like 'unexpectedness', they can give only indirect evidence that points towards a particular hearing. The direct evidence for 'incorrigible statements' is in the details of each individual's objectively inaccessible hearing.

Babbitt had something to say about this, too. In considering Schenker's 'conceptions' in a 1952 review of Felix Salzer's *Structural Hearing*, he states that 'validity' is dependent upon

whether, after having become aware of these conceptions, the listener does not find that they may not only codify his previous hearing but extend and enrich his perceptive powers by making listening more efficient and meaningful, by 'explaining' the formerly 'inexplicable,' and by granting additional significance to all degrees of musical phenomena.[19]

---

18 David may have been trying to present his evidence. Babbitt's quote is drawn from Paul Henry Lang (ed.), *The Creative World of Mozart* (New York: Norton, 1963), p. 62 (Bruce Samet, who first directed my attention to the example, also discovered the source of this quotation):

> Such a chromatic ascent dominates the first part of the development in the *Andante* of the G-minor Symphony (K. 550; 1788). The section begins with a unison B♭, continuing the dominant sound from the end of the exposition. An unexpected C♭, heard first in unison (as E-flat minor VI), is harmonized as a subdominant of the tonic minor.

More typically, the meaning of such predicates is presumed to be self-evident. In many such instances, if a speaker is asked for evidence, the rejoinder is something like 'That's the way I hear it', which renders the original statement 'indiscussable' and thereby 'indefensible' to Babbitt. I would limit the range of that claim to 'indiscussable with that individual' and therefore 'indefensible in that instance'.

19 Babbitt, review of Felix Salzer, *Structural Hearing*, in *Journal of the American Musicological Society*, 5/iii (1952), p. 261.

Following this reasoning, an assertion is justified by its enriching effect on hearing – on its codifying or changing it.

This suggests that the most fundamental evidence for an assertion is a determination – which is often made almost immediately – whether a description captures aural qualities of an event convincingly. If a description is *evocative*, this constitutes strong empirical evidence in its favour. If it is not evocative, it is likely to drop from thought. 'Unexpectedness' passes this empirical test for David. It fails for Babbitt, who indicates his reasons.

But if an observation like David's is a report of a hearing, can it be faulted? I think it can, because, although a hearing cannot be denied, the report of a hearing may be obscure or imprecise. In such a case, the report can be improved.

For example, 'singular', in the sense of odd or peculiar, seems a little closer than 'unexpected' to how the C♭s sound to me: although C♭ or B♭– C♭ has occurred before, *these* C♭s sound strange. In saying this, I have picked up *something* in David's observation – it does not seem dead wrong to me. In fact, it seems likely that he merely misplaced the unexpectedness, asserting it of C♭ rather than of its manner of occurrence or its outcome (the development's harmonic path), which he does describe. Stating the reasons in such a case might have clarified the precise source of the otherwise only vague sense of unexpectedness, and sharpened the claim, the hearing, and the analysis.

Nevertheless, 'unexpected' is imprecise, and 'singular', replacing 'unexpected', swallows it up. That, too, will be swallowed up by a richer and even more precise characterisation of how the C♭s are singular.

As I hear them, bar 53's C♭s are portentous: charged with some inchoate – perhaps even threatening – meaning. They have the qualities of events that we describe as portentous, events that are themselves peculiar, dramatic and inexplicable, and that also point towards some significant, impending event. The situation is signalled by discomfort, anxiety, even worry about a loss of control. Calling portentousness into play predicts while it asserts: it points towards the future but, disconcertingly, gives little clue about what, precisely, can be expected. In bar 53, the C♭s intimate that something (untoward, even unexpected) is about to happen, and, true to the prediction heard in the portentous sounds, the C♭s in bar 56 set that something in motion.

This description invites you to match your hearing with mine or to imagine a new hearing that could be described by you in the same terms; in this respect it is like David's. It requires your active participation to (re)construct the hearing: you must make the imaginative leap necessary to discover the correlations between the musical events and their figurative description – if you can and will.[20] I have pointed the way by elaborating the senses in which I mean 'portentous', but I have not pointed to the features of the piece that elicit my hearing – which is the sort of evidence Babbitt had in mind. Still, if your hearing matches mine, my description, following the Babbitt of 1952, provides a means, however implicit, to codify it. If you can imagine such a new hearing, my description 'extends and enriches [your] perceptive powers'.

This is, of course, no formal test; it leaves a lot unsaid, assumes a lot about the similarity of people's conceptions – takes a lot on faith. But it is the sort of pragmatic test that must suffice in the rough and tumble of everyday talk about music. In particular, personal statements, if evocative, can be more useful than more formal discourse in, say, conveying ideas about how to play a passage, and they are judged by the changes wrought in the performance under their influence. If such a statement is formulated effectively, then the individual to whom it is directed can create a performance in terms of it. That performance is the evidence for the descriptive adequacy of the statement: a desired change indicates an adequate characterisation. Though not formally explicit, such discourse had better be intersubjective and useful.

It is just such pragmatic considerations that determine the value of an analysis for Babbitt:

there are an infinity of analytical expressions which will generate any given composition, and one moral of this casual, but undeniable, realization is that the relation between a formal theory and its empirical interpretation is not merely that of the relation of validity to truth (in some sense of verifiability), or of the analytic to the synthetic (be this or not an untenable dualism or dogma of empiricism), but of the whole area of the criteria of *useful, useable, relevant, or significant characterizations*.[21]

Both the assertion and its evidence must be claims worth making.

Rereading Babbitt suggests, among other things, that an 'incorrigible' statement can be rehabilitated if the individual who makes it takes care to render it capable of evaluation. It can be made intersubjective, usually by giving evidence that supports the interpretive statement. If such evidence is given, other individuals can determine whether the statement is both sensible and worthwhile: that is, whether the model proposed by the

---

20 See Ted Cohen, 'Metaphor and the Cultivation of Intimacy', *Critical Inquiry*, 5/i (1978), pp. 8–12.
21 Babbitt, 'Structure and Function', p. 14 (emphasis added).

attribution creates a hearing that incorporates, with precision and richness, those aspects of the sounds the reader cares about.

'Incorrigible' statements that interpret musical events can be an acceptable, if not indispensable, form in which to frame observations about how a piece is heard to go.[22] They may express a personal insight, but that is not unusual or very different from many less controversial analytical interpretations.[23]

The evidence

Analytical discourse operates in a primarily verbal field. For its purposes, it is important that participants be reasonably certain of the intersubjectivity of their descriptions, that meanings are shared and that those descriptions pick out the same features of pieces for everyone. Thus, it is desirable to adhere to the rules of intellectual courtesy that 'scientific' language and method codify.

In the case under consideration, this means producing the evidence by which my description of the C♭s can be tested. The reasoning inherent in the attribution has already been partially revealed in my exposition of the features of portentousness that the Mozart invokes. This complex of features can be correlated with a complex of musical features.

I hear the C♭s in bar 53 as portentous because of the C♭s' (unexpected) manner of occurrence there. They are singular, being unaccompanied, unharmonised in low-register octaves, in strings alone (see Ex. 3.1). Furthermore, they transform the movement's opening motive, whose initial leap is shrunk to a semitone and whose functional emphasis is reversed so that the pitch of the anacrusis is decorated by the pitch of the repeated note.[24]

22 David Lewin's remarks on analyses as poems and the poetics of analysis in 'Music Theory, Phenomenology, and Modes of Perception', *Music Perception*, 3/iv (1986) are pertinent here. See especially pp. 382–9.
23 The foregoing rationale for analysis is related to an account of the aim of analysis I have given in 'The "Endless Round"', *Perspectives of New Music*, 31/i (1993), pp. 306–14, according to which analyses are a 'medium of intersubjective exchange', by which I mean that analyses are 'the means to change and refine hearings and therefore that, when analysts write analytical texts, we are offering readers the possibility of recreating a hearing that we have found worthwhile' (p. 307).
24 Patrick McCreless ('Syntagmatics and Paradigmatics: Some Implications for the Analysis of Chromaticism in Tonal Music', *Music Theory Spectrum*, 13/ii (1991), pp. 167–72) takes Babbitt's complaint about David as a point of departure for an analysis of the Andante from the point of view of C♭ that identifies many of the same events as the analysis presented here, though the interpretive context is quite different.

Example 3.1   Mozart, Symphony No. 40 in G minor, K. 550,
second movement, bars 53–5

Having been the *only* thing happening for a bar, C♭ then continues for
a second bar. In bar 54, instead of an imitative entrance, the winds erupt
dramatically in an A♭-minor chord in quavers widely spaced above and
around the upper octaves of the strings' C♭; halfway through the bar, the
violins leap high into the A♭ chord. Clearly, C♭ and its surroundings have
changed, and, furthermore, these changes signal a turning point.[25]

25 David Lewin (private communication) has offered a refinement:

The portentous character *begins* for me with the *upbeat*, not with the C♭. The
unison strings on the B♭ thicken and darken (especially the violins' IVth strings)
the sound of the violas' IIIrd string, that we are used to. The bowing over B♭–C♭
contributes to the effect too – of course it condenses the bow of m. 2 in the bass,
but it also – and more immediately for me – contrasts with the one-bow-per-note
texture of the opening measure-with-pickup. Even the bass and viola of m. 44 are
detached bows (though the chroma is slurred in the winds there). In any case, as
ideal 'conductor', I want the portentous quality to *be* there on the *pickup* to m. 53
(B♭), and *not* to suddenly emerge at the *barline* of m. 53 (C♭), changing the timbral

The 'contextualities' of C♭

Despite the evidence I have advanced to support my description, which goes quite far, I think, to answer Babbitt's criticisms, another of his concerns refuses to be ignored. No matter how persuasively I have described the C♭s or how inclusively my description encapsulates the particulars of the events at that point, to say that the C♭s are portentous is also to make claims about the piece in which the C♭s can sound portentous. I must go on to embed the passage in the 'contextualities' of the piece.

Babbitt's citation of bar 2 discerns a relation among C♭s; my description, and even David's, allude to a connected line of thought hovering behind the isolated ascription. Bar 2 suggests the conventional characterisation of certain types of musical events as foreign elements; further examination identifies a succession of C♭s throughout the piece. And that in turn suggests the expansion of the conventional notion into a story about C♭ as a rather daring immigrant adjusting to an alien culture.[26] Unlike an 'incorrigible statement', standing apart and demanding that empirical evidence be provided, the incorrigible claims of this tale interweave with the exposition of the empirical data to make the fabric of the account.[27]

The tale takes shape around a kernel incorporating (at least) being alien and surviving in unfamiliar surroundings, as well as temporally more shaped ideas of acclimatisation to those surroundings, and, perhaps, eventual assimilation. While some parts of this framework are relatively constrained, others seem more flexible; none is absolutely fixed in its expression. As the account develops, C♭'s qualitative and functional peculiarities motivate refinements in the immigration scenario. Acclimatisation, for example, often includes disparity between one's position in one's

gesture across the slur. The C♭, in other words, is to some extent the *fruit* of a portentous timbral transformation on the B♭ at the last [quaver] of m. 52, as well as – maybe even more than – a portentous thing in itself.

A further point, brought to mind by Lewin's fine reading of timbral details, is the different qualities that C♭–B♭ takes on in exactly that register, beginning in bar 2.

26 David Lewin's account of F♯/G♭, within the drama that is the first movement of Beethoven's Symphony No. 5 ('Music Theory, Phenomenology, and Modes of Perception', pp. 389–90), characterises its pitch class even more directly.

27 See Fred Everett Maus, 'Music as Drama', *Music Theory Spectrum*, 10 (1988), pp. 56–73 on narrative in musical description, in which he describes how an analysis of the beginning of Beethoven's String Quartet, Op. 95 'mingles standard music-theoretical vocabulary with other sorts of description' (p. 69).

ethnic and one's adopted community. More rarely, this disparity or other tensions in the situation lead to some overt reaction that can be accounted for by delving into questions of character. Thus the stereotypical immigrant becomes an individual, reflecting the idiosyncrasies of C♭'s role in the Mozart.

In telling my tale, I will be on dangerous ground, because I conceive of the immigrant C♭ as animate and motivated – but I intend to stay here.[28] My underlying contention is that musical structure can be modelled in terms of patterns in other domains of experience, including motivated action, with useful and significant analytical results.[29]

At its first occurrence in bar 2, C♭ seems a somewhat alien member of the little crowd clustering towards B♭ in the bass, one that draws attention away from the second imitative entrance. Foreigner though it is, it can already be identified as a version of C that intensifies the voice-leading resolution to B♭; this is the most likely status C♭ could have in E♭ major. Nevertheless, C♭'s foreign origins are unmistakably audible, and, given the absence of any other fifth of the chord at that point, it hints at ii$_5^6$ in E♭ *minor*.

When C♭ recurs in bar 11, it is in surroundings that recast bars 1–3. The crowd that had clustered towards B♭ now arranges itself in a meas-

28 Even if the ground is dangerous, I do not stand alone. Among the analytical narratives I might cite, in addition to Lewin's analysis of the first movement of Beethoven's Symphony No. 5 and Maus's analysis of the Beethoven Quartet opening, are Edward T. Cone's analysis of Schubert's *Moment musical* in A♭, Op. 94/vi in 'Schubert's Promissory Note: An Exercise in Musical Hermeneutics', in Walter Frisch (ed.), *Schubert: Critical and Analytical Studies* (Lincoln: University of Nebraska Press, 1986), pp. 11–30; David Lewin's analysis of Schubert's 'Auf dem Flusse' from *Die Winterreise* in '*Auf dem Flusse*: Image and Background in a Schubert Song', ibid., pp. 126–52; and Leo Treitler's analysis of the Andante of Mozart's Symphony No. 39, K. 543 in 'Mozart and the Idea of Absolute Music', in *Music and the Historical Imagination* (Cambridge, Mass.: Harvard University Press, 1989), pp. 176–214. In all of these, figurative language facilitates lively depiction of the moment-by-moment, detailed progress of the piece under consideration; though I will be characterising only selected moments in the Andante of Mozart's Symphony No. 40, my narrative is meant to characterise those moments in detail. By contrast, Anthony Newcomb's 'Once More "Between Absolute and Program Music": Schumann's Second Symphony', *19th-Century Music*, 7/iii (1984), pp. 233–50, relates a story of the whole symphony in the outlines of emotive descriptions, which, like the outline of motivic development he is tracing, change over relatively longer spans and are described in broader terms. The differences between the contrasting characterisations of language and analytical viewpoint just given suggest questions about the diversity of 'incorrigible' language that must, for now, be deferred.

29 I have also addressed the mutual conceptual influence of musical and non-musical description on each other in three other papers: 'Musical Images as Musical Thoughts: The Contribution of Metaphor to Analysis', *In Theory Only*, 5/v (1981), pp. 29–43;

ured line that spans the imitative procession. C♭ is more poignantly piercing and prominent in its new register and timbre, as well as its duration and, most importantly, its delay of B♭. While remaining a voice-leading conformist, C♭ asserts its E♭-collection outlandishness.

After a cadence on V of B♭ in bar 27, C♭ arises in a tonally ethnic community that occurs within the region of – that is, within a prolongation of – B♭'s V.[30] The music passes fleetingly through D♭ major towards E♭ minor (bar 31) where C♭ makes an apparently ephemeral appearance – to be replaced again by C♮ (bar 32). However, when the tendencies of the tonal culture begin to clarify in bar 33, C♭ reappears as both a voice-leading precursor to the tonic triad's B♭ and as the root of IV$^6_5$ in the harmonic assertion of the area's G♭ tonal nationality. As it turns out, G♭ is the bass of an augmented-sixth chord returning to B♭'s V, and the community's subordination to the principal tonal culture is affirmed.

The E♭ minor-G♭ major region arises more clearly within a further prolongation of V of B♭ in bars 44–6. C♭, in a trill's fancy dress, is conspicuous in the position of the seventh of G♭'s dominant.

Thus, C♭ seems to have found comfortable surroundings that duplicate its native culture, implied in bar 2's reference to ii$^6_5$, and in which it continues in its traditional role as precursor to B♭. It is C♭'s relation to its companions – leading to B♭ – that is consistent whatever its surroundings. That point of contact first enabled it to immigrate and continues to provide it with a functional status in both the larger culture of E♭ major and in the ethnic E♭ minor-G♭ major region. Thus E♭ major seems to accommodate its foreign element and C♭ seems to find a settled place in its unfamiliar surroundings.

C♭'s character has also shown itself in its travels. First, in the alien culture and again in the ethnic region, it quietly took up its place. Then, in the second of each pair of appearances, it evidenced a tendency to draw attention to itself.

The music of bar 53 exaggerates that tendency as C♭ becomes the sole object of attention. Still in a diatonic environment, it gains status as the bass of a iv^6 that proceeds to V. But its migration to the bass in the costume of the pulsating quaver motive (described in detail above) portends an upcoming development or departure from its accommodating surroundings. And, when, in bar 56, C♭ strikes out on a different path, it

'Beethoven as Dramatist', *College Music Symposium*, 29 (1990), pp. 8–18; and 'Two Types of Metaphoric Transfer', in Jamie C. Kassler (ed.), *Metaphor: A Musical Dimension* (Paddington, NSW: Currency Press, 1991), pp. 1–12.

30 This use of the notion of tonal region is, of course, akin to that of Schoenberg.

thereby abandons both its identity as precursor to B♭ and the diatonic and harmonic status it has achieved. It fulfils the implicit drama of bar 53–5's portentous changes by wrenching free of its voice-leading role.

By uprooting itself from its diatonic enclave, C♭ gives impetus to a rising chromatic bass that advances by dominant–tonic pairs through D♭, E♭ and F minor. The line culminates in a prolonged G-major chord on the verge of C minor. By this point, C♭ has become too radically foreign and undergoes yet another change of costume, a metamorphosis that reverses bar 56's wilful C♭–C♮, giving it a more 'natural' form. In the transformation (bars 64–6), the upper voice C♯–B♮ line mimics the old C♭–B♭, promoting C♭ (now B♮) to the note of resolution.[31] C♭ has, for the moment, ceded its position to C♯ and its identity to B♮ in order to survive in an environment – even more alien than E♭ major – in which it finds itself at the centre – the furthest point – of the development.

C♭'s evident urge to transform its environment in bars 53 and 56 precipitates *its* transformation by its environment. The course of the piece turns back to E♭, and C♭ reappears in bar 73 – in what is by now, from C♭'s point of view, more familiar territory – leading to B♭ just as the recapitulation begins.

C♭'s behaviour in the recapitulation will be exemplified by reference to only two of its appearances. In bar 99, C♭ recurs at the opening of what will become a tonicisation of C♭ major whose cadence is averted by C♭'s reinterpretation as the bass of an augmented-sixth chord in bar 105 (comparable to bar 31). It appears that C♭ has succeeded to the leadership of its community; that the community has a distinctive position in the larger culture; and that this position is mediated by C♭, which thus achieves greater prominence in the E♭ community as well. This position, while traditional, must be held by an individual from the parallel minor culture. Thus C♭ is assimilated by E♭ major, and, at its final appearance in bar 115, it participates in a voice-leading summary of the C♭–C♯–B♭ voice-leading implied in bar 2 and heard as either C♭–B♭ or C♯–B♭ throughout the movement.[32] C♭ has been, so to speak, naturalised, though its foreign accent remains.

Evaluation

The foregoing exposition is itself an analysis in the conventional music-theoretical sense, if not in the conventional music-theoretical style. The

---

31 C♮–B♮ also has a history, beginning in bar 5.
32 A more complex review of C♭ *vs.* B♮ occurs in bars 83–5, where the original C♭ motive

predicate 'portentousness' has crystallised into an interpretation of the events not only of bar 53, but of its anacrusis through to at least bar 56, that distinguishes the many facets of the events that contribute to the span's structure of dramatic change.[33] Situating the C♭s among portentous events reifies their features and relations in a particularly pungent and insightful way: it makes sense of them in ways not formerly possible. I could have pointed out which patterns fuse in bar 53's C♭s without reference to 'portentousness', but to capture the intensities and interactions of the passage's qualities in precisely *that* fusion along with its sources in patterns from the past and its intimation of future events – its teleology – I needed a description as rich as 'portentous'.

The interpretation ascribes a certain significance to 'the event at precisely its own moment of occurrence, at its own tonal level, and in its relation to other such events and to the work as a whole'. It suggests a strategy for hearing not only the highlighted events but also the lines of development in which they participate, which is to say that it provides a means of codifying and enriching the hearing of the whole piece. It yields 'useful, useable, relevant, or significant observations'.

The immigrant's tale contrasts in both its structure and its scope with portentousness. Whereas portentousness incorporates a conceptual structure that is covert in the original statement, the conceptual structure of the immigrant's tale is revealed in the process of its telling. It *begins* life as an analysis.

The story spans – intermittently – the whole piece, weaving in portentousness along the way. Some episodes in the analytical tale might seem more simply conceived than that of bars 53–6 – a few features creating a sketch – but each episode contributes qualities and rhythms to a progression whose accumulation is directed towards accounting convincingly for C♭'s participation in the piece.

is heard stretched out in the high register (as in bars 10–11), but partially transposed to include B♮–C♮.

33 In fact, some readers may be wondering what the fuss is about, since portentousness, for them, is literally and unproblematically a quality of the music. Though I have been calling these predicates figurative, because the semantic questions are closely related to questions about metaphor, such readers and I might be able to agree to calling them fictional. (This possibility came to mind during a conversation with Kendall Walton.) If fictional predicates, when used in novels, have their consequences within the world created by the novel rather than in the real world, fictional predicates, when applied to musical works, have their consequences within the world created by the musical work. On the subject of fictional truth, see Kendall Walton, *Mimesis as Make-Believe: On the Foundations of the Representational Arts* (Cambridge, Mass.: Harvard University Press, 1990), pp. 195–204.

Thus, the narrative requires evaluation as a whole to determine whether it is a coherent representation – whether it tells a good story – and the analyst faces all the problems in carrying out this task that are faced in carrying out any discourse-level analysis. Truth is replaced by the plausibility of the narrative. The nature and quality of the evidence, over the longer spans of the narrative, are dependent on a different and less straightforward notion of what counts as observable, because the interpretation of such spans depends less on identifying atomic observables than on relating and integrating the observables into hearable progressions.

For example, one must consider not only how 'uprooting' pertinently characterises the C♭s just at bar 56 but also how it is a salient characterisation of the crisis in C♭'s voice-leading and scale identification, and thus of the version of tonality projected by this piece. It must account for the radical sound of the voice-leading's behavioural change, and this can be accomplished only in relation to this episode's place in the continuity of the narrative about the stream of the piece's events. Thus, the question, finally, is whether the immigrant's tale plausibly reflects the entire succession of C♭ events (to take the perspective of the piece) or the C♭ line of reasoning (to take a listener's perspective), and this can be evaluated only over the extent of the whole analytical tale.[34]

The story of the indomitable immigrant C♭ is more than just an amusing vehicle for visualising an analytical issue: how the points of contact between C♭ and E♭ major eventually resolve C♭'s initial disparity. It is a fertile method for addressing, to borrow another line from Babbitt, 'my eternal concern with the musical composition's accruing progress in time' while also describing the complexities of the single event – returning to Babbitt, 'the fusion of a stream of lines of values', 'a composite simultaneity, a point of polyphonic confluence of lines, of values of time points, metrical frames, dynamics, durations, timbres, etc.'[35] Because to explain how C♭ inflects E♭ major in terms of the immigrant's tale (or to describe how bar 53's C♭s are portentous) is to draw on a *model* just as surely as any scientist does.

The ideas associated with an immigrant, evoked by C♭'s relation to E♭ major early in the analysis of the piece, long before the tonal argument

---

34 In fact, I doubt that any isolated statement about a piece can be more than provisionally justified, if our standard of analytical adequacy is the characterisation of events just as and where they are in a particular piece and in that piece alone.

35 Babbitt, 'Responses: A First Approximation', *Perspectives of New Music*, 14/ii–15/i (1976), p. 9.

matured, provided the initial *relational logic* for closer examination. Under closer examination, the model's stereotypical framework left room to refine and modify its fit to the contextually defined identity of this piece. Character traits became models for contextual traits as ideas about an individual who is consistent but resilient enough to change in order to survive came to model the consistency of C♭'s pitch function as well as its C-major inspired transformation. The analytical tale reflected the continuity and qualities of C♭'s interaction with the tonality of E♭ major. A hearing of the piece developed and was increasingly enriched and refined as the generic became the particular immigrant.

Conclusion

Incorrigible statements are indeed personal, and verifiable only individual by individual, but they can be precise in their contextual claims, even meeting Babbitt's relevant standards of explanatory adequacy, and they are justifiable if they yield a sufficiently rich analysis. They can be expressed intersubjectively; they can uniquely specify the musical events; and they can be 'useful, useable, relevant, or significant' characterisations. They may not answer an aesthetic or emotional need for cognitive purity, but pragmatically speaking, they *are* used – even by Babbitt – and we will get further in understanding musical 'concept formation' as it 'involves those problems of intersubjectivity and of verbal utterances as empirical data'[36] by including them in our investigations.

This paper bears a complicated relation to Milton Babbitt's methodological work. It adopts his analytical goals, but, to achieve them, demotes the claims about '"scientific" language', by which he is best known, in favour of the other half of that famous duality, '"scientific" method'. In particular, Babbitt himself has indicated how the 'incorrigible personal statement' can be rehabilitated by providing evidence. If one accepts his prescription, analytical sedatives can be transformed into interpretations of musical contextualities that stimulate us to 'extend and enrich [our] perceptive powers'.

36 Babbitt, 'Structure and Function', p. 13.

Decisions

4

Criteria of correctness in music theory and analysis

JONATHAN DUNSBY

The title 'Criteria of Correctness' is an immediate departure from overall consideration of 'Theory, Analysis and Meaning'; but not a diversion. Writing recently about 'extravagance', W. V. Quine noted how 'a frequent cause of overstatement is diffidence: wondering whether what one is about to say is worth hearing. So one embellishes it a bit, not quite deliberately.'[1] A discussion of music-analytical 'meaning' without supporting technical illustration would, at least in my hands, be far too much of an embellishment, an intellectual extravagance. 'Correctness', however, has a modest urgency about it, as a standard that gives us the confidence to publish our work, and the confidence to impede the dissemination of work we don't like. The idea 'don't like' is simply not good enough in, for instance, research supervision, or in the refereeing of potential publications. At the other end of the scale, we are unlikely to say of a piece of analysis or of an analytical theory, 'I can prove this to be true'. 'Correctness' is somewhere in between. The reason it is of great import is obvious from the question: 'If we came to the conclusion that what we were achieving as theorists and analysts was probably not correct, would we be prepared to stop doing it?' Recently, calls of this kind have been made entirely seriously. Alan Street, for example, has argued for an 'allegorical' approach which

dissolves the last vestige of articulate theory: adherence to a distinct system. Whatever the individual case, it designates no preferred method or approach. In spite of this, allegory does not simply give up all hope of constructive insight. On the contrary, it is to keep alive the prospect of disinterested truth that allegorical understanding deliberately resists the use of convenient conceptual props.[2]

This chapter originated in papers delivered at the Society for Music Theory, Oakland, California, in 1990 and at City University, London, in 1991.

1 W. V. Quine, *Quiddities: An Intermittently Philosophical Dictionary* (London: Penguin, 1990), p. 58.
2 Alan Street, 'Superior Myths, Dogmatic Allegories: The Resistance to Musical Unity', *Music Analysis*, 8 (1989), pp. 77–123. See especially pp. 120–1.

The sort of correctness that alarms Street appears to be that which relies on mere consent for its truth value, a formalism that may be a veil protecting an underlying vacuity, the mere application of standard analytical methods, and the ready acceptance of standard analytical dicta. One example of this 'correctness' is a theme running through various of my own publications, in which it is pointed out that the aesthetic concept of the 'masterpiece' is fundamental to Schenker's work, and that without it Schenkerian technique is merely a set of, to use Street's well-chosen words, 'convenient conceptual props'. It is 'correct' as it were, politically, but artistically it is not so.

In looking for criteria, one must take account of a certain scatter in the 'analysis' of music, which has its 'superior myths' (Street), its small number of hegemonies, but within which the close observer can detect substantial differences of practice. One feature the hegemonies have in common is that they meet with resistance, and I welcome the fact that it is fashionable – hardly needs to be defended – to examine the nature of the resistance at least as closely as the nature of the phenomenon itself.

Hegemonies

What is it in significant theories that stimulates genuine, informed antagonism? My question is designed to expose the nature of the problem of truth in this discipline, without prejudging whether the problematics will be heterogeneous, or in clear focus. The procedure for exposure is, inevitably as far as I can see, to invoke some opinions. I invoke Schenker, Forte, Nattiez and Cone for symbolic reasons that will emerge later.

The problem in Schenker, so it is said, is that our response to the repertoire becomes overdetermined. Few musicians can reasonably be expected actually to perceive music in performance in an authentically and fully Schenkerian way. Among recent thinkers I would judge that Nicholas Cook, above all, has exposed this problem through his detailed studies of how analysis actually works, and how the musical imagination works.[3]

The problems with the Forte of 1973, so it is said, are that no-one can reasonably be expected actually to perceive music in performance through the frame of reference offered by the pitch-class set, and that some empirical qualities of the music which are fully scrutable are not

3 See Nicholas Cook, *A Guide to Musical Analysis* (London: Dent, 1987) and *Music, Imagination, and Culture* (Oxford: Clarendon Press, 1990) respectively.

entailed in, and may even be contradicted by, pc-set segmentation. Thus the repertoire becomes underdetermined.[4]

The problem with semiotic analysis of the kind familiar from Nattiez and his followers, so it is said, is that our response to the repertoire becomes underdetermined, for the actuals of experience are insufficiently encompassed by the provisionality of semiotic theory. We are asked to give up our dominant intuitions about the empirical data.[5]

The problem about what Cone called 'beyond analysis', so it is said, is that the theorist may refuse to accept that some empirical qualities of music are essentially inscrutable. Melodic ascent and descent, for example, are distinct and not interchangeable, therefore we simply must analyse their intention and effect, and not throw in the sponge as Cone seems to invite us to do in contemplating, for example, the inverted version of the beginning of Schoenberg's Piano Piece, Op. 33a.[6]

The objects of antagonism in the above are thus as follows: over-determination, underdetermination, empirical dominance, and empirical defeatism. Thus there are two underlying reasons why original theoretical thinking may find disfavour – thinking that has sufficient impact to become the cause of worthwhile professional debate, yet that may be found to be 'incorrect': on the one hand, in the matter of determination it may be because one is told too much or told too little altogether about the piece, the repertoire, the age or the culture; and on the other hand, empirically, it may be because one is told too little or told too much in relation to what one believed in the first place.

I think it follows that arguments about determination can be taken more seriously than arguments about empirical status, for the former avoid arguing about an entity with reference to a further entity that may prove to be more complex. In other words, if I think a particular music theory is wrong because it is over- or underdetermined, I ought to be able to fault it purely theoretically, without reference to any opinion of analytical results which calls for empirical evidence.

4 In this case, there is a fascinating historical record, for Forte himself exposed and resisted the critical response to his theory in 'Pitch-Class Set Analysis Today', *Music Analysis*, 4 (1985), pp. 29–58.

5 The most recent example of this kind of resistance to Nattiez is in Raymond Monelle's *Linguistics and Semiotics in Music* (Chur, Switzerland: Harwood, 1992). 'This theorist renounces ideology and established ideas', writes Monelle of Nattiez, typically painting in black and white a highly nuanced body of thought, 'and calls for patient and painstaking observation. The call is imperative, even if his own results are of limited scope.' (p. 126)

6 Edward T. Cone, 'Beyond Analysis', in Benjamin Boretz and Edward T. Cone (eds.), *Perspectives on Contemporary Music Theory* (New York: Norton, 1972), pp. 72–90.

Now, is this argument in fact a hand-washing, reductionist conceit that enables me to eliminate the dirty but exciting empirical world of real-life music? In a sense, I have no doubt that it is, for truth is the first casualty of one kind of philosophising – recall Aristotle's eternal 'truth' that 'all is not what it seems'. Yet the examples were chosen, as was said, for symbolic reasons: no-one in generous mood could object to them as leading cases in this field. They are in fact doubly symbolic, for not only do they represent a shared value system among music theorists, but it would be difficult, in my view at least, to find other examples inside that value system that could lead to a different kind of reduction. These are the myths, and all myths are of their type. Wherever I turn in recognisable music theory of the last hundred years or so the story is the same, if the yardstick is not what I myself think, but rather the response of others as it appears to me. Let it be clear, by the way, that this emphasis on observation is not a semiotic position. I am not concerned here with exegesis; indeed, I continue to hope for the development of a hermeneutical semiotics.

Resistance

Considering what level of argument is offered so far, how is it that such a broad brush can be taken in depicting a discipline in which most of us, as teachers and researchers, pride ourselves on knowledge of the differences, of the minutiae that cleave Schenker from Salzer, Forte from Perle, to the uncomprehending amazement of the cartoon historical musicologist? When we debate in our curriculum meetings, and ultimately in our journals and our books, whether to place emphasis in graduate school next year on *Basic Atonal Theory*[7] or on pc-set genera, are there real matters at issue, or is this the self-gratifying circularity of a corner of academe, it mattering only to itself?

I do think that music theorists need to use a broad brush as well as counting the angels, and that the main weakness of the discipline is that it does not recognise its own wider importance. Generally, the kind of question to be asked is, for instance: does the quality of music theory in the twentieth century significantly exceed the quality of general philosophical thought during the period? Even if it is a question that has not occurred to many music analysts and theorists, it is one that we must, in the end, answer. By way of illustration: it was not that long ago that

7 John Rahn, *Basic Atonal Theory* (New York: Longman, 1980).

Kerman seized the imagination of learned musicians with the opportunity to 'get out' of analysis.[8] Kerman doesn't share the view that we ought to be able to fault a theory without reference to analytical results. Indeed he comes close to priding himself in this notorious essay on penning the actuals of his own experience, without realising that, as it were, the diary of a luscious evening of musical musing at the beach is, literary matters aside, of little interest, and of none at a theoretical level. His very own particularity was saddening, for the journalistic flair of his title coupled with the historical shrinkage in his actual words seems to me to have done more harm than good. The impressionable student now thinks there is authority to say that (i) Schenker is probably not worth years of study, and (ii) in vocal music the text matters most, or at least it must always be taken into account – how I am supposed to do that when practising the triplets of *Der Erlkönig* at 7.00am is not specified, nor is the more tricky matter on the same continuum of what is to take place at the 9.00am harmonic analysis class. There is a lesson in this for every conspicuous music theorist and theoretical commentator: what is the *worst* use to which your work may be put?

These last remarks have taken us, not further from the question of truth, but through the ethical corollary of theoretical practice, the matter of its purpose and effect. If one believed, as Hans Keller did, that there actually were a fundamental ethical imperative in music-theoretical practice, in analysis, then it could not be sidestepped. But it was only Keller's dogged focus on criticism, indeed on communication ultimately at the cost of the very possibility of neutral contemplation, that pushed him to such an interpersonal extreme. Similarly, I cannot chastise Rudolph Réti – to take a remarkably worthy case – for some ethical failure in his theoretical vagueness, or, to use my terminology, in his theoretical underdetermination.

If truth is the first casualty of activity, and if all is not what it seems, and if we are not plagued here by ethical questions, what sort of purchase do practitioners have on the discipline of music theory? The answer to that question depends on when and where it is asked, why and by whom, and very often how and for what reason. It is hard to imagine a more contingent question in a more contingent context. Still, I think history teaches us that something can be said.

Any groundswell of opinion brings with it notions of correctness. The

8 Joseph Kerman, 'How We Got into Analysis, and How to Get Out', *Critical Inquiry*, 7 (1980), pp. 311–31.

American music theory groundswell has brought notions of correctness that are characterised by logical consistency of observation and explicit awareness of received scholarly opinion – coupled sometimes with justification of the particular cultural focus of the enterprise. These notions of correctness seem to me alarmingly strong. We forget that whereas the 'logic' that exerts such a force in standards of correctness has existed since the earliest recorded days of our civilisation, so also have formal procedures such as rhetoric, which supported that civilisation strongly for a long time and died out only relatively recently, probably at great cost to the coherence of our endeavours. We also forget in our courting of scholarly grace that a sixteenth-century theorist's mention of one or another Greek authority was just as important, just as significant, as may be my own reference within a contemporaneous one-hundred-strong footnote club. The very contemporaneity of scholarly protocol is a sign of dissolution. Indeed, some might say that in recent times scholarly protocol has itself become the central criterion of correctness in music theory and analysis. The tendency has been to judge what is new mainly by the placing and setting of its arguments against the yardsticks of others more or less contemporaneous.[9]

Continuities

However, it is becoming much less clear what is and what is not correct, as the passing orthodoxies of the 1960s and 70s have been challenged in the 1980s. We can see this in repertoire – opera studies for example, which often call for comment not on organic masterpieces but on highly valued compositional misjudgements, as Carolyn Abbate recently, and memorably, reminded us.[10] It can be seen, too, theoretically: in Allen Forte's new theory of pitch-class set genera; in David Lewin's overarching work on a theory of musical space; even in Carl Schachter's emblematic article 'Either/Or', which brings an idea of undecidability into the heart of the Schenkerian stronghold.[11] Here we shall propose that

---

9 Argument and illustration on this point may be consulted in my article 'Music Analysis: Commentaries', in John Paynter et al. (eds.), *Companion to Contemporary Musical Thought* (London: Routledge, 1992), pp. 634–49. In this current text, I am of course a victim of my own diagnosis, Aristotle on his own being no cure: the only defence needed is deliberation.

10 See Carolyn Abbate and Roger Parker (eds.), *Analyzing Opera: Verdi and Wagner* (Berkeley: University of California Press, 1989).

11 Allen Forte, 'Pitch-Class Set Genera and the Origin of Modern Harmonic Species', *Journal of Music Theory*, 32 (1988), pp. 187–270 (see also Forte's 'Debussy and the

two crucial areas merit investigation, and they are, after all, the obvious ones: language and cognition.

There does not appear to be among linguists the passionate interest in the behaviourist or mentalist study of verbal language that once there was, and music theory needs to look to newer models if it needs models from elsewhere. We have heard papers and read articles in the last few years to give the impression that American theory is only just discovering the delights of structuralism as it illuminated literary studies several decades ago. It does seem more important to engage music theory with the post-structuralist tradition that is now well ensconced, and indeed in the spirit in which this volume itself is published. Where the criteria may shift will depend, however, on what I think are the toughest questions of all, such as I asked above about philosophy (and the literary and language studies than flow in its wake). Lawrence Kramer's *Music and Language* dramatised the issues and led to a flow of abuse from 'real' musicians concerned at the possible inflow of less than edified thinking from other disciplines.[12] The essential step, in my view – the first step, at least – is to evaluate exo-musical ideas endogenously. How good, for instance, is Bloom's theory of poetic influence as a poetic theory? Is it a better theory of poetry than Meyer's theory of style development is a theory of music? Unless one is first convinced of that, and can convince other musicians, there is nothing correct and nothing to correct.[13]

Whether music theory needs models from elsewhere in the field of cognition is an otiose question, for the world of cognitive science and

Octatonic', *Music Analysis*, 10 (1991), pp. 125–69); David Lewin, *Generalized Musical Intervals and Transformations* (New Haven: Yale University Press, 1987) and *Musical Form and Transformation: 4 Analytic Essays* (New Haven: Yale University Press, 1993); Carl Schachter, 'Either/Or', in Hedi Siegel (ed.), *Schenker Studies* (Cambridge: Cambridge University Press, 1990), pp. 165–79.

12 Lawrence Kramer, *Music and Language* (Berkeley: University of California Press, 1984). The most recent deep discussion of Kramer's work I have come across is in David Griffiths' 'Song Writing: Poetry, Webern, and Musical Modernism' (PhD dissertation, King's College, University of London, 1993). The author finds Kramer's approach 'amusing' (p. 14). But it is more sinister than that if it clears the way ahead for further 'parlour games' in the name of musical hermeneutics.

13 In 'Towards a New Poetics of Musical Influence', *Music Analysis*, 10 (1991), pp. 3–72, Kevin Korsyn appropriates Bloom by asking 'Can we perform the same kind of deliberate misreading *on Bloom*, reading him as if he were talking about *music* instead of *poetry*? I think that within certain limits we can.' (p. 12; Korsyn's emphasis) And why should we want to? '[To allow] music analysis to recover the element of fantasy that is as necessary to theorizing about art as it is to artistic creation.' (p. 61) But if we know what it is we want to recover, why not just go ahead and do it? What was wrong with the way Wagner analysed Beethoven's String Quartet, Op. 131, in 1870? (See also Alan Street's comments on Wagner's analysis, this volume, p. 166. [Ed.])

artificial intelligence must necessarily impinge on how we think and how we formulate questions about our activity. It implies no disrespect to those engaged in the development of computer-based musical grammars and simulations to say that I believe the first wave of a new kind of relationality in our dealings with the musical score was evident even in Fortean pitch-class set theory. The personal computer offers the possibility of even further shifts in our imagination, and these are as unforeseeable as they may prove to be important. One criterion for correctness offered by this arises through a re-animation of the role of depiction in musical thought: it is precisely the fantasy of poetic response to music that writers such as E. T. A. Hoffmann entrenched in the nineteenth-century European consciousness of musical discourse, and, if it was lost sight of here and there in the modern age, the ghost in the microchip may be bringing it back.[14]

The now-famous CD-ROM of Beethoven's Ninth Symphony is the obvious example to consider, since it brings us into contact with the work in a strictly unprecedented way, indeed altering our impression of what the 'work' is in our memory of all its manifestations and in the expectations we bring to it anew.[15] It would be easy game to comment on how this CD-ROM offers us, in conventional ways, the music-analytically trite; but it is also certain that it opens up a new way of relating to the music, and the possibilities in the technology are vast enough to carry right through the continuum of entertainment, education and enlightenment, to new forms of correctness.[16] Quine, again, discusses the modern proliferation of artificial languages, observing that they proliferate 'much as the old artificial languages did, and the joy of tinkering is again no doubt a factor'.[17] On the one hand Quine is here at his laconic best; on the other, this is a perhaps unintentional tribute to the continuity of culture.

14 Cf. the author's comments on the work of Kevin Korsyn (n. 13). [Ed.]
15 Robert Winter, *Beethoven's Ninth Symphony* [multimedia reference work] (Los Angeles: Voyager, 1988) [CD-ROM publication MEC0138].
16 I would like to say, not having done so elsewhere, that there is some element of 'depiction' even in pc-set work, computerised or not. I have often felt, looking at monster charts and long runs of figures, a sense of connection with the 'work' itself; there is no getting away from the fact that the printer is spewing out what it is only because – and exactly because – Webern, say, wrote those notes back then. This is not to imply that 'anything goes', which would be ironic if not perverse under my title. However, and on the contrary, even these sorts of depiction can seem to have more substantive connection with the artistic content of the music than might the critical judgements of some Jo Musicologist.
17 Quine, *Quiddities*, pp. 12–13.

Although I undertook to consider only two factors, it would be wrong to evade the question of the creative environment. How music theory should deal with new art is not only a formally necessary consideration but also, I suspect, likely to be an indicator of its transformed survival, for music theory has always fed on new music. If it fails to do so now, this may be said to be an indictment of new music, though I have never believed the Meyer theory of cultural stasis, which post-modern composers seem to be disproving every day in any case.[18] However that may be, we have to decide whether to apply different criteria to the contemporary repertoire, as Edward Cone has urged us to do in a passage that will probably continue to be much quoted:

Although for practical purposes [analysis] cannot ignore compositions of the recent past, its pronouncements must be considered preliminary. Analysis today should ideally concern itself with works of no less than a decade ago. Works of art need that much time to begin taking their place in history and tradition; analysts need it in order to be secure from both the shock and the seductiveness of novelty.[19]

There is a kind of austere, East Coast correctness to this, call it rectitude perhaps, in hoping to ensure that artistic bombshells are safely defused before we look at what used to make them tick; in any case we must doubt whether chronological newness or oldness is part of our actual musical experience; and in any case too, if the fundamental problem in music theory were indeed its constant dalliance with music less than ten years old, our musical environment would be a pretty healthy one.

A last gasp

I trust that my departure from 'meaning' has led, if by only a few paces, to some terms for debate. I feel that there is a common instinct among those concerned with music theory and analysis that we are entering some sort of post-modern abandonment of critical orthodoxies. The challenge is likely to be, not the undecidability diagnosed by the deconstructionists, but a non-decidability that arises when theoretical commitment gives way to pseudo-artistic confusion. It would be wasteful if the credibility gained for theorising in the last few decades were to be lost in another post-Romantic onslaught in the name of pan-cultural freedom and the freedom of individual experience.

18 Jonathan Cross, this volume (p. 186), takes a contrasting view of Meyer. [Ed.]
19 Edward T. Cone, *Music: A View from Delft* (London: University of Chicago Press, 1989), p. 7.

5

Ambiguity in tonal music: a preliminary study

KOFI AGAWU

An unlikely example: Beethoven's Fifth Symphony

Beethoven's Fifth Symphony begins with a four-note motive containing two pitch classes, G and E♭. In the universe of major and minor scales (including melodic, harmonic, and natural minor as distinct constructs), these two pitch classes belong to three major keys and eleven minor keys. You could say, therefore, that the opening is ambiguous in the sense that it gives rise to two or more harmonic meanings. It would be an extraordinary listener, however, who claimed to hear simultaneously fourteen different harmonic meanings at the beginning of Beethoven's Fifth. Once a context is taken into account – and by 'context' I mean a series of additional texts – ambiguity dissolves into clarity. After all, this is a work in C minor, its opening plays with and against the Classical convention of beginning, the four-note motive is sequentially repeated on pitch classes F and D, and so on: these kinds of observation serve to eliminate most if not all of the alternative meanings. This does not mean that there might not be a network of harmonic meanings associated with this particular opening. But how does one construct such a network? Are some meanings stronger than others, some implications more potent than others? Is it enough to know, or do listeners need voluntarily to incorporate additional meanings into their experience of the inaugural motive? Are there reliable ways of choosing preferred meanings, or is the choice of context essentially an ad hoc move?

Few analysts of tonal music can claim ignorance of these kinds of issues. Attempts to analyse chromatic harmony, metric and hypermetric structures, and formal and generic constraints: these attempts often en-

This is a revised version of a paper read at the University of British Columbia in March 1992 and at the Eastman School of Music in December 1992. Critical comments received on both occasions, as well as from Ingrid Arauco, Matthew Brown, Patrick McCreless, Roger Parker, David Rosen and Arnold Whittall, have been helpful to me in preparing this version.

counter equivocal situations, equivocality being attributed to the phenomenon itself rather than to the tools with which that phenomenon is to be grasped. Yet, with few exceptions, theorists have been reluctant to embrace the notion of ambiguity as a phenomenon in its own right and to theorise it explicitly. Could it be that there is a basic contradiction between the explanatory impulse of theory and the resistance to explanation implicit in an ambiguous phenomenon? Is there not, in short, something contradictory about the notion of a 'theory of ambiguity'?

Twenty years ago, when the canonisation of techniques of musical analysis was still in progress, one might have answered both questions with a decisive 'yes'. Today, however, things look different. Two particular developments are worthy of mention. First, spurred on by some of the more radical developments in French and American literary theory, especially those that place plurisignification, indeterminacy and undecidability at their centre, recent thinking in analysis has begun to embrace the liberal and exploratory motivations of literary theory.[1] A second development is the completion – to the extent that such things are ever completed – of the process of canonisation, enabling us to begin interrogating the canon. As Proctor and Riggins put it in connection with Schenkerian theory:

Now that [the Schenkerian] condition is fairly stable, we are in the position of doing what we always do with orthodoxies: we question them, look for their weaknesses, and perhaps end up rejecting them in favor of something else.[2]

To state the historical sequence another way: a period in which tonal music was understood as subtending single meanings ('essences', 'basic shapes' and 'fundamental structures') has now been supplanted by a period in which music's multiple meanings or inherent ambiguities dictate the terms of theory and analysis. And the retrieval of that multiplicity necessarily entails an embrace of methodological pluralism.

The aim of this chapter is to take another look at the concept of

1 For examples see Robert Snarrenberg, 'The Play of *Différance*', *In Theory Only*, 10/iii (1987), pp. 1–25; Arnold Whittall, 'Analysis as Performance', in *Atti del XIV Congresso della Società Internazionale di Musicologia* (1987), pp. 654–9; Alan Street, 'Superior Myths, Dogmatic Allegories: The Resistance to Musical Unity', *Music Analysis*, 8 (1989), pp. 77–123; Patrick McCreless, 'Roland Barthes's *S/Z* from a Musical Point of View', *In Theory Only*, 10/vii (1988), pp. 1–29; Lawrence Kramer, *Music as Cultural Practice, 1800–1900* (Berkeley: University of California Press, 1990); and Carolyn Abbate, *Unsung Voices: Opera and Musical Narrative in the Nineteenth Century* (Princeton: Princeton University Press, 1991).
2 Gregory Proctor and Herbert L. Riggins, 'Levels and the Reordering of Chapters in Schenker's *Free Composition*', *Music Theory Spectrum*, 10 (1988), p. 102.

ambiguity as it might apply to the analysis of tonal music of the common-practice era. My main point – stated much too directly and therefore inaccurately at the outset – is that the concept of ambiguity is meaningless within the confines of an *explicit* music theory. While such a view might at first sight appear counterintuitive, perhaps even bizarre, I hope to support it by showing, not that multiple meanings do not exist in tonal music (how could they not?) but that, once the enabling constructs of music theory are brought into play, equivocation disappears. Why, then, has current thinking in musicology, and to a lesser extent theory, embraced – almost unhesitatingly – notions of ambiguity and undecidability? The answer, I suspect, lies in a political motivation, and I will make a comment about this at the end of the chapter.[3]

What is ambiguity?

There are two prominent types of ambiguity in natural language: lexical ambiguity and grammatical ambiguity. An example of lexical ambiguity is the word 'port', which could mean 'harbour' or a 'kind of wine'.[4] Another

---

3 The literature on ambiguity in music is on the whole analytical rather than theoretical in orientation. For a typology, strongly influenced by William Empson's *Seven Types of Ambiguity* (Harmondsworth: Penguin, 1961), see Thomas Clifton, 'Types of Ambiguity in Schoenberg's Tonal Compositions' (PhD dissertation, Stanford University, 1966). An informal commentary in which familiar instances of ambiguity such as incomplete chords, diminished-seventh chords, pivot chords, enharmonic equivalence, major/minor interplay and metrical ambiguities are identified may be found in Leonard Bernstein, 'The Delights and Dangers of Ambiguity', in *The Unanswered Question* (Cambridge, Mass.: Harvard University Press, 1976), pp. 193–259. See also: Jonathan Dunsby, *Structural Ambiguity in Brahms: Analytical Approaches to Four Works* (Ann Arbor: UMI Press, 1981); William Thomson, 'A Functional Ambiguity in Musical Structure', *Music Perception*, 1 (1983), pp. 3–27; Cheryl Noden-Skinner, 'Tonal Ambiguity in the Opening Measures of Selected Works by Chopin', *College Music Symposium*, 24 (1984), pp. 28–34; Roland Jordan and Emma Kafalenos, 'The Double Trajectory: Ambiguity in Brahms and Henry James', *19th-Century Music*, 13/ii (1989), pp. 129–44; Carl Schachter, 'Either/Or', in Hedi Siegel (ed.), *Schenker Studies* (Cambridge: Cambridge University Press, 1990), pp. 165–79; and Kenneth Delong, 'Roads Taken and Retaken: Foreground Ambiguity in Chopin's Prelude in A-flat, Op. 28, No. 17', *Canadian University Music Review*, 11/i (1991), pp. 34–49. For a theoretical study which proposes 'a computational model of cognition based on the process of identification and parsing of ambiguous musical events using music of the Common Practice period', see Jonathan Berger, 'A Theory of Musical Ambiguity', *Computers in Music Research*, 2 (1990), pp. 91–119. Also of interest in its overriding concern with multiple harmonic meanings is Charles J. Smith, 'The Functional Extravagance of Chromatic Chords', *Music Theory Spectrum*, 8 (1986), pp. 94–139.

4 This discussion is based on the article 'Ambiguity' by Patrizia Violi and Wendy Steiner

---

is 'mouth', which designates 'organ of body' as well as 'entrance of cave'. The former example involves the use of homonymous lexemes, the latter of polysemy. A grammatically ambiguous sentence is one 'to which there is assigned more than one structural analysis at the grammatical level of analysis'.[5] If I refer to 'beautiful girl's dress', I could mean either 'the dress of the beautiful girl' or 'the beautiful dress of the girl'. Similarly, in the sentence 'Tom didn't know if he had passed the exam', the pronoun 'he' may or may not be reflexive. Again, Chomsky's famous example, 'Flying planes can be dangerous' can mean either that 'Planes which are flying can be dangerous' or that 'To fly planes can be dangerous'. Here we have an example of transformational ambiguity, in which a sentence is derived from two or more different underlying structures. Although music exhibits features akin to both lexical and grammatical ambiguity, it is the latter that is more widespread. The crucial point is that 'anyone claiming that a word or expression is ambiguous must . . . be ready to specify the senses that they wish to distinguish'.[6]

By analogy, a musical situation is ambiguous if it gives rise to two or more meanings.[7] If, for example, I say of an excerpt from *Parsifal* that it is harmonically ambiguous, I must be ready to specify the competing meanings. Furthermore, I must be prepared to specify the plausibility of each meaning in relation to every other meaning. More formally, we might say that a musical situation is ambiguous if and only if its two (or more) meanings are comparably or equally plausible, leaving the listener undecided about their future significance. While the matter of comparable or equal plausibility may seem unnecessarily binding to those who wish to revel in an endless play of musical signifiers, it is an unavoidable theoretical move insofar as limits have to be set and a context has to be specified. Suppose I say that the opening of Beethoven's First Symphony, in addition to tonicising F as IV, also promises, by enharmonic equivalence, a move to E because the C^7 chord could technically later function as a German sixth, you might think me somewhat insane: 'the connection is far-fetched', you would say. 'There is no precedent for this

in Thomas A. Sebeok (ed.), *Encyclopedic Dictionary of Semiotics* (Berlin: Mouton de Gruyter, 1986), vol. 1, pp. 23–6. For a formal and rigorous philosophical study, see Israel Scheffler, *Beyond the Letter: A Philosophical Inquiry into Ambiguity, Vagueness and Metaphor in Language* (London: Routledge and Kegan Paul, 1979).

5 Violi and Steiner, 'Ambiguity', p. 23.

6 Anthony Flew, *Dictionary of Philosophy* (New York: St Martin's Press, 1979), s. v. 'Ambiguity'.

7 Note, incidentally, that the definition itself is ambiguous because open-ended: 'two or more' = 2 . . . n.

in the Beethoven literature', or 'you could not physically hear both things', or 'that is not a very musical way to hear'. Clearly then, some inferences are historically plausible, others less so, some are stylistically pertinent, others less so, and some are theoretically sound, others not. In an ideally ambiguous situation, the interplay among potential meanings will fail to tilt the balance and thus produce a genuine state of undecidability in the listener.

I do not know of any musical situation that elicits this sort of undecidability. Such situations are, of course, conceivable in the abstract, but they are quickly 'disambiguated' in concrete musical situations. Once a specified context and a specific metalanguage intervene, and given that we are always in context and always in (meta)language, the interpretation of a musical event as ambiguous in the strict sense becomes untenable.

Although they are liable to be confused in ordinary discourse, ambiguity and vagueness do not mean the same thing. If vagueness is defined as 'the existence of indefiniteness in the meaning of a word, expression, or statement',[8] then it is not immediately clear what musical vagueness might be. While an ambiguous musical situation is one that enables the analyst to specify two (or more) alternative meanings, a vague musical situation is presumably one in which the meanings are not sufficiently well-formed to be specifiable. It is conceivable that 'spatial' parameters such as timbre and texture may support some uncertainty in articulation, but I doubt whether the 'temporal' parameters of rhythm, harmony and melody can do the same. It may be that music's apparent lack of a stable semantic dimension paradoxically undermines its potential for supporting vagueness. If we grant, at least provisionally, the possibility of musical ambiguity, we must eliminate the corresponding possibility for musical vagueness.

Consider a final example given by the philosopher C. S. Peirce in illustration of indexical signs or indices, of which pronouns form a major category:

a. A replied to B that he thought C (his brother) more unjust to himself than to his own friend.

---

8 Flew, *Dictionary of Philosophy*, s. v. 'Vagueness'. It might be argued that the basic condition of language is one of ambiguity, and that all linguistic usages have the potential to signify in a multiplicity of ways. This is a valid viewpoint – we can never hope fully to control the semantic field of any individual word. If we grant ambiguity at the level of object language, however, we have to deny ambiguity at the level of metalanguage in order to ensure sufficiency in communication about technical matters. For the

b. A replied to B that he A thought C (his A's brother) more unjust to
                         B   B's
    himself A than to his A's own friend.[9]
        B   B's
        C   C's

The challenge is to eliminate ambiguity in the (conceptual) transition from sentence a to sentence b. Observe the gradual accumulation of multiple meanings as sentence b unfolds, a process analogous to the 'composing out' of a simpler proto-structure (sentence a). There is no need to rehearse this well-known generative process here except to note a paradox in the relationship of deep to surface structure. In one sense, the progression from background to foreground is a progression from an ambiguous, lifeless and abstract proto-structure to a concrete, unambiguous and unique structure. In another sense, however, the foreground, in its particularity, is multiply interpretable, and therefore requires the postulation of an unambiguous background in order to be deciphered.

How might the principle of Peirce's example apply in the analysis of tonal structure? Considered in relation to the diachronic aspects of tonal structure, Peirce's example may resemble situations in which an initial ambiguity persists until the end of the given musical sentence or passage. In general, however, tonal structures, if they exhibit ambiguity, do so in an irreversible ambiguity-to-clarity order. The rhetorical premise seems to privilege a clear ending, leaving the most functional ambiguities for the beginning and middle. If an event or process termed 'ambiguous' persists, the fact of its persistence confers on it a referential status such that, as the work unfolds, ambiguity is not compounded but eliminated. The convention of closure, prescribed as a norm for all tonal structures, further privileges an ambiguity-to-clarity over a clarity-to-ambiguity progression. While the latter stance is, of course, available in the abstract, it is not normally encountered in actual works, unless the clarity-to-ambiguity pattern occurs in the context of a larger clarity-to-ambiguity-to-clarity progression. If the most extended and equivocal moments are thus 'contained', then what can we mean when we speak of musical ambiguity? Might the use of the phrase represent an (unconscious) attempt to mystify what is clear?

only way I can assert that 'language is inherently ambiguous' is to assume a degree of clarity in the assertion itself.
9 Charles S. Peirce, 'Logic as Semiotic: The Theory of Signs', in Robert E. Innis (ed.), *Semiotics: An Introductory Reader* (Bloomington: Indiana University Press, 1982), p. 15.

Example 5.1   Chordal summary of Song 12 from
Schumann's *Dichterliebe*, bars 1–13

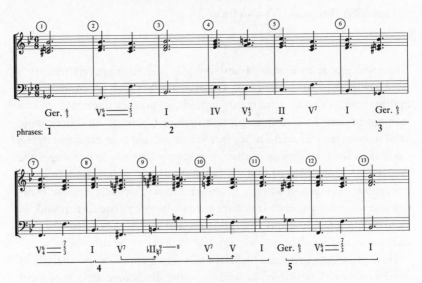

A plausible example: Schumann's *Dichterliebe*,
song 12, bars 1–13

As an illustration of the ostensibly self-evident and commonsensical understanding of ambiguity, let us consider the first thirteen bars of
Schumann's song, 'Am leuchtenden Sommermorgen', the twelfth of his
Dichterliebe cycle. Ambiguity is thought to reside in the harmonic narrative, specifically in the play between the synonymous German sixth and
dominant seventh chords (see Ex. 5.1 for a chordal summary of the
passage).

Schumann's song begins with an arpeggiated sonority that unfolds at a
relatively slow tempo and in two different registers. What is the chord,
and what might it mean? Since it sounds like a seventh chord, I might
infer two meanings: V^7 of B (major or minor), or German-sixth of B♭
(major or minor). If I am familiar with Schumann's harmonic practice, in
particular with his opening strategies, I am unlikely to regard the two
alternatives as equally plausible. On statistical grounds, a V^7 meaning is
more likely than a German-sixth meaning. But I may not wish to allow
statistics to determine what I choose to expect, in which case I will insist
on retaining the two possibilities. In other words, knowing what usually
happens should not lead me to discount what *could* happen. The percep-

tion of ambiguity thus depends on the kind of baggage that I bring or wish to bring to the auditing process.

Some might wonder whether it is good to diagnose ambiguity on the basis of hearing a single chord – might we not be better served by a context of, perhaps, two chords? Here we encounter another paradox. The construction of context depends, of course, on what the analyst wishes to show. Since a seventh chord is more particular (phenomenally speaking) than a good old major or minor triad, I could start drawing inferences right from the start. Had I not been presented with a musical term of such particularity, I would have insisted on some kind of relationship as the irreducible minimum unit for drawing harmonic inferences. (In linguistic terms, the former view is weighted towards the paradigmatic, the latter towards the syntagmatic.) The point, then, is that if I claim to perceive an event or set of events as ambiguous, I must not only specify but *justify* the context that I have constructed to enable that perception.

How does one model ambiguity during a real-time audition of the opening of Schumann's song? By the end of the first phrase, and irrespective of what my initial expectations were, I understand (in retrospect) the function of the opening chord as an augmented sixth. Does ambiguity then exist only in prospect, never in retrospect? This cannot be the case, for to interpret a musical event as ambiguous does not mean that I do not know its meaning, or that there are innumerable possibilities for its meaning; the claim is rather that the event remains ambiguous *after* a reflective analytical exercise. The 'I do not know' type of ambiguity is a weak kind, one that need not detain us here so long as ours is a theory-based context. Ambiguity in the stronger sense is a product of *both* prospective and retrospective views. After several hearings, I know (of course) what happens to the opening chord, but I might still choose to model a hearing in which the dual meaning of the opening chord plays an important part. I might argue that the richness of the experience derives not from not knowing what the resolution of the opening chord is going to be but from self-consciously enacting a state of harmonic ignorance, from temporarily unknowing what I already know. When the chord resolves on the downbeat of bar 2, I obtain foreground assurance of the chord's German-sixth function but I do not lose the complementary 'background' sense of a denied V^7 function, which will be implemented in bars 8–9. This dual meaning exists in what Derrida would call a 'violent hierarchy', and although some analysts may choose not to weigh the relative potentials of the two meanings, others will insist on doing so.

If we regard an ambiguous musical event as one that gives rise to a multiplicity of undifferentiated meanings, then of course the opening of the Schumann song, like numerous other openings, is ambiguous. But if we differentiate among meanings, and acknowledge their hierarchic formation on the basis of internal (structural) and/or external (stylistic) factors, then this opening is not ambiguous. Note, then, that as we specify context, listener baggage and segmental level, we are effectively contextualising ambiguity by showing that its constituents are hierarchically rather than non-hierarchically formed.[10]

One model for harmonic progression in the song is a Riemannesque three-stage progression from dominant preparation through dominant to tonic chords. (In Ex. 5.1, each of the five 'phrases' includes this progression, although there are overlapping boundaries between phrases 1 and 2 and between phrases 3 and 4). Once the pattern of harmonic progression has been established, the process of drawing inferences becomes more as well as less complicated. It becomes more complicated because every time the pre-dominant chord is struck, I might predict that the entire pattern will be unfolded. Any ambiguities inherent in the first presentation of the pattern will therefore remain operative in subsequent presentations. The process is at the same time less complicated, because experience tells me that each subsequent repetition of the pattern will be different since each repetition occupies a unique moment in musical time. This larger expectation for change may well conflict with the internal expectations generated by the pattern itself. Moreover, any time an intertextual correlation is activated by a given event or set of events, the parameters for drawing inferences multiply and the process grows in complication.

Consider the chord in the second half of bar 6. At least two interpretative possibilities are suggested. First, if I privilege recurrence, then I will assume that I am hearing a German-sixth chord again. I might further reason that phrase 3 will function as the symmetrical equivalent of phrase 1 (phrase 2 was different from phrase 1). Second and alternatively, the fact that phrase 2 is a harmonic and durational expansion of phrase 1 could signal further recomposition in phrase 3. Note, however, that unless I am viewing these harmonic events from the most privileged posi-

10 The process I am describing here has been analysed in more formal terms by David Lewin in his 'Music Theory, Phenomenology, and Modes of Perception', *Music Perception*, 3/iv (1986), pp. 327–92. See also the discussion in Leonard B. Meyer, *Emotion and Meaning in Music* (Chicago: University of Chicago Press, 1956) and, *via* a series of preference rules, Fred Lerdahl and Ray Jackendoff, *A Generative Theory of Tonal Music* (Cambridge, Mass.: MIT Press, 1983).

tion possible – that of the transcendental signified – I will *not* find the analytical situation undecidable. For if I am schooled in the periodic structure of Schumann's songs, or in the Romantic protocol of beginning, I will know which of my competing meanings is the more plausible (in this case, my first). The more of such knowledge I bring to the interpretative process, the less ambiguous I am likely to find a given passage. Ambiguity, according to this view, is either a pre-theoretical, 'I don't yet know' phenomenon, or a pronouncement in a transcendent, 'I know it all' vein. While the former cannot hold much interest for analysts, the latter is a position that not even the most confident analyst would admit to holding.[11]

Another plausible example: Mozart's Symphony No. 40 in G minor, K. 550, first movement, bars 1–23

It could be argued, contrary to Carl Schachter's claim that it is 'in the sphere of harmony . . . that the most frequent and difficult problems [of interpretation] arise',[12] that the understanding of rhythm and metre present even more formidable problems. Many such analyses acknowledge instances of ambiguity. In one of the clearest articulations of the problems of rhythmic analysis, Lerdahl and Jackendoff include several structural descriptions of passages in which ambiguity plays an important role.[13] One of these, the opening of Mozart's Symphony in G minor, K. 550, is described as a 'not untypically complex' passage, and serves to illustrate some of the problems of large-scale metrical analysis. In what senses are the first twenty-three bars of Mozart's symphony metrically ambiguous? Are the two (or more) meanings equally or comparably plausible, even given the disambiguating effects of context and performance?

Lerdahl and Jackendoff's interpretation consists of a preliminary analysis of bars 1–9 on six metrical levels followed by a reading of the large-scale metrical structure of bars 1–23 incorporating the previous analysis. The preliminary analysis (Ex. 5.2) reveals a predictable mode of organisation from the quaver level and beyond. Up to the two-bar level,

---

11 To consign something to the category 'pre-theoretical' is, of course, to court disaster since, in some views, we can never be 'outside' theory. Throughout this paper, I use 'theory' in this all-embracing sense as well as in the more specific sense of an explicit organising framework (e. g. Schenkerian theory). I believe the two uses to be self-explanatory in context.

12 Schachter, 'Either/Or', p. 166.

13 Lerdahl and Jackendoff, *A Generative Theory of Tonal Music*, pp. 40–3, 64–7, 90–6, 142–5.

Example 5.2   Lerdahl and Jackendoff's metrical analysis of Mozart's
G minor Symphony, K. 550, first movement, bars 1–9

there appears to be no metrical problem. That is, strong and weak beats or groupings of beats alternate in regular fashion. Things look different, however, when we listen as far as bar 23 (Ex. 5.3). If we allow thematic and tonal returns to indicate large spans, then we might interpret the return of the opening theme in bars 21–3 as bearing an accent on the highest level. Whilst this location of a high-level accent does not alter the rhythmic pattern established from the beginning on quaver and crotchet levels, a distinct problem arises on the minim level. More precisely, a simple alternation of strong and weak will not do; somewhere along the line, a strong–strong or weak–weak pattern must intervene in order to maintain the larger accentual pattern.[14]

Invoking a distinction of Andrew Imbrie's between 'conservative' and 'radical' hearings, Lerdahl and Jackendoff provide two interpretations of the passage. A conservative hearing retains the pattern of strong–weak alternation until the last possible moment. In a radical hearing, by contrast, the listener makes the necessary adjustment as soon as new (i. e. conflicting) evidence is presented. Radical and conservative hearings of

14 This problem is unique to Lerdahl and Jackendoff's theory, which disallows successive downbeats. The problem does not arise in rhythmic theories that have no such prohibition. See for example William Rothstein, *Phrase Rhythm in Tonal Music* (New York: Schirmer, 1989), pp. 58–63 for a discussion of 'successive downbeats'.

Example 5.3   Lerdahl and Jackendoff's metrical analysis of
Mozart's G minor Symphony, K. 550, first movement,
bars 1–23, showing alternative interpretations A and B

the Mozart passage, marked A and B respectively in Ex. 5.3, are identical
until bar 9 and become one again in bar 13. The divergence occurs in
bars 9–13. If I hear conservatively, I will hear the downbeats of bars 9, 11
and 14 (deleting bar 13 – or rather collapsing it into a two-bar unit) as the
main beats on the two-bar level; if, by contrast, I hear radically, I will
experience the accents on the downbeats of bars 10, 12 and 14, the

discrepancy occurring between bars 7 and 13. In short, while a conservative hearing balances the account at the conclusion of the passage, a radical hearing pays its debt in advance.

Is this a genuine case of ambiguity? Is the situation undecidable? Lerdahl and Jackendoff say 'yes'. In fact, they not only acknowledge ambiguity but refuse to choose between the two interpretations:

> We will refrain from choosing between these competing alternatives; suffice it to say that in such ambiguous cases the performer's choice, communicated by a slight extra stress (in this case, at the downbeat of either bar 10 or bar 11), can tip the balance one way or the other for the listener.[15]

A footnote then directs the reader to recordings of this piece in which alternative accentuations may be heard. No recording is cited, however, which 'refrains from choosing between . . . competing alternatives'.[16]

Putting aside the relative technical merits of each analysis, we note that practically every performance and every hearing of the G minor Symphony prefers one of the two interpretations. The only hearing that uses neither interpretation is a non-hearing. So, whereas the theorist can afford to sit on the fence, the performer cannot. Performers are, of course, not unaware of ostensibly ambiguous situations. At the moment of execution, however, they must decide one way or other and convey their interpretation with conviction.[17] Now, if an actual performance makes this

15 Lerdahl and Jackendoff, *A Generative Theory of Tonal Music*, p. 25.
16 Cf. Bruce B. Campbell's claim (review of Janet M. Levy, *Beethoven's Compositional Choices: The Two Versions of Opus 18, No. 1, First Movement* (Philadelphia: University of Pennsylvania Press, 1982), in *Journal of Music Theory*, 29/i (1985), p. 193) that:

> ambiguity in music does not really exist. Some musical phenomena can be understood in several ways – a popular example is the diminished-seventh chord – but surely one of the functions of analytical insight is to show how all but one of the apparent or 'theoretical' possibilities are artistically untenable in a given context. Without a firmly fixed point of view, it is difficult to maintain any perspective or coherent vision. An analysis, after all, is an opinion of how to hear a piece. Certainly, the performers have to decide where the music is going (how does one perform ambiguously?), and the composer *had* to know where he was going. . . . A powerful analytical system, such as Schenker's (regardless of whether his method can account for all details of a composition), will at least be able to relate the details with which it *is* concerned (in Schenker's case, voice-leading) to the larger structure, and thereby resolve any and all matters of seemingly local 'ambiguity' – certainly no mean accomplishment.

17 I leave out of consideration the possibility that a performer, fully aware of an ambiguous musical situation, performs in such a way as to convey the ambiguity. I have my doubts as to whether this kind of 'neutral' playing is possible. (See also the remarks of Bruce B. Campbell quoted above, n. 16 [Ed.]) Here, perhaps, is one difference between a score and a performance, the idea being that a score enshrines a multiplicity of potential interpretations while a given performance instantiates only one of those

demand on the performer and on the listener, it seems likely that the analyst of large-scale metrical structure – who is, after all, concerned with a relatively immediate level of structure – will face similar problems. To 'refrain from choosing between . . . competing alternatives' is to refuse to take advantage of the disambiguating functions of theory; it is to retreat from the practice of theory. It is, of course, perfectly legitimate for Lerdahl and Jackendoff, as theorists, to concern themselves with possibilities rather than prematurely getting their feet wet with probabilities. I insist only that the force of such an authorial plot be acknowledged, so that we do not mistake the refusal to choose for the absence of a mechanism for choosing.

Reading ambiguity (1): William Thomson's theory of 'functional ambiguity' *or* Thomson's error

Proceeding from the view that 'the condition of ambiguity is readily analyzable, its nature amenable to theoretical formulation', William Thomson proposes 'to assemble an embracing theory of musical ambiguity'. Here is his straightforward and unproblematic definition of ambiguity:

When a music event, whether small or large, projects equivocation, implying no clear syntactic meaning or two or more potential meanings, I call this an instance of *functional ambiguity*.[18]

Ambiguity, according to this view, occurs on all levels of structure, and can either mean vagueness ('implying no clear syntactic meaning') or point to multiple meanings. (Here, we can dispense with the 'vagueness' category both in the light of remarks made earlier and because Thomson is unable to provide an example of such.) Ambiguity and clarity exist in a necessary dialectical relationship. Although Thomson, following David Epstein,[19] acknowledges cases of 'ambiguity as premise', the usual procedure, he says, is for ambiguity to issue from clarity. Thomson acknowledges the intentional use of ambiguity by composers, and notes the apparent paradox by which a musical event may 'suggest ambiguity' without itself being ambiguous.

It will be clear from even this preliminary definition that a proper

possibilities. It should be noted, however, that in so far as any reading of the score – including a silent one – is ontologically possible only as a remembered or imagined performance, the gap between score and performance may be ultimately untenable.
18 Thomson, 'Functional Ambiguity', p. 3.
19 David Epstein, *Beyond Orpheus* (Cambridge, Mass.: MIT Press, 1979). Chapter 3 is entitled 'Ambiguity as Premise'.

Example 5.4   William Thomson's abstract demonstration of metric
ambiguity resulting from contradictory stress and contour patterns

study of musical ambiguity requires at least a statement about what music
is. Thomson does not venture a comprehensive definition of music, but
allies himself with those aestheticians and theorists who see music as
'non-referential' or as meaning (music) itself (Hanslick, Stravinsky,
Hindemith and Meyer). This 'means itself' is then elucidated as a form of
hierarchical processing, a concept influenced by Meyer but distinct from
Schenkerian notions of hierarchy.

Thomson's theory of ambiguity rests on a proposition of 'parametric
noncongruence': when parametric processes in a musical situation are
non-congruent there is potential ambiguity. More specifically, 'if within
the total event at least two properties are noncongruent, then structural
ambiguity is a latent potential'. Further, 'if pairs of noncongruent properties coincide, either simultaneously or serially, ambiguity becomes a
result of high probability for the perceptive listener'. The theory, presented in a series of loose statements, rather than made concrete in the
form of logical or symbolic propositions, is then illustrated by means of
an abstract example in which contradictory patterns of stress and contour
change are said to produce metric ambiguity. Ex. 5.4 reproduces one of
Thomson's examples of ambiguity.

There are two preliminary points to be made about this theory. First,
'parametric noncongruence', far from being a departure from a putative
norm of parametric congruence, is in fact the norm of musical structure.
Eugene Narmour's network analyses, elaborated recently by Robert
Gjerdingen, make this clear.[20] Although the dynamics of networks remain
to be specified, it is clear that non-congruence is not restricted to such
cases as interrupted cadences (which Thomson mentions) but may include perfect and imperfect cadences, as well as stable and unstable por-
tions of a work. We might go even further and claim that parametric non-

20   See Eugene Narmour, *Beyond Schenkerism: The Need for Alternatives in Music Analysis*
(Chicago: University of Chicago Press, 1977) and Robert Gjerdingen, *A Classic Turn
of Phrase: Music and the Psychology of Convention* (Philadelphia: University of Pennsylvania Press, 1988). See also Richard Smith, 'Foreground Rhythmic Structures: A
Preliminary Study' (MMus dissertation, King's College, London, 1987).

Example 5.5   Thomson's illustration of metric
ambiguity in Debussy's *Danse*

congruence appears to be the inescapable condition of any expressive art. Schenker's reference to a 'tension of musical coherence' may be read as a hint at this precarious balance among musical parameters.[21]

Second, the only possibly significant cases of ambiguity cited by Thomson are based on abstract examples. The excerpt quoted in Ex. 5.4, composed specifically for the occasion, behaves differently from most tonal pieces. If ambiguity exists only as an abstract phenomenon, to be invented as foil for ordinarily non-ambiguous real works, then ought we not to acknowledge this fabrication as what it is, namely, a useful theoretical tool, not a property of any given work? There are, in fact, ways of disambiguating the structure quoted in Ex. 5.4 by examining the beginning and ending of the pattern, by following the built-in circle-of-fifths pattern, by extracting a polyphonic melody from the complex, and so on. Thomson does not assign numerical weights to the determining functions of individual parameters, and so encourages the view that parameters are weighted equally. While this democratic pattern may serve the purposes of analysing a musically restricted structure, it creates severe problems in a tonal work with real harmonic, melodic or rhythmic content.

Consider Thomson's analysis of four bars from Debussy's *Danse* (see Ex. 5.5), cited as 'a clear example of . . . bi or polymetric rhythm'. The two metres are $\frac{3}{4}$ and $\frac{6}{8}$ and are conveyed in the left and right hands respectively. Thomson concludes that the metre of the piece is 'functionally ambiguous'. It might be argued, however, that the primary metre of the piece is an unequivocal $\frac{6}{8}$, communicated in the rate of harmonic change, in the quaver pulsation in the left hand, and – paradoxically

21 Heinrich Schenker, *Free Composition*, trans. and ed. E. Oster (New York: Longman, 1979), p. 6. It is possible – although this is not made clear in the article – that Thomson is referring to a degree of non-congruence over and above that which normally exists in musical structure. In that case, it seems necessary, in building a 'theory of functional ambiguity', to explore the continuities as well as discontinuities between normal conditions and those that obtain in the specific works analysed.

though it may seem – in the tension between the momentary triple grouping of the right hand (bars 1–2) and the permanent duple grouping of the left. For since the definition of metre frequently entails some sort of challenge, however brief, to its normative regularity, the so-called ¾ of the right hand is not a comparable, equally valid metre but the aggregate of a set of effects heard within the overriding ⁶⁄₈ metre. One would have to ignore the resultant rhythm in order to find this a 'functionally ambiguous' metric situation.

Let us be clear that one can reject the interpretation of this example as an instance of bi-metric rhythm without denying the rich contrasts of articulation and grouping within the governing ⁶⁄₈ metre. Many propositions for musical ambiguity seem to founder on this very point. To say that there is a hierarchic formation in the metric situation here is not to deny the existence of subsidiary meanings. It is rather to challenge the reading of the passage as metrically undecidable.[22]

Reading ambiguity (2): Carl Schachter's 'Either/Or' or the impossibility of Schenkerian equivocation

Unlike Thomson's theory of functional ambiguity, which is built on a generally defined conception of musical structure as a form of 'hierarchical processing', Carl Schachter's exploration of analytical alternatives is firmly anchored in Schenkerian theory. Such situating of limits allows Schachter stronger theoretical grounds on which to discuss musical ambiguity. In my reading, Schachter's study is a spectacular demonstration of the impossibility of apprehending ambiguity once the enabling con-

---

22 In a number of analyses, Thomson undercuts his own argument by giving the edge to one or another formation. For example, the opening of Debussy's *Prélude à 'l'après midi d'un faune'* is said to be tonally ambiguous because of the strong presence of the tritone C♯–G:

> Both pitches serve as points of tentative repose, for they represent agogic accents and contoural outer limits. And yet the uncomplementary harmonic relationship of C♯ and G, forming a tritone, provides no edge to one or the other pitch as harmonic focus. They are merely two pitches of contoural and rhythmic prominence, one of which, the C♯, enjoys slightly greater contextual and durational advantage. ('Functional Ambiguity', p. 8)

From an initial assertion that the tritone 'provides no edge to one or the other pitch as harmonic focus' Thomson ends by acknowledging that C♯ 'enjoys slightly greater contextual and durational advantage'. In other words, the context makes possible the resolution of the ambiguity. Often, when analysts infer ambiguity from a particular situation, it is not because they have no way of deciding but because they refuse to make the decision.

structs of theory have been explicitly invoked. The antithesis between theory and ambiguity is nowhere better illuminated.

It should be said at the outset that Schachter is sceptical not so much of the phenomenon of musical ambiguity but of its pervasiveness. After outlining a method for choosing between three different harmonic interpretations of the first eight bars of Chopin's Mazurka in G♯ minor, Op. 33, No. 1, Schachter comments as follows:

This is not to deny the possibility that ambiguity and multiple meanings might exist in tonal music; they certainly do exist. But their function, in my opinion, is more narrowly circumscribed than some analysts, perhaps misled by false analogies to language, seem to believe.[23]

Schachter is right to warn against uncritical borrowings of methods for finding ambiguity from linguistic and literary studies. What is puzzling about this statement is the confident assertion that 'ambiguity and multiple meanings . . . certainly do exist'. This is puzzling because, as I will show in a moment, Schachter's own argument amounts to a decisive vote against the plausibility of musical ambiguity.

The ruling metaphor of Schachter's essay is a 'fork in the road', which conveys a more dynamic (i. e. time-dependent) view of tonal process than Thomson's spatial 'parametric noncongruence'. Schachter reports the ways in which an analyst makes decisions when confronted with ostensibly equivocal situations. Part of his aim is to clarify this process by showing what additional – but not external – factors might be invoked in order to resolve the ambiguity. While Thomson understands 'functional ambiguity' as an irreducible residue of a finished work, Schachter's 'fork in the road' presents the analyst with a choice which he or she can (must?) make.

Like Thomson, the only unequivocal cases of ambiguity offered by Schachter are abstract ones. About the white-note progression quoted in Ex. 5.6, Schachter asks whether IV or I is the 'correct' reading. While 'the arid surface of our abstract example can provide decisive confirmation for neither interpretation', a concrete piece 'can give us reasons for our choice'. Does this imply that ambiguity is best viewed as an abstract principle, useful on remote levels of structural organisation as a fiction, foil, or metaphor for understanding the particularities of actual works? If so, then some acknowledgement of this catalytic role should be made in order to avoid confusion. Schachter, too, provides evidence in support of

23 Schachter, 'Either/Or', p. 169.

Example 5.6   Carl Schachter's abstract example of alternative
harmonic interpretations of the same harmonic progression

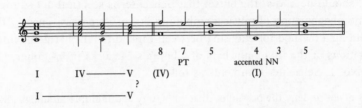

the view that as soon as we enter into the details of an actual musical work, ambiguity recedes in our perception.

There is something programmatic about Schachter's 'Either/Or' title, for rather than pursue genuine alternatives, he provides, I fear, mostly weak alternatives that are promptly discarded. Has Schachter set up straw alternatives? In the end, do we really have forks in the road? It seems that, although his rhetoric includes references to 'a true double meaning' and 'genuine ambiguity', none of Schachter's analyses demonstrates a final-state awareness of ambiguity.[24]

Consider the analysis of the first eight bars of Chopin's Mazurka in G♯ minor, Op. 33, No. 1, quoted in Ex. 5.7. Although Schachter entertains the possibility that there might be at least three viable interpretations of harmony and voice-leading in this phrase (see the three-level Roman numeral analysis shown beneath the quoted passage), he quickly discards the second and third, finding the first 'the only tenable interpretation'. His preferred interpretation is one that takes account of the motivic shape of the music. Stated as a general rule: given two equally valid but mutually exclusive harmonic interpretations of a passage, prefer the one that is richer in motivic content. Whether this is a good or bad preference rule is not the point here. The point is rather that Schenkerian theory makes possible the postulation of such a rule. Analysts may therefore not facilely invoke undecidability when confronted with three apparently equally valid interpretations of a passage. They might look to complementary domains for 'disambiguating' factors.[25]

---

24 It is perhaps an indication of a basic unease about the concept of ambiguity that many writers feel a need to use words like 'true', 'genuine', 'real' in describing situations of ambiguity. Schachter, and Lerdahl and Jackendoff, use such words frequently.

25 It would be a narrow view of Schenkerian theory that restricted its purview to what Schenker actually said. For one thing there are often gaps between what Schenker said and what he did. For another, there is enough dynamism in Schenkerian concepts to

Example 5.7   Schachter's demonstration of three different interpretations
of harmony in bars 1–8 of Chopin's Mazurka, Op. 33, No. 1

This is a crucial point in the debate about ambiguity: one group
refuses to march on, satisfied that the situation is undecidable, and leaving individual listeners to make up their minds in private; the other
group insists that the march continue, assured that there is a way out.
Schachter's own view about how to deal with this apparent impasse is
instructive. Rejecting as 'erroneous' the belief that the three alternative
analyses of Ex. 5.7 'are equally good', he insists on the following:

enable extension. The fact that such 'extensions' have not yet been formalised does not
mean that they are not part of the theory. In the muddy waters of motivic and
thematic analyses conducted within a Schenkerian framework, for example, we, of
course, await such a process of formalisation, but individual practices (including that
of Schenker himself) suggest that a high premium is placed on 'rich' and unsuspected
motivic relationships. For a recent critique of 'gaps' between Schenkerian theory and
practice in the matter of motivic analysis, see Richard Cohn, 'The Autonomy of
Motives in Schenkerian Accounts of Tonal Music', *Music Theory Spectrum*, 14/ii
(1992), pp. 150–70.

One of the three readings is truer to the Mazurka as a unique and individual work of art than are the other two, which can be considered valid only from a perspective that takes in general aspects of tonal structure but that excludes the specific features of the piece's design.[26]

It is unlikely that there will be disagreement about Schachter's view that analysis must go beyond 'general aspects of tonal structure' to illuminate 'specific features of the piece's design'. In a sense, that has been the project of tonal analysis all along. The pursuit of that goal logically entails the contextualisation of ambiguities encountered at earlier stages of the analysis. Just as no two works, however similar, can ever be 'the same', so no two readings of a work, however similar, can ever terminate in undecidability. Only if one consciously withholds the texts of context can one reach such an outcome. The decision as to how many more texts to bring into view is, alas, motivated by ethical, pragmatic, political and economic factors, not by epistemological concerns.

Finally, it is worth noting that Schachter, too, fails to situate as unequivocally as possible the limits of ambiguity. This is easily accomplished by juxtaposing an actual or hypothetical passage that is unambiguously clear with one that is not. In most analyses, clarity is assumed to be self-evident. Thus one term of the binary opposition is strategically left under-explicated. But since notions of clarity and ambiguity are inextricably linked, it is theoretically unacceptable to assume the meaning of one of the terms. To do so, in fact, amounts to mystifying (deliberately?) that term. I suspect that this is a strategic omission, for it is entirely possible that, abstractly-composed examples aside, no musical situation in a tonal work is unequivocally clear. It is in the nature of interdimensional interaction that while some dimensions close, others remain open. Never do all dimensions proceed in parallel fashion. If by 'clarity' we mean a particular state of interdimensional tension, then we must be ready to specify the equations that distinguish these relatively clear structures from relatively unclear ones. The clarity/ambiguity dialectic therefore urgently demands explication in order to counter the true but trivial proposition that either all tonal music is clear or all tonal music is ambiguous.

The politics of musical ambiguity

The issues raised by ambiguity are of course far too numerous and complex to be adequately discussed in a short essay like this. (I have said

26 Schachter, 'Either/Or', p. 169.

nothing about ambiguity of form, textural ambiguity, timbral ambiguity, ambiguity in other tonal musics, and so on.) My aim, however, has been merely to sketch the problem. My position may be summarised in the form of four simple propositions:

1   Theory-based analysis necessarily includes a mechanism for resolving ambiguities at all levels of structure;

2   An analysis that terminates in undecidability represents a conscious or subconscious retreat from theory;

3   While ambiguity may exist as an abstract phenomenon, it does not exist in concrete musical situations;

4   In situations of competing meanings, the alternatives are always formed hierarchically, making all such situations decidable without denying the existence of multiple meanings.

At a time when the guiding motto in contemporary humanistic thought appears to be 'nothing *but* ambiguity',[27] it would seem reactionary in the extreme to present an argument against ambiguity. Obviously, the impulse to adapt this motto to musical study is neither free of value nor innocent of an interest in what Milton Babbitt would call 'mere fashionability'.[28] While perfectly harmless in themselves, programmatic calls for scholars of tonal music to place ambiguity and indeterminacy at the centre of their efforts have not yet had the salutary effect of encouraging the production of theory-based analyses of ambiguity. Perhaps *ambiguity in the strong sense* is waiting to be discovered by theorists interested in formalisation. Until then, we will continue to live with an apparent desire to mystify what is not unclear and thus to reproduce the gulf between language and metalanguage, between, on the one hand, our embrace of linguistic undecidability as an exciting and liberating concept, and, on the other, our undiminished aesthetic attachment to a notoriously decidable tonal repertoire.

27 Violi and Steiner, 'Ambiguity', p. 25.
28 Milton Babbitt, preface to Epstein, *Beyond Orpheus*, p. ix.

6

Systems and strategies: functions and limits of analysis

ANTHONY POPLE

Historians of analysis have identified a broad range of musical purposes and functions with which the term has been associated. Ian Bent's renowned survey shows that within living memory 'analysis' has by turns been, at the very least, a pragmatic adjunct to composition, an informal source of learning for concert-goers, and a rigorous academic discipline for the study of scores and sketches.[1] Is it the range of such activities that defines analysis, or is analysis a closely delimited discipline whose essence is to be found within the respective scope of these and possibly other activities?

If the former alternative seems truer, this must at least partly reflect a historical dimension to the question – or, more specifically, to the attempt to answer it. Within the limits imposed by the impossibility of objective description, it is reasonable to suppose that a change in the meaning of 'analysis' need not of necessity affect the musical meaning with which analysis is concerned. For this to hold, however, the musical meaning must be meaning observed rather than meaning prescribed. In other words, while an empirical component of analytical activity might be capable of meeting this condition, insofar as it is entirely personal, the analysis must lose all pretensions to objectivity when it begins to affect patterns of interpretation elsewhere (e. g. by being read). So long as one conducts analysis for oneself, in private, one can remain a Clark Kent; by writing it down, on the other hand, one assumes the mantle of Superman, who can change the world. Thus emerge the critical and didactic aspects which seem to pertain to all written analysis, whether conceived in humility or with a Toveyesque presumption of authority. Critical and

Earlier versions of this paper were presented at the University of Nottingham, 1989, the Society for Music Theory, Oakland, 1990, and at City University, London, 1991. I should like to thank Alan Marsden and Robert Samuels for their comments.

1 Ian Bent, *Analysis* [The New Grove Handbooks in Music] (Basingstoke: Macmillan, 1987); this book is based on Bent's article 'Analysis', in Stanley Sadie (ed.), *The New Grove Dictionary of Music and Musicians* (London: Macmillan, 1980), vol. 1, pp. 340–88.

didactic modes of writing invite antagonism: when Joseph Kerman told his colleagues 'how to get out' of analysis in the early 1980s,[2] he was aiming at an easy target.

Systems (i): analysis or *reportage?*

There remains, perhaps, the personal, empirical aspect, but under closer examination this becomes elusive. The existence of empiricism as a *modus operandi* is not in doubt, but the idea of its being 'untainted', as outlined extravagantly above, cannot seriously be maintained. In other words, recognition depends on prior knowledge – it is a process that cannot simply start, but must start *from somewhere*. Kerman saw the symptoms of this in the unacknowledged critical positions, generally concerned with the acceptance of a canonic set of 'masterpieces', that lay behind some analyses he did not much enjoy. (One may usefully elaborate his position a little by pointing out that the use of masterpieces as the objects of analysis also relates to the didactic.)

Ideas of prior knowledge and subsequent processing invoke the principle of a flow of control through a complex system. Attempts to describe or model such systems are inevitably constrained by human ingenuity; and the fact that the terms 'top-down' and 'bottom-up' are frequently used for this purpose ought not to be taken to imply a strictly hierarchic conception. In line with Kerman's complaint, one might broadly characterise as 'top-down' any strategic move from a stated or unstated critical position to the body of statements which constitute a given analysis,[3] but this would be to imply that the strategic move is necessarily one which leads from simplicity to complexity. There is something to be gained instead by characterising the orienting context as a set of assumptions; for it is clear that assumptions can be complex as well as simple, and – no less importantly – that assumptions can be 'low-level' as well as 'high-level'. Among the issues that follow from this I should like to identify two at this stage. First, that by positing a collection of high-level assumptions, rather than a single definitive headline, one opens up the question of whether the items thus collected are themselves related hierarchically or heterarchically. Second, that the identification of low-level givens as a

---

2 Joseph Kerman, 'How We Got into Analysis, and How to Get Out', *Critical Inquiry*, 7 (1980–1), pp. 311–31.
3 The word 'statement' is used very broadly here: to include graphics, for example, and with the understanding that a single linguistic formulation may embody the statement of two or more distinct propositions.

focus of debate demands that the cognitive status of basic music-theoretic constructs be examined, and that a bottom-up flow of control – whether hierarchic or heterarchic or both – also be brought into consideration.[4]

Whether presented inductively (bottom-up) or deductively (top-down), the relationships between the constituent statements of an analysis are frequently organised hierarchically in accordance with theoretical models. Theories of form, for example, tend to be hierarchist and top-down; post-Cooper/Meyer theories of rhythm and metre tend to be hierarchist and bottom-up, and frequently exemplify the potential of strictly hierarchical theories to be organised as rule systems.[5] Schenkerian theory, though less formal, promotes a particular way of mapping processes of deduction and induction onto its hierarchy of 'structural levels',[6] but its deductive or inductive character is disputed. It is a notable characteristic of the revisionist post-Schenkerian theories of Proctor and Riggins, on the one hand, and Forte and Gilbert, on the other, that the former is essentially top-down while the latter is essentially bottom-up.[7]

In *Free Composition*, Schenker himself specifically excludes unidirectionality, making it clear that 'young artists, who are mainly dependent upon imitation' would nonetheless be misguided to ask whether one 'need . . . only vary some fundamental structure in order to arrive at the foreground of, say, a symphony':

The concept of the fundamental structure by no means claims to provide specific information about the chronology of creation; it presents . . . the *strictly logical precision in the relationship* between simple tone-successions and more complex ones. Indeed, it shows this . . . not only from the simple to the more complex but also in reverse, from the complex to the simple. . . . The secret of balance in

4 This leaves the naive simple-to-complex argument sidelined, but then that is no more than it deserves. Whether one heralds a move from naivety to sophistication, or castigates a move from straightforwardness to obfuscation; whether one places the broadly critical or the formally analytical at the pejorative end of the equation; whether one assumes a top-down or a bottom-up process is being described: all these are political stances. As such, they are of great significance, but they are ploys in a meta-game that, if inescapable, is at least deferrable.

5 For example, Grosvenor Cooper and Leonard B. Meyer, *The Rhythmic Structure of Music* (Chicago: University of Chicago Press, 1960); Fred Lerdahl and Ray Jackendoff, *A Generative Theory of Tonal Music* (Cambridge, Mass.: MIT Press, 1983), chapter 4.

6 The distance between Schenker's own writings and formalist music theory, and the authenticity of terms such as 'structural level', are charted by Robert Snarrenberg, this volume, pp. 29–56.

7 Gregory Proctor and Herbert Lee Riggins, 'Levels and the Reordering of Chapters in Schenker's *Free Composition*', *Music Theory Spectrum*, 10 (1988), pp. 102–26; Allen Forte and Steven E. Gilbert, *Introduction to Schenkerian Analysis* (New York: Norton, 1982).

music ultimately lies in the constant awareness of ... the motion from fore-ground to background or the reverse.[8]

Schenker maintains here that an analysis is capable of presenting some kind of essence of the work without making claims about the way in which it was composed; but at the same time he makes claims in general about the way in which composers think. If an analysis lies outside time, both in that it 'presents ... relationship[s]' and in its avoidance of spe-cifically chronological claims, the idea of 'constant awareness' – which, the context indicates, is an attribute of the 'genius' while composing or extemporising – is, rather, an indication of the richness of the thought processes involved. Another passage takes up the key idea of 'motion' between levels:

As a motion through several levels, as a connection between two mentally and spatially separated points, every relationship represents a path which is as real as any we 'traverse' with our feet. Therefore, a relationship actually is to be 'tra-versed' in thought – but this must involve actual time. . . . Today one flies over the work of art in the same manner as one flies over villages, cities, . . . rivers, and lakes. This contradicts not only the historical bases of the work of art but also . . . its inner relationships, which demand to be 'traversed'.[9]

Among other things, this indicates a belief that the traversal 'in thought' of such relationships is available to others than the composer. Reaffirm-ing the critical/didactic function of analysis as an enabler of such thought, Schenker also distances this facility from the listening act: even 'musicians of talent', he tells us, 'have not yet learned to hear true coher-ent relationships'.[10]

That an analysis does not directly describe a process of listening is obvious, despite the origins of the personal/empirical aspect in real or simulated listening and the potential, through the critical/didactic aspect, for analysis to condition real or simulated listening. There are in any case very many different ways of listening: in the opera house, for example, some members of the audience may be straining for the words, others waiting merely for the high Cs; the singers may be listening for their cues, while the journalists may be focusing on the quality of the voices. There may even be some musicologists in the house, indulging in what

8 Heinrich Schenker, *Free Composition*, trans. and ed. E. Oster (New York: Longman, 1979), p. 18.
9 Ibid., p. 6. The translation is disputed however (see Jonathan Dunsby, 'Heinrich Schenker and the Free Counterpoint of Strict Composition', *Research Chronicle*, 16 (1980), p. 144).
10 Cf. Robert Snarrenberg on the concept of the master analyst, this volume, pp. 53–4.

Nicholas Cook terms 'musicological listening' – 'any type of listening to music whose purpose is the establishment of fact or the formulation of theories'[11] – but, as he makes clear, this too covers many possibilities. At the very least it can include recognitions made within different (but, axiomatically, connected) domains or parameters of music, thus implying a heterarchic interaction which necessarily undermines the strictness of supposedly hierarchic rule-like relations by introducing extraneous factors into ideally hermetic systems. Indeed, the interconnectedness of parameters means that observations from one musical domain may inform the context for the operation of rules in another domain at virtually any level, so that the integrity of any and every such rule system is irretrievably compromised. The problematic interactions between the four limbs of Lerdahl and Jackendoff's theory, which have been widely discussed,[12] offer a concise example, but both the conciseness and the problems are also something of a counter-illustration, since it must be assumed that normal listening is less problematic than the process their theory generates, and at the same time less granular than the theory itself.

A useful starting-point may be provided by speculating on the manner in which generic inductive and deductive flows of control within a complex network might interact in real-time listening.[13] The straightforwardness of the time constraints involved means that the density of layering in a bottom-up hierarchical process will condition how its high-level propositions may, or conversely may not, inform the top-down operation of other processes. This is shown schematically in Fig. 6.1: a loose inductive hierarchy will construe high-level recognitions more quickly than a dense one, and so may provide a context enabling the latter to operate top-down and bottom-up simultaneously within a larger network. For example, as a process of listening is initiated, low-level cues of outstanding salience may allow the general stylistic context to be induced very quickly – e. g. 'Sonata-Allegro movement, early nineteenth-century Germanic, minor mode' – and these will set top-down constraints on the operation of the more detailed processes by which the progress of the music may be followed more closely. Conversely, the fast bottom-up recognition of the

11 Nicholas Cook, *Music, Imagination, and Culture* (Oxford: Clarendon Press, 1990), p. 152.
12 See, for example, Michael Baker, 'A Computational Approach to Modeling Musical Grouping Structure', *Contemporary Music Review*, 4 (1989), pp. 311–25.
13 The following outline model is indebted to discussions with Alan Marsden and John Self. See Alan Marsden and Anthony Pople, 'Modelling Musical Cognition as a Community of Experts', *Contemporary Music Review*, 3/i (1989), pp. 29–42, and 'Towards a Connected Distributed Model of Musical Listening', *Interface*, 18 (1989), pp. 61–72.

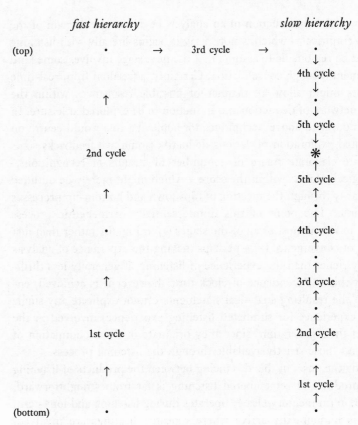

Figure 6.1   Outline protocol for heterarchic interaction between hierarchies

NB The paths shown here are understood as fragments of a larger network, the deductions/inductions between nodes being traversed in parallel through successive time-cycles

Sonata-Allegro movement-type (in this instance) is itself conditioned, top-down, by prior knowledge – belonging elsewhere in the network – normally given as composer-title information or inferred from the context in which the music is heard. Indeed, and in general, the point at which recognition is made comes precisely where inductive and deductive paths converge (a notional example is shown by an asterisk in Fig. 6.1). The linear flow of *reportage* in listening is, according to this view, bound to be a volatile mix of recognitions in different 'domains' and at different 'levels'.[14]

14 Cf. Otto Laske's use of verbal protocols and his treatment of analysis as 'output' in 'KEITH: A Rule-System for Making Music-Analytical Discoveries', in M. Baroni and

Insofar as the construction of an analysis begins in the domain of the personal/empirical – which is not to say it begins literally with listening – it might be reasonable to assume that the next stage involves some kind of refinement through consolidation. Certainly, a freedom from real-time constraints might allow all manner of possible resonances within the complex network of deduction and induction to be explored at leisure. In the terms outlined above, techniques for achieving this would centre on the repeated exploration of various deductive/inductive feedbacks so as to generate elaborate traces of a number of strands of recognition – chronologically linear within the score – which might merely be outlined fragmentarily through the meeting of top-down and bottom-up processes in real time. The point of this quintessentially hermeneutic process would be to reveal most or all of the stages (•) in Fig. 6.1 rather than just the point of convergence (∗) – perhaps making the experience of analysis inherently richer than the experience of listening, if generally less thrilling.[15] But this transcendence of clock time, however it is achieved, ensures that the resulting analytical statements cannot explicate any single listening experience (or simulated listening experience) involved in the process of their generation, since they originate in the accumulation of data beyond those strictly available through the listening process.

Locating the onset of this distancing between the products of listening and the products of remembered listening is far from straightforward, since short-term memory clearly operates during listening and long-term memory is undoubtedly active where repeated hearings are involved. Nonetheless, it is clear that such a distance *is* opened up by the cultural component of listening: Eric Clarke, exhorting his readers to 'mind the gap', points out that

there is a tendency to confuse *cultural norms* (such as the norms of formal design) which are established by convention, with *perceptual norms* which are the consequence of the characteristics and limitations of perceptual systems. This . . . potentially leads to the absurd situation in which attempts are made to account for socio-historical conventions in terms of innate perceptual characteristics (for

L. Callegari (eds.), *Musical Grammars and Computer Analysis* (Florence: Olschki, 1984), pp. 165–99.
15. This distinction between listening and analysis recalls Walter J. Ong's distinction, in *Orality and Literacy* (London: Methuen, 1982), between the dynamics of oral and literate thought – the former being characteristically 'formulaic and aggregative', the latter 'analytical' [sic]. Just as an author has a technological advantage over an orator, so an analyst should have time to sift through genuine and simulated listening experience, 'erasing' and 'recasting' it in the mind or on paper so as to create a differently coherent account of musical understanding.

114

example, accounts of Western tonality based solely, or heavily, on psycho-acoustics or auditory physiology).[16]

If it is apparent that 'cultural norms' must be active, through long-term memory, in almost any kind of listening by someone who knows what music is, it is certainly the case that such norms will be most fully invoked during instances of Cook's 'musicological listening'. Nor can there be any doubt that the real or simulated listening at the heart of the personal/empirical domain of music analysis is a musicological listening in precisely the sense that '[its] purpose is the establishment of fact or the formulation of theories'. And it is in keeping with the reflexive character of the whole process that those 'cultural norms' most saliently involved in the proto-analytical type of 'musicological listening' are the low-level 'facts' of established, long-term music theory.

Systems (ii): theory or representation?

Viewed in this light, certain aspects of analytical music theories – such as the way they tend to promote the hierarchical organisation of raw obser-vations, or their fragmentation across various parameters which are inte-grated in musical understanding[17] – make it easy to cast theory in the villain's role, as something which corrupts the innocence of the personal/empirical. But it can be argued that, within the framework set out above, the reflexivity that 'makes sense' of listening also implicates another kind of theory – quite personal in nature, *pace* the question of 'universals' – which, no less than the more explicit kind, infiltrates the impossibly pure empiricism of observation. When observation becomes recognition – and cognitivism, in its strongest form, would say it cannot be otherwise – then the critical/didactic aspect already exists, albeit within the per-sonal.[18] If the 'pure' personal/empirical must be regarded as an ideal, there arises the question of whether in this sense the private, implicit type of theory is in some way preferable to the public, explicit kind. It would be wrong to equate the former with cognitive music theory, since such theory is also – obviously – explicit; the fact that a theory makes psychological claims is not enough. But a useful if lesser distinction may be made between explicitly or palpably cognitive theories and 'don't care'

16 Eric F. Clarke, 'Mind the Gap: Formal Structures and Psychological Processes in Music', *Contemporary Music Review*, 3/i (1989), p. 11.
17 See Marsden and Pople, 'Towards a Connected Distributed Model'.
18 This conclusion would be differently nuanced by those who maintain that the indi-vidual is socially constructed.

theories, or even ostentatiously non-cognitive theories. The question of preferability is then one of pragmatics, and turns ultimately on the priorities of the critical/didactic domain.

The comprehensiveness of explicitly cognitive theories of pitch representation is attested to by the quantity of work reported in Krumhansl's survey.[19] It is interesting to compare these formalisms with the artefacts of long-term music theory. Consider, for example, the Deutsch-Feroe algebraic system which notates pitch successions using 'alphabets' which correspond to chromatic scales and arpeggiated triads;[20] or the Terhardt-Parncutt 'psychoacoustical model of the root(s) of a musical chord' – which is so closely related to Rameau's theory of the Fundamental Bass;[21] or Shepard's double-helical representation of pitch relations, in which the metrics of chromatic scale, circle of fifths and octave equivalence are combined.[22] The psychological claims are explicit in only one of each pair, but the artefacts of long-term music theory are, at the very least, not contradicted. If the reaction of musicians to these competing formulations is likely to be in favour of the familiar ones, the tautology lurking behind this merely confirms the implicit psychological status of such artefacts also: it is reassuring rather than worrying when musicians complain that psychologists tell them nothing they don't know already.

A contrasting example is Alexander Brinkman's binomial representation of non-enharmonic pitch classes.[23] This makes use of some (though by no means all) of the integers between 0 and 116: D♯, for example, is represented by 31 (i. e. pitch class 3, note class 1, where C = 0), and E♭ by 32 (pitch class 3, note class 2). The representation is constructed in an entirely logical manner with a view to its practical implementation on a microcomputer, and as such is entirely successful. But other no less practical alternatives are possible. For example, one may take D as a not entirely arbitrary zero and derive note classes as positive and negative

19 Carol L. Krumhansl, *Cognitive Foundations of Musical Pitch* (Oxford: Oxford University Press, 1990).

20 Diana Deutsch and John Feroe, 'The Internal Representation of Pitch Sequences in Tonal Music', *Psychological Review*, 88 (1981), pp. 503–22.

21 Richard Parncutt, 'Revision of Terhardt's Psychoacoustical Model of the Root(s) of a Musical Chord', *Music Perception*, 6 (1988), pp. 65–93. For a critical discussion of this in relation to the theories of Rameau, Hindemith and others see William Thomson, 'The Harmonic Root: A Fragile Marriage of Concept and Percept', *Music Perception*, 10 (1993), pp. 385–415.

22 Roger N. Shepard, 'Structural Representations of Musical Pitch', in Diana Deutsch (ed.), *The Psychology of Music* (London: Academic Press, 1982), pp. 343–90.

23 Alexander R. Brinkman, *PASCAL Programming for Music Research* (Chicago: University of Chicago Press, 1990), pp. 132–3.

-7	-6	-5	-4	-3	-2	-1	0	1	2	3	4	5	6	7
etc. Db	Ab	Eb	Bb	F	C	G	D	A	E	B	F#	C#	G#	D# etc.

Figure 6.2   A system of non-enharmonic note classes

integers using the cycle (not circle) of fifths (see Fig. 6.2).[24] In this system, diatonic collections are contiguous and enharmonically equivalent note classes are equal, *modulo* 12.[25] How is one to decide between the merits of such representations? David Huron, in a comprehensive examination of this question, points out that 'it is impossible to represent all properties of a signified even in the extreme case where a signified itself is used as its own signifier', and indicates the importance of pragmatic considerations:

Although two representation systems may be logically homologous, practical considerations affect their utility . . . Hence it is vital to consider what properties distinguish a good representation scheme from a poor one. Unfortunately it is not clear that such properties can be deduced *a priori*. It is primarily through experience with different schemes that it has become evident how one scheme is superior to another and what principle of design distinguishes the good from the bad.[26]

Huron's idea of practical experience in such cases is not restricted merely to questions of programming convenience or computational parsimony. On the contrary, his approach is semiological, and he arrives thereby at the conclusion that 'Good representations are . . . unique . . . mnemonic . . . consistent . . . reversible . . . terse . . . non-cryptic . . . structurally isomorphic . . . context-free . . . idiomatic . . . explicit . . . optional [and/or] extendable.' Under the second of these headings, he addresses the explicitly cognitive issue of memorability directly:

An obvious human failing is our disposition to forget. A good representation will display mappings between signifiers and signifieds which are easily remembered.

24 Taking D as zero introduces flats at −4 and sharps at +4, and reaches the extremes of double flats and double sharps at ±17. In other respects this system is similar to one proposed by J. Timothy Kolosick in 'A Machine-Independent Data Structure for the Representation of Music Pitch Relationships: Computer-Generated Musical Examples for CBI', *Journal of Computer-Based Instruction*, 13/i (1986), pp. 9–13. (I am grateful to Alan Marsden for drawing this to my attention.)
25 If n is a note class, then the equivalent enharmonic pitch class p is found according to the formula $p = (n + 2) \times 7 \bmod 12$.
26 David Huron, 'Design Principles in Computer-Based Music Representation', in Alan Marsden and Anthony Pople (eds.), *Computer Representations and Models in Music* (London: Academic Press, 1992), p. 16.

At least seven types of mnemonic relationship can be identified: *literalism, initialism, pictorialism, operational mapping, semantic convention, isotonic convention,* and *topographical correspondence.*[27]

Brinkman in fact appears to claim mnemonic status for his binomial representation, stating that the system is 'easy to read' because 'the last digit always indicates the spelling . . . and the preceding digits give the [pitch class]'.[28] While this depends on the reader knowing that the last digit is detachable, as well as being fluent at reading pitch class integers, the more important point is that Brinkman concurs with Huron in recognising the force of the criterion itself.

Perhaps the most readable system available for the purpose under discussion is after all another binomial system, in which the first element is a note class represented by an alphabetic letter from the list A–G, corresponding to the pitch classes 9, 11, 0, 2, 4, 5 and 7, and the second element is a modifier taken from the list [♭♭, ♭, ♮, ♯, ×], corresponding to decrements or increments from −2 to +2, to be applied to the pitch class. The system proposed in Fig. 6.2 facilitates certain arithmetical processes, and might be thought preferable to Brinkman's as an *internal* representation for purely computational purposes. But, as the comparison with the familiar system makes plain, it has little viability as a *external* representation (the kind with which Huron is concerned) because it is extremely unmemorable. In principle, Brinkman's system is only marginally less memorable than the conventional system: its principal defect is simply that it is unfamiliar. Specifically, in Huron's terms, the second element of a Brinkman binomial term is straightforwardly related to the first element of the more familiar system through an isotonic mapping; the major distinction is that the first element of a Brinkman term (the pitch class) does not correspond to anything found in the familiar system. The point is not that the pitch class integers are unfamiliar in themselves, which to many they are not, but that the conjunction of elements *is.*

A more intriguing example is Forte's set class system, which is considerably more familiar than Brinkman's binomial representation[29] – to analysts at least – and yet is nonetheless apparently unmemorable, as Joel Lester has observed:

I have found Forte's names useful when using his lists (e. g., to see whether a given set is Z-related or to locate quickly the complement of a given set) or his

27 Ibid., p. 17.
28 Brinkman, *PASCAL Programming for Music Research*, p. 132.
29 Allen Forte, *The Structure of Atonal Music* (New Haven: Yale University Press, 1973).

various graphics. But the names themselves are as arbitrary as numbers on foot-ball uniforms . . . I do not know any theorists familiar with Forte's names who remembers [sic] more than a handful of them.[30]

The functionality of the system is not in doubt, and its organisation is (almost) perfectly logical;[31] moreover, the first element of the two that make up each set class name satisfies Huron's mnemonic criterion, being a literalism for the number of distinct pitch classes constituting the set. Lester's point hinges on the arbitrariness of the second element (the ordinal number). This derives from a ranking of the interval class vectors of like-sized set classes;[32] as such, it might be thought to have the poten-tial to correlate with a cognitively salient feature such as the 'level of dissonance', but no such correlation appears to have emerged in the literature despite twenty years of use by analysts. It might be argued that Forte's system has no need of memorability, because it makes no claims about the ways that collections of pitch classes are held in memory. In this sense, it is not a *theory* at all. But, as Huron points out:

the most powerful types of representations will attempt to make explicit precisely what the signifiers represent – and in doing so, tacitly expose those potential signifieds present in the artifact which are absent from the representation. To represent is to interpret; and to represent well is to lay plain the interpretation.[33]

In the case of Forte's system, this does not apply at the level of the individual set class names, but rather at the systematic level, where, as Huron says, 'a representation system as a whole may be viewed as a signifier for a particular assumed or explicit explanation'.[34]

It is at this level that Forte's system has suffered from a recurrent criticism that centres on its supposed contradiction of certain long-term music-theoretical 'facts' (e. g. concerning the distinction between major and minor triads) by the use of inverse 'equivalence' to define set class-es. The problem itself is easily obviated through the introduction by Rahn, Solomon and others of 'T_n' (rather than 'T_n/T_nI') set-classes,[35] but

---

30 Joel Lester, letter to the editor, *Journal of Music Theory*, 36/ii (1992), p. 405.
31 For complete inner consistency, by Forte's own rules for the determination of the 'best normal order' (*The Structure of Atonal Music*, pp. 3–5), set-classes 6–Z28 and 6–Z49 should be exchanged.
32 As is well known, the Z-paired set classes are anomalous in this respect, since they do not have adjacent ordinal numbers.
33 Huron, 'Design Principles', p. 32.
34 Ibid., p. 38.
35 John Rahn, *Basic Atonal Theory* (New York: Longman, 1980); Larry Solomon, 'The List of Chords, Their Properties and Use in Analysis', *Interface*, 11/ii (1982), pp. 61–107.

criteria for deciding between these alternative systems seem not to be widely agreed. It may be, in line with Huron's conclusion, that the near-arbitrariness of Forte's ordinal numbers (in terms of 'potential signifieds present in the artifact') signifies an interpretation which would argue that the set classes, however named, are virtually unmemorisable. This may be true of the 200 or more classes taken as a group, but it is clearly the case that some set types, such as triads, are highly recognisable and well remembered. Reading an analysis that uses Forte's representation, then, requires some kind of suspension of normal belief: as Jonathan Dunsby puts it, in a broader context, the problem is 'that some empirical qualities of the music which are fully scrutable are not entailed in, and may even be contradicted by, pc-set segmentation'.[36] To analyse a musical passage or work in this way, then, is to pursue a particular strategy on behalf of the critical/didactic mode – a top-down strategy that, perhaps because it is so very straightforward in its assumptions ('In 1908 a profound change in music was initiated when Arnold Schoenberg . . . deliberately relinquished the traditional system of tonality, which had been the basis of musical syntax for the previous two hundred and fifty years.')[37] reaches straight into the personal/empirical and is likely to arouse antagonism.

This is certainly in marked contrast to the kinds of critical writing that employ such densely layered high-level assumptions that their strategic sweep, in the terms sketched in Fig. 6.1, remains distanced from the inductive levels – a kind of writing, in other words, that is characterised by the anecdotal treatment of musical detail using music theories of various kinds in an *ad hoc* manner. Such writing is of course also likely to arouse antagonism; the question is, can these different antagonisms be resolved?

Strategies: method, or . . . ?

The distinction made above between a representation and a theory ought to be highly pertinent to this question. Something which does not theorise about how musical entities are amenable to thought ought not directly to arouse antagonism. But, as Huron points out, this distinction between representation and theory cannot be fully maintained; it is a difference in degree rather than in kind. So, for all that Forte's system (to continue with it by way of a specific example) is functional, concise and

36 Jonathan Dunsby, this volume, pp. 78–9.
37 Forte, *The Structure of Atonal Music*, p. ix.

logically organised, its support in some basic mathematics well documented, and its primarily taxonomic intention well stated, it is taken for something else and has met with difficulties. This phenomenon is exacerbated by the constitution of music analysis as a genre in which the critical/didactic component is prominent: when people read something called 'music analysis' they assume that they will be 'told something about the piece', which implies not merely that the terms used will constitute a theory rather than a representation, but that this distinction will apply in a non-trivial way. Some sort of imaginary negotiation is necessary, therefore, between an analyst and his or her assumed readership, so that the specific analytical observations, brought forth necessarily by introspection, can have the potential to be integrated with other peoples' prior knowledge. The kind of critical writing that remains tangled up in its own high-level assumptions, and so deals with musical detail in an anecdotal fashion, is in fact likely to be acceptable in these terms, insofar as such anecdotal observations will scarcely contradict the reader's own impressions. Writing of this kind certainly 'tells us something'; but, to those who expect the strategic sweep of analysis to range constructively through to the personal/empirical, what it tells us may not seem to be 'about the piece'. Conversely, work which is excessively bottom-up, however carefully aligned with cognitive theory, may remain tangled in the empirical and fail to cross other than trivially into the critical/didactic domain; it is certainly 'about the piece', but may 'tell us' little or nothing.

These two types of failure may be contrasted as, on the one hand, critical writing that fails to be didactic, and on the other, empirical writing that fails to be personal. But is it reasonable to expect analytical writing to range comprehensively across all of these? If analysis is to draw on the experience of one musician in order to inform the experience of another – notably, to condition future listening experience, either real or simulated – it must do so in a reasonably concise manner. The strategic sweep of analysis moves in one way or another between empirical 'how to follow it' musical knowledge – which is procedural – and summary (i. e. 'analytical') musical knowledge – which is declarative. Certainly, the procedural knowledge that is needed to listen (or 'follow') music is widely shared; but as with all such knowledge it is learned relatively slowly. The role of the critical/didactic here – in other words, why people need music analysis – is to provide declarative (categorical) insights in order to bring forward this learning process; but these must correlate with what they already know or believe in order for the didactic function to be fulfilled. It is reasonable to hope that music theory might assist analysts in achieving this, but the usual manner in which such theories are expounded, through a combination of exemplars with narrative, means that they are neither straightforward pattern-matching systems – which might assist in meshing new analytical observations with recognised empirical or critical positions – nor genuine rule-based systems – which might accomplish the strategic move between these domains in a reliable way. On the contrary, the function of the theoretical narrative is generally to provide both an informal rule-system in consideration of the specific exemplars and to give an indication of meta-rules to assist in correlating these with other musical observations. This leaves the pragmatics exposed but ill-defined, and promotes the very strong possibility that the organisation of empirical observations – so as to constitute a Schenkerian middleground, for example – will in practice tend to reflect the pattern of other Schenkerian middlegrounds (in this instance) rather than generate new categorical knowledge of entities identified through extended contemplation. That is to say, if the analyst uses primarily his or her experience of analysis to organise a reading, rather than his or her experience of the piece at hand, then the period of contemplation will not engage fully with empirical knowledge of the music (as readers might reasonably expect) but will lead merely to the mundane recognition of categorically different kinds of entity defined by theory.

Of course, analyses that present such results – which reflect precisely the phenomenon of 'method' being pursued for its own sake – remain of interest to those for whom the theoretical categories concerned are themselves interesting and meaningful. To the extent that this implies an inward-looking elitist position, it had little to recommend it even before advice was offered on 'how to get out' of analysis; but, at the same time, there is a need to maintain intellectual and professional integrity in a discipline which claims the didactic among its functions. Indeed, a constructive broadening of focus need not throw out the baby of insight – whether empirical or critical – with the bathwater of misappropriated 'method'. David Clarke, for example, has shown how theories of the psychological present may be correlated with the tiny focus of foreground Schenkerian analysis if this is done in a way which concentrates on local harmonic events and leaves the recognition of larger linear motions to more remote levels.[38] And at the other end of the scale, critical issues far broader than those Schenker permitted himself to discuss, or his mute

38 David Clarke, 'Structural, Cognitive and Semiotic Aspects of the Musical Present', *Contemporary Music Review*, 3/i (1989), pp. 111–31.

Ursatz to suggest, have been addressed over a number of years by those who have sought to move beyond party-line post-Schenkerian dogma – particularly in relation to late tonal music and early music – even while maintaining a conventionally analytical outlook.

It may assist in keeping these two fruitful domains of insight in focus – personal/empirical and critical/didactic – to think of each analysis itself as a kind of theory that proposes a way in which the music in question might be better understood by other musicians. The consequences for method are less tangible, though one might argue that this double focus, in itself, constitutes some sort of methodological principle. It is of course important to be wary of the latent biases on critical and empirical viewpoints that follow from particular analytical methods, but even more important – because more productive – to turn such biases to advantage within a broader strategy. Behind this possibility lies the fact that one may circumscribe the notion of 'analysis' independently of the methods through which analysis has come to be pursued. Identifying analysis in this way through its functions and aspects inevitably suggests that the limits of analysis should be seen in terms of those functions and aspects, rather than in terms of methodological collisions or deconstructionist impasses. As we 'rehabilitate the incorrigible',[39] one might say, we ought also to 'discourage the debilitating'.

39 I allude to the title of Marion Guck's chapter in this volume (pp. 57–73).

Texts

7

Debussy's significant connections: metaphor and metonymy in analytical method

CRAIG AYREY

Structure/discourse

Contemporary music analysis struggles with a dualism. The production of increasingly rigorous and sophisticated systematic theories of structure continues, while a more recent and contentious turn to post-structuralist literary theory questions both the products of the analytical canon and the very assumptions on which structuralist theories, in the widest sense of the term, are based. This dualism within theory has been accommodated and valorised in various ways: as confrontation, rejection, or assimilated into the vogue for secure and unperturbing comparative analysis. The latter is the least fertile: it takes refuge in the postmodern 'solution' to all confrontation – its highly prized pluralism – so that the existence of contrasting or contradictory analyses not only represents the fragmentation of contemporary culture but is essential to it. The intellectual shift that this entails tends to displace the analytical project from the analysis of works to the criticism of analytical discourse, that is, to the analysis as text, to the metacritical analysis of analyses.[1] Undoubtedly, this flight into postmodernism has increased our understanding of theory as an activity, but the opening up of a field of limitless commentary risks occluding works themselves. Postmodern stratagems can be endlessly fascinating, but since their repeated undoing of interpretation often leaves the musical work untouched their analytic fallout is elusive, even evasive. Simply to 'question', 'interrogate' or 'scrutinise' the 'musical fact' (in Molino's sense)[2] is not in fact intrinsically post-modern, and at worst can

1 For a theoretical defence of the necessity of comparative analysis see Jean-Jacques Nattiez, 'The Concepts of Plot and Seriation Process in Music Analysis', trans. C. Dale, *Music Analysis*, 4 (1985), pp. 107–18; and 'Existe-t-il des relations entre les diverses méthodes d'analyse?', in Rossana Dalmonte and Mario Baroni (eds.), *Secondo convegno europeo di analisi musicale* (Trento: Universita degli studi di Trento, 1992), pp. 537–65.
2 Jean Molino, 'Musical Fact and the Semiology of Music', trans. J. A. Underwood, *Music Analysis*, 9 (1990), pp. 113–56.

appear to be merely a weak response to the challenges of critical modernity, challenges that can only be met by less etiolated versions of post-structuralist thinking.

That said, Debussy's music is notoriously resistant to theory-based analysis and therefore attracts metatheoretical questioning of the analytical results obtained by traditional methods. This 'resistance' has to do with the received view of Debussy as a seminal composer of the twentieth century, innovator, iconoclast, and above all the originator of modernist modes of musical structure. Applications of modern analytical techniques therefore relegate Debussy to the status of a predecessor. Whether refracted through Cone's Stravinskian structural categories[3] or stratified in an often dichotomous conjunction of voice-leading and pitch-class set structure,[4] the historicity of Debussy's style is consigned to a half-world of either/or straining for the overflowing presence of both/and. Setting aside *Jeux* and *En blanc et noir* – that is to say, as the exceptions that prove the rule – Debussy emerges from such studies as both regressive and progressive, simple and complex, as the very image of the *post-*modern artist in whom the point at issue – ambiguity – is resolved into a comfortable plurality. There is some truth in our postmodern view: the tension of style, the pluralism of structural procedure are self-evident. But if Debussy were to be reviewed as a nineteenth-century composer, would this too constitute a retreat to a more comfortable position? Quite the opposite: specious modernity (Debussy as proto-Stravinsky) would give way to true modernism. Like the early modernist poets – Yeats, Pound, Eliot – Debussy's well-documented reactionary position toward the nineteenth century is not the only precondition of innovation: his originality is doubly centred, conservative (Wagner and Mallarmé) and iconoclastic (the early Stravinsky). Debussy's modernism, and continuing modernity, depends on this thoroughly questioning, subversive duality. Debussy is, dare one suggest, a deconstructive composer, to whom deconstructionist principles apply:

Instead of a simple 'either/or' structure, deconstruction attempts to elaborate a discourse that says *neither* 'either/or', *nor* 'both/and' nor even 'neither/nor', while at the same time not totally abandoning these logics either. The very word

3 See Neela Delia Kinariwala, 'Debussy and Musical Coherence: A Study of Succession and Continuity in the Preludes' (PhD dissertation, University of Texas at Austin, 1987).
4 See Richard E. Parks, *The Music of Claude Debussy* (New Haven: Yale University Press, 1989).

deconstruction is meant to undermine the either/or logic of the opposition 'construction/deconstruction'.[5]

Some explanation is necessary for this leap from one conceptual universe to another. Although it might be true to say that all significant music is deconstructive in the sense suggested by Johnson, this image can only come into focus mediated by theory. This is strikingly evident in late nineteenth- and early twentieth-century music where music theory accurately reflects, often unwittingly, the features of the early modernist condition, elevating 'neither/nor' onto the positive plane of discontinuity, that is to say affirming the value of pure opposition. But this also seems too comfortable a position: however oppositional structures are created, we lack descriptions of their moment-to-moment continuity. To put it simply, music theory is often oblivious to the fact that opposition itself is a relation, a mode of connection between disparate units. On the other hand, the classic oppositions in the analysis of structure – part/whole, continuity/discontinuity, similarity/opposition – are conventionally re-examined and resolved (or at least tamed) in the context of a metacritique that draws its procedures from precedents in post-structuralist literary theory. Among the three oppositions I have listed, opposition itself is present in an opposed pair. Questions of terminology apart ('opposition' is perhaps a synonym for 'dissimilarity'), opposition is accorded a special place in musical structure as both the ground of theoretical concepts and as one of its functions. It is therefore marked in the problematic of theory, and because it has a privileged role in Debussy's music and thought,[6] is a point of correspondence between the general theoretical issues described here and Debussy's characteristic structural procedures.

Fissures and blindness in structural analysis attest to the value of self-reflective commentary and to the necessity of the recent turn to metatheory. But it would appear that an awareness of the provisional and contingent nature of all statements about music, of all positions, is increasingly paralysing the impulse to analyse. As Derrida himself reminds us, the critical impulse must go beyond interrogation:

We have to question the form of questioning. I would say that deconstruction is affirmation rather than questioning, in a sense which is not positive: I would

---

5 Barbara Johnson, *A World of Difference* (Baltimore: The Johns Hopkins University Press, 1987) p. 12.
6 This issue is considered in Jonathan Dunsby 'The Poetry of *En blanc et noir*', paper delivered at the Journées Claude Debussy, City University and Institut français, London, 1993.

distinguish between the positive, or positions, and affirmations. I think that deconstruction is affirmative rather than questioning; this affirmation goes *through* some radical questioning, but is not questioning in the final analysis.[7]

'Questioning' in music theory rarely leads to affirmation: paradoxically, perhaps, this constitutes an aspect of de Man's 'resistance to theory',[8] in the sense that the adoption of non-positivist modes of discourse in music analysis often betrays the avoidance of the pressing analytical issues it is intended to confront; consequently, its ground – the musical work (insofar as that can be said to exist independently of its reflection in analytical discourse) – is marginalised. If the few published applications of the post-structuralist methods of, for example, Barthes, Derrida and de Man have achieved anything it is the deconstruction of the 'dogmatic allegories' of analytical writing.[9] The heart of the problem, though, lies in the attempt to use the deconstructive idea in analysis itself. One such attempt, Robert Snarrenberg's exploration of Derrida's strategy of *différance*, the combination of the operations of differing and deferring, all too easily dissolves analytically into Meyer's implication-realisation model.[10] The issue here is whether the difference between an application of Derrida's strategies and Meyer's model is important. If it is not then there is little to be gained.[11] That this theoretical connection can be made, however, is highly significant. It raises the question again of whether music *itself* is amenable to deconstructive strategies, but in a different form: is the reinscription of one mode of discourse in the terms of another telling us something about a musical work, as well as about theoretical representations of it?

This question cannot be answered easily. First, I think, some aspects of existing theories must be rethought even if good counter-arguments could be developed within them. Snarrenberg's application of *différance* is an example: whatever the objections from within the generative model he employs, or from outside – in the form of other models that could explain the issues at stake in more familiar terms – there will be no escape from closed systems on the one hand, and flabby pluralism on the other.

---

7 Imre Saluzinsky, *Criticism in Society* (London: Methuen, 1987), p. 20.
8 Paul de Man, *The Resistance to Theory* (Minneapolis: University of Minnesota Press, 1986).
9 See, for example, Alan Street, 'Superior Myths, Dogmatic Allegories: The Resistance to Musical Unity', *Music Analysis*, 8 (1989), pp. 77–123.
10 Robert Snarrenberg, 'The Play of *Différance*', *In Theory Only*, 10/iii (1987), pp. 1–25.
11 For a critique of Snarrenberg, 'The Play of *Différance*', see Robert Samuels, 'Derrida and Snarrenberg', *In Theory Only*, 11/i–ii (1989), pp. 45–58.

In the quotations above, Johnson and Derrida argue radically for a middle way, a method that offers systematic procedures but is predicated on the notion of ambiguity. And if plurality in this sense is to be placed at the heart of theory, one strategy is to reformulate our descriptions of music itself: replace 'structure', as the essential musical fact, with 'discourse'.

Discourse should be understood here as inscribed within music, not only as (in Nattiez's *Music and Discourse*) the sum of music's descriptions and interpretations.[12] The language model of structuralism can be retained (it cannot be ignored), but with a difference: it must go beyond the linguistic to the metalinguistic, from the structure of language to the structure of discourse. This move reduplicates Derrida's elucidation of the 'structurality of structure'. 'Structure' in Derrida is a concept, and a concept is, as Deleuze and Guattari remind us, a composite 'figure'.[13] Structure must therefore be redefined as 'structurality', the intellectual construction of structure:

Structure – or rather the structurality of structure – although it has always been at work, has always been neutralized or reduced, and this by a process of giving it a center or of referring it to a point of presence, a fixed origin. The function of this center was not only to orient, balance and organise the structure – one cannot in fact conceive of an unorganised structure – but above all to make sure that the organising principle of the structure would limit what we might call the *play* of the structure.[14]

This concept of structure corresponds to what we know as 'pure' structure in the positivist sense. But since this objective, neutral structure is perpetually redefined, Derrida writes that:

the entire history of the concept of structure . . . must be thought of as a series of substitutions of center for center, as a linked chain of determinations for the center. Successively, and in a regulated fashion, the center receives different forms or names. The history of metaphysics, like the history of the West, is the history of these metaphors and metonymies.[15]

At the point when the structurality of structure is radically questioned

---

12 See Nattiez, *Music and Discourse*, trans. C. Abbate (Princeton: Princeton University Press, 1990), p. ix.
13 Gilles Deleuze and Felix Guattari, *Qu'est-ce que la philosophie?* (Paris: Les éditions du minuit, 1991), pp. 21–37.
14 Jacques Derrida, 'Structure, Sign, and Play in the Discourse of the Human Sciences', in *Writing and Difference*, trans. Alan Bass (London: Routledge and Kegan Paul, 1978), p. 278.
15 Ibid., p. 278.

('when the structurality if structure had to be thought . . .'),[16] the centre
is undermined to the extent that structure must be reconceived as discourse:

This was the moment when language invaded the universal problematic, the
moment when, in the absence of center or origin, everything became discourse –
provided we can agree on this word – that is to say, a system in which the central
signified, the original or transcendental signified, is never absolutely present
outside a system of differences.[17]

Discourse, as the recognition of the world as a system of differences
erasing the centre (origin, central signified), entails the awareness of the
substitutions and displacements (respectively, metaphor and metonymy)
of one centre for another. Thus Derrida defines the fundamentals of
structuralist linguistics, the 'rupture' in the history of structurality with
which he is concerned ('the moment when language invaded the universal problematic'). But his siting of discourse and structuralism in the
same location, as equivalent, sits oddly in relation to music theory in
which structuralist procedures are neutral, taxonomic and corrigible,
while discourse is subjective, mobile and ambiguous. Derrida's equivalence is therefore split into opposed fields. While he can analyse the
illusory unity of signifier and signified in Lévi-Strauss,[18] structuralist
music theory tends to ignore the signified altogether, the dimension that
has begun to be recaptured for music only in discourse.[19] Derrida's discussion of the sign in Lévi-Strauss's structuralism, though, emphasises
that 'play' is an essential element, a play of signifiers that supplements 'a
lack on the part of the signified';[20] the liberating arbitrariness of the
signifier in semiotics demands that the signified maintains its totalising
function as the 'centre'.

The origin of the disparity between Derrida's reading of semiotic relations and those of music theory lies in the theoretical opposition within
the latter: musical semiosis is either introversive, as pure structure, or
extroversive, as psychological and cultural meaning.[21] The mismatch of
this theoretical frame with Derrida's is that the descriptive methods of

16 Ibid., p. 280.
17 Ibid., p. 280.
18 Ibid., pp. 280–93.
19 See, for example, Carolyn Abbate, *Unsung Voices: Opera and Musical Narrative in the
   Nineteenth Century* (Princeton: Princeton University Press, 1991), and Nattiez, *Music
   and Discourse*.
20 Derrida, 'Structure, Sign, and Play', p. 289.
21 This widely accepted opposition was formulated explicitly by Roman Jakobson. For a
   concise discussion see Nattiez, *Music and Discourse*, pp. 111–18.

structuralism control and limit the playful mobility of Derrida's signifiers, while musical discourse frees up and plays with the limited, even rigid, 'centrality' of Derrida's signifieds. It would seem that this reversal of functions that Derrida allows us to recognise arises from the methodological separation in music theory of the two dimensions of the sign, and therefore from a certain blockage of their connections. By emphasising the signifier, structuralist theories reduce the *linguistic* signifier, the model, simply (but logically) to patterns of sound comprising similarities and oppositions (its phonological aspect). Jakobson's formalist definition of the 'poetic function' of language – the projection of the principle of equivalence of the axis of selection [paradigm] into the axis of combination [syntagm][22] – is similarly drained of content if the signifying dimension is ignored, by which I mean the potential relation of signifiers *via* identical or equivalent signifieds.[23] On the other hand, theories of discourse have been absent in modern music theory except for the recent fashionability of narrative.[24] Why this should be the case is no mystery: 'discourse' demands a focus on the musical signified, the most elusive and problematic dimension; 'narrative' is attractive because it reinstates the domain of the signifieds, reconstructing the unity of the sign by giving each musical signifier a referent, and permits the analyst – usually with relief – to interpret. The autonomist/referentialist debate is thereby sustained, dressed up in our own *fin-de-siècle* conceptual clothes which allow both positions to be held as valid.

What might appear to be an ideological transgression is given some support in Barthes's description of music as an isologic language. Discussing the role of the semiological signifieds in isologic systems, he writes:

the signified has no materialisation other than its typical signifier; one cannot therefore handle it except by imposing on it a metalanguage. One can for instance ask some subjects about the meaning they attribute to a piece of music by submitting to them a list of verbalized signifieds . . . whereas in fact all these

22 Roman Jakobson, 'Linguistics and Poetics', in Thomas A. Sebeok (ed.), *Style in Language* (New York: MIT Press, 1960), p. 358.
23 In 'Linguistics and Poetics' Jakobson himself emphasises phonology at the expense of the signifieds, which has led to a rather narrow application of the 'poetic function' to musical structure. For a demonstration of the analytical potential of the phonological model see David Clarke, *Language, Form, and Structure in the Music of Michael Tippett* (New York: Garland, 1989).
24 See, especially, Abbate, *Unsung Voices*. A critique of recent theories of musical narrative is found in Nattiez, 'Can One Speak of Narrativity in Music?', trans. K. Ellis, *Journal of the Royal Musical Association*, 115/ii (1990), pp. 240–57.

verbal signs for a single musical signified ought to be designated by one single cipher which would imply no verbal dissection and no metaphorical small change.[25]

The first sentence of this description can be invoked to justify traditional applications of the phonological model, and the second to support the discourse model. But a more radical reading is possible: if music comprises a pure relation of signifiers then it seems reasonable to suppose that at some stage one or many of the signifiers will masquerade as signifieds, as referential entities, reinstating the play of the signifiers as Derrida's supplement for the lack on the part of the signified, to compensate for its very instability. The only outstanding question here is that of metalanguage. Obviously, an appropriate metalanguage cannot be concerned only with semantics, since the re-reading of Barthes I have proposed conflates the functions of the signifier and signified and locates the semantic (i. e. referential) dimension in the signifiers. But this allows discourse in Derrida's specific sense – the system of differences that recognises metaphorical and metonymic displacements and substitutions – to be tested as a model for musical structure where, I suggest, it properly belongs. If the model is taken from literature (not simply language) it is metalinguistic; and if the metalanguage must be appropriate to the structure of discourse, to tropes and figures, then the most appropriate metalanguage is rhetoric.

Language/rhetoric

Differentiating language from metalanguage, structure from discourse, is normally to make a general distinction between the literal and the non-literal (or figurative). The analysis of musical structure, though, transcends the oppositional nature of such distinctions in that what are usually asserted as literal structural relations within a work are always open to non-literal discursive readings. Even neutrally-descriptive methods contain this feature: two identical or equivalent units, for example, can never be literally equivalent since the repetition is always functionally non-equivalent to that which is repeated, and the function of the repeated unit is redefined in relation to its repetition. The tinge of the literal in structuralist methods therefore depends on an assumption about the nature of the relation of musical events, and in another context on the

25 Roland Barthes, *Elements of Semiology*, trans. A. Lavers and C. Smith (Boston: Beacon Press, 1967), pp. 45–6; translation modified.

assumption that an analysis is a literal representation, a picture of its object. But in Derrida's classic discussion of the non-literal (as metaphor) at the origin of language,[26] even the language model is accepted to be fundamentally metalinguistic. If the non-literal is inescapable, then rhetoric demands our attention.

By 'rhetoric' I do not mean the 'old Rhetoric' (described by I. A. Richards as 'the rationale of pleadings and persuadings') but a 'revised rhetoric' that 'must undertake its own enquiry into the modes of meaning . . . on a microscopic scale by using theorems about the structure of the fundamental conjectural units of meaning and the conditions through which they and their interconnections arise'.[27] I find this particular definition attractive because it is centred on the non-literal ('fundamental *conjectural* units of meaning'), while insisting on analytical methods (in the form of 'theorems') that can be elaborated to reveal the structure of units and their relations ('interconnections'). The generality of Richards' definition entails that all rhetorical theorems will depend on a particular, individual reading of structural relations and that the rhetorical categories to which they are ascribed will depend on the nature of this reading. As William Empson emphasised, discussing poetic ambiguity:

two statements are made as if they were connected, and the reader is forced to consider their relations for himself. The reason why these facts should have been selected for a poem is left for him to invent: he will invent a variety of reasons and order them in his own mind. This, I think, is the fundamental fact about the poetical use of language.[28]

The essential question here is the degree of resemblance. Whether Empson's 'statements', or two musical events, are equivalent or opposed, similar or different, is a decision for the reader/analyst. Opposition, however, is the both more creative and problematic relation. Richards writes, glossing Empson:

As the two things put together are more remote, the tension created is, of course, greater. . . . bafflement is an experience of which we soon tire, and rightly. But, as we know, what seems an impossible connection, an 'impractical identification',

---

26 Derrida, *Of Grammatology*, trans. Gayatri Chakravorty Spivak (Baltimore: The Johns Hopkins University Press, 1976) pp. 271–80. Further discussion of this topic is found in Michael Payne, *Reading Theory: An Introduction to Lacan, Derrida, and Kristeva* (Oxford: Blackwell, 1993).

27 I. A. Richards, *The Philosophy of Rhetoric* (New York: Oxford University Press, 1965), pp. 23–4.

28 William Empson, *Seven Types of Ambiguity* (Harmondsworth: Penguin, 1961), p. 25.

can at once turn into an easy and powerful adjustment if the right hint comes from the rest of the discourse.[29]

Here 'tension' is the crucial term because it instates resemblance *within* opposition as the essential feature of all figurative language; the degree of tension is greatest in what Kenneth Burke calls the 'four master tropes', metaphor, metonymy, synecdoche and irony.[30] Of these, I select metaphor and metonymy as the most apposite for musical structure; synecdoche and metonymy are often indistinguishable, while irony is sustained on a macroscopic scale and not in the microscopic relations of discursive units.[31]

In Aristotle's formulation, metaphor dominates many other figures, including metonymy, because they all involve the substitution of one term for another and some aspect of semantic resemblance.[32] Lacan's definition is only slightly less broad: metaphor is 'one word for another'; metonymy is a matter of 'word to word connection' within the signifying chain.[33] Quite simply, this definition identifies metaphor as paradigmatic and metonymy as syntagmatic – as in Lacan's source, Jakobson's 'Two aspects of language'.[34] Jakobson equates metaphor with the paradigmatic plane of language and metonymy with the syntagmatic plane, since they comprise relations of similarity and contiguity respectively. Taking his own example: a metaphor for 'hut' is 'den', since this is a relation of similarity ('one word for another' in Lacan); a metonym for 'hut' is 'thatch', since this is a relation of contiguity (that is, 'thatch' is a property of the thing it stands for). In the metonym two terms are positionally contiguous because there is a constant genitive relation between them (for example, 'thatch of the hut'), corresponding to Lacan's 'word to word connections'. There is no such relationship available in metaphor ('den of the hut', for instance, is nonsensical unless 'den' is read as a culturally-

---

29 Richards, *The Philosophy of Rhetoric*, pp. 125–6.
30 Kenneth Burke, 'Four Master Tropes', in *A Grammar of Motives* (Berkeley: University of California Press, 1969), pp. 503–17.
31 See Walter Nash, *Rhetoric: The Wit of Persuasion* (Oxford: Blackwell, 1989), pp. 117–29.
32 Aristotle, *The Art of Rhetoric*, trans. H. Lawson-Tancred (Harmondsworth: Penguin, 1991), pp. 224–5 and pp. 234–41. For a full discussion of Aristotle's view see David E. Cooper, *Metaphor* (Oxford: Blackwell, 1986).
33 Jacques Lacan, 'The Agency of the Letter in the Unconscious or Reason since Freud', in *Ecrits*, trans. A. Sheridan (London: Tavistock, 1977), pp. 156–7.
34 Jakobson, 'Two Aspects of Language and Two Types of Aphasic Disturbances', in Roman Jakobson and Morris Halle, *Fundamentals of Language* (The Hague: Mouton, 1956), pp. 69–96.

specific North American metaphor, in which case the whole phrase becomes metonymic).

The origins of this distinction are of course in Saussure's definition of associative (that is, paradigmatic) and syntagmatic relations: but metaphor and metonymy are not absolutely identical with them. Positional similarity, which Jakobson defines as 'the capacity for two words to replace one another' is common to both the paradigm and metaphor; positional contiguity, on the other hand, is the possibility for two words to combine with one another[35] – as in syntax, which is solely a syntagmatic function. The pervasiveness of positional similarity presents a difficulty, since metonymy obviously also relies on positional *similarity* and therefore on a paradigmatic relation – a feature which erases the distinction (at this level of description) between it and metaphor. Jakobson, therefore, must make a distinction between positional and semantic relations in order to maintain the contiguity inherent in metonymy. Thus, the difference between metaphor and metonymy is said to be a difference between *semantic* similarity and *semantic* contiguity.[36] This reinforces the metaphorical relation of 'den' and 'hut' as semantically similar, and the metonymic relation of 'thatch' and 'hut' as semantically contiguous; but it removes the simple identification of the two tropes with the paradigm and the syntagm, and constitutes a second level of description.

This second, semantic level is essentially the domain of the signifieds, in which there is no syntagmatic organisation (as Lacan recognised, at least implicitly). It is therefore paradigmatic; for the construction of the tropes to be established, any two terms must be regarded as paradigmatically equivalent within the structure of the trope (this is the origin of Richards' 'tension' as a primary discursive function). And this is why Lacan observes that metaphor and metonymy both involve some degree of semantic contiguity: metaphor, in Françoise Meltzer's paraphrase of Lacan's dispersed discussion of the topic, is said to be 'contiguous within a large field' (i. e. the paradigm) so that, for example, 'Volkswagen' and its metaphor 'prancing steed' are contiguous within the field of transportation.[37] Metaphor is thus metonymised in Lacan: the connection between the terms in the example given is made by the interpreter (Empson's 'reader') and is not inherent in the comparison as it is

35 See Russell Grigg, 'Metaphor and Metonymy', *Newsletter of the Freudian Field*, 3/i–ii (1989), p. 60.
36 Jakobson, 'Two Aspects of Language', pp. 254–5.
37 Françoise Meltzer, 'Eat your *Dasein*: Lacan's Self-Consuming Puns', in Jonathan Culler (ed.), *On Puns: The Foundation of Letters* (Oxford: Blackwell, 1988), pp. 156–63.

in true metonymy. Semantics, now established as an interpretative construction, allows Lacan to conceive metaphor and metonymy as located primarily in the domain of the signifieds, with the proviso that metaphor eventually crosses the 'bar' between signifier and signified to reach the repressed referent of the trope. But Lacan also maintains that metaphor must not be seen as analogy, a 'non-contiguous figure which insists upon totality',[38] which maintains a one-to-one correspondence with the signifieds at each point in the discourse. By revealing, in effect, a merging of distinctions between metaphor and metonymy on Jakobson's semantic level,[39] Lacan reveals its discursive superfluity (Derrida's 'lack on the part of the signifieds'). This has informed my reading of Barthes's conception of music as an isologic language: that is to say, matching the rhetorical modes of musical and psychoanalytic discourse – similarly mobile and ludic (exhibiting 'free play' in Derrida's sense) – is productive, since both are essentially concerned with the activity and relations of the signifiers, in which the signified is elusive or perpetually retreats to the position of a further signifier. As Lacan writes of psychoanalytical discourse, 'the signifier, as such, signifies nothing': 'experience proves it – the more the signifier signifies nothing, the more indestructible it is',[40] and thus for the speaker the signifier takes over the function of the signified. Additional theoretical support for this correspondence is found in Paul de Man's discussion of rhetoric in Proust, where de Man finally concludes that Proust's typical strategy is to collapse the aspect of 'necessity' in metaphor ('the inference of identity and totality'[41] inherent in resemblance) into contiguous, metonymic relations of 'chance' – a contingent, purely relational contact of terms – so that, through repetition and recontextualisation across large units of discourse, metonymy controls metaphor: metaphors masquerade deceptively as 'figures of necessity', when in fact they are also 'figures of chance' (metonymies).[42]

Since the interpreter constructs the specific tropic relation of terms, metaphor and metonymy, like all other tropes, are essentially heuristic devices. For musical structure, Jakobson's formulation, although overly schematic, is useful because it offers a systematic description of discur-

38 Meltzer, 'Eat your *Dasein*', p. 159
39 Lacan's reinterpretation of Jakobson is outlined in Grigg, 'Metaphor and Metonymy'.
40 'The signifier, as such, signifies nothing' – Lacan, in *The Psychoses: The Seminars of Jacques Lacan, Book 3, 1955–1956*, ed. Jacques-Alain Miller, trans. R. Grigg (London: Routledge, 1993), p. 185.
41 de Man, 'Semiology and Rhetoric', in *Allegories of Reading: Figural Language in Rousseau, Nietzsche, Rilke and Proust* (New Haven: Yale University Press, 1979) p. 14.
42 de Man, 'Reading (Proust)', in *Allegories of Reading*, p. 67.

sive structure in theory. But these broad theoretical synopses can be instantiated only in relation to specific examples. Confronting Jakobson with the Prelude of Debussy's *Pelléas et Mélisande* in the light of Lacan and de Man, I use only the concepts of positional similarity and contiguity (which pertain specifically to the relation of signifiers) and I restrict this application initially to melody, a first (though not necessarily primary) level of structure in which positional relations are clearest. 'Position' here must become a fluid concept (a 'figure', in fact): while positional similarity (metaphor) is observed primarily within the paradigm and positional contiguity (metonymy) within the syntagm (as in Jakobson), it will be seen that contiguity also exists among the paradigms, that is in oppositional units; this reflects the pervasiveness of positional similarity noted above. More strikingly, this merging reveals specific instances of the tendency of metaphor to resolve into metonymy as Lacan and de Man lead us to expect, and demonstrates the detail of Richards's instatement of resemblance within opposition.

Similarity/contiguity

Nicolas Ruwet's analysis of the Prelude[43] together with Nattiez's revisions[44] is displayed paradigmatically in Ex. 7.1. Ruwet groups the nine paradigms (a–i) as far as possible into units of equal duration (1.111, 1.112, etc.), and the resultant paradigmatic relations are described as forming 'a dialectic of the repeated and the non-repeated'.[45] Many objections to this analysis are possible, but a by-product of Nattiez's revisions (shown as transformations in brackets on the example) has particular interest here. Units e and e' are a single unit in Ruwet, while units f, f', g and i are all transformations of earlier units. Thus, Ruwet's analysis attempts to duplicate the pattern f, f, g (h, h, i) when in fact, as Nattiez shows, the transformations (marked 'T') would break it up. Nattiez's revisions also reveal that there is apparently no new material in bars 16–20. (Bar 20 is in effect the end of the Prelude: the curtain rises during bars 21–3, a section which is clearly both cadential and transitional.) These revisions unravel the relentlessly metaphoric character of Ruwet's analysis: connections among the units are minimal because these

43 Nicolas Ruwet, 'Note sur les duplications dans l'œuvre de Claude Debussy', in *Langage, musique, poésie* (Paris: Seuil, 1972), p. 91.
44 Nattiez, *Fondements d'une sémiologie de la musique* (Paris: Union générale d'éditions, 1975), p. 252.
45 Ruwet, 'Note sur les duplications', p. 91.

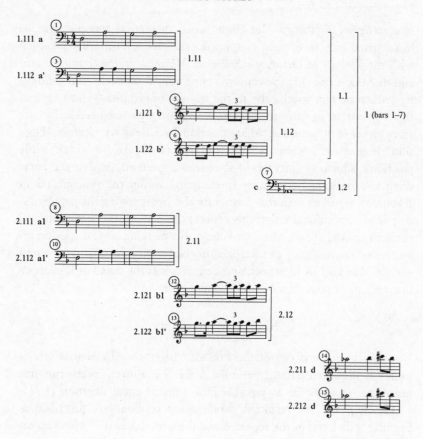

Example 7.1 (cont. opposite)

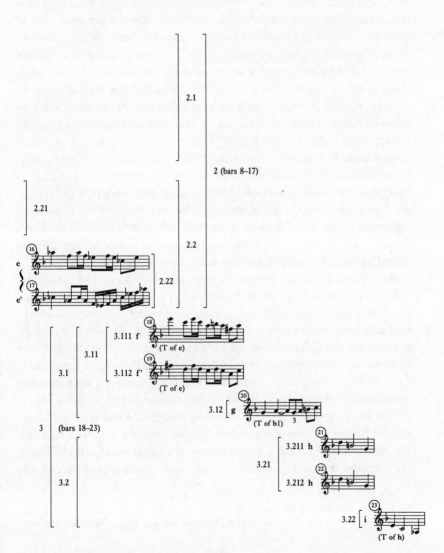

are either exact repetitions or simple transformations exemplifying the features of similarity and totality in Lacan's 'metaphor'. And Ruwet obscures the primary feature of the 'leitmotives' in *Pelléas* (at least four of which are present in the Prelude) – that each can be transformed, metonymically, into another. Nattiez's revision of bars 16–23 moves towards this metonymy, in that the equivalence of units e, e', f and f' points to a greater number of more complex transformations, and thus a chain of 'word to word', unit to unit connections. Nattiez's own analyses (that of Debussy's 'Syrinx', for example)[46] are consistent with this tendency to reveal metonymic connections: the paradigms are larger, the transformations more numerous, to the point where a separate table of melodic variables is required to capture the complexity of the relationships. Thus, metonymic connections can be present within a paradigm, but only if the equivalence of units is seen as multivalent. At this stage, then, it would appear that a metaphoric paradigmatic analysis may be defined as one in which there is a proliferation of paradigms (as in Ruwet) and a metonymic analysis as one characterised by fewer, but larger, more inclusive paradigms. However, larger paradigms also tend toward metaphor because they assert positional similarity. Provisionally, it seems clear that metaphor is resolved into metonymy as a result of the analytical reduction of tension between units, the erasure of difference. As I will show later, oppositions must be maintained if this analytical reduction to the 'same' is to be resisted; on the other hand though, it will become evident that such interpretative control cannot always be sustained against the insistence of the musical work.

Ruwet's analysis, too, merges the relations of similarity and contiguity. While the analysis is primarily metaphorical (characterised by positional similarity) and each paradigm is characterised by the ability of one unit to replace another either as repetition or transformation, no attempt is made to represent the different functions of the units except in the 'dialectic' of repeated and non-repeated units indicated by the three large segments 1, 2, 3 and their constituents. Ruwet's commentary, however, adds a further dimension to the analysis. In particular, the large unit e (bars 16–17, indicated by the curly bracket combining Nattiez's e and e') is problematic for Ruwet because it is purely a *harmonic* repetition (over a bass B♭): his view of bars 16–17 as a single unit is significant because it challenges the metaphoric character of the analysis insofar as bars 16–17 are clearly

---

46 Nattiez, 'An Analysis of Debussy's *Syrinx*', in *Toronto Semiotic Circle: Monographs, Working Papers and Pre-publications*, 4 (Toronto: Victoria University, 1982), pp. 1–35.

melodically processive, positionally contiguous, and therefore metonymic. The same could be said of bars 18–19 (units f and f', over a bass A), and to a lesser extent bars 21–3 (h, h, i). Ruwet's appeal to harmonic duplication (by which he means 'contiguity') in bars 16–17 as a criterion for melodic metonymy is distinct from the harmonic structure of paradigms a–d because each of these involves a repeated harmonic progression: although it would seem that progression is a metonymic property, here the repetition itself renders the progression static and metaphoric, whereas in Ruwet's description the units in bars 16–17 are processive because there is continuity in the harmonic domain. In Ruwet, then, the two large sections in the Prelude, bars 1–15 and bars 16–23, can be defined respectively as primarily metaphoric and metonymic. That this division cuts across the more obvious division at bar 14 (unit d) is a feature of structural ambiguity addressed in Exx. 7.2 and 7.3.

Are bars 1–15 as non-processive as Ruwet maintains? Ex. 7.2 shows a paradigmatic analysis according to three criteria in descending order of priority: (i) the first note (D, G, A♭); (ii) emphasis of the second beat of the bar; (iii) melodic shape. This reveals that the units of bars 1–10, which all begin with D, form a large paradigm in which a process can be observed: that is, the processive emphasis of the second half of the bar and then the second beat of the bar (indicated by the dotted line) through register (in bar 1), repetition (bar 3), syncopation (bar 5), and the dotted upbeat (bar 6). Bars 12–13 show the same process operating on the G–A shape of bars 8–9. This shift from the first to the second bar of the opening unit (bars 1–2) in bars 7–8 reveals a *processive* rather than a dialectical function for the repetition of the opening material. That is, the repetition in bars 8–10 is required to begin the process that will propel the structure of the Prelude. The shift to the G–A leads to the new transposition on A♭ (bar 14) where the melodic shape (the rising tone) is retained but now loses the second-beat emphasis and is followed by a transformation. In this first paradigm (bars 1–13) there is a mixture of metaphoric and metonymic features. Positional similarity (as metaphor) exists in conjunction with positional contiguity (as metonymy), but none of the units is completely static: each contributes to the primary process of transformation – the emphasis of the second beat – and therefore the structure is primarily metonymic.

The second large section (bars 14–19) is similarly metonymic, but in a more restricted sense. The transformations beginning at bar 16 are taken from the new element in bar 14 (the augmented second C♯–B♭) and are therefore shown (as by Nattiez) to involve continuous transformations of

Example 7.2

144

a single, large-scale melodic shape. (A more detailed analysis is required to capture the real structure of this section; see below). In bar 20, though, there is a return to the G–A paradigm, and bars 21–3 incorporate features of both paradigm I (beginning on D, second beat emphasis) and paradigm II (the descending third). Thus, bars 21–3 are placed in both paradigms, as an explicit example of the complexity of metaphoric relations (since there is no positional contiguity, but complex positional similiarity). In this and other similar cases where a double entry seems necessary, such paradigmatic over-determination demonstrates the truth of de Man's 'metaphor' in which a chance conjunction in the syntagm (here bars 19 and 21) masquerades as a 'necessary' paradigmatic relation.

The paradigmatic analysis of the second half of the Prelude (see Ex. 7.3) is essentially metonymic because it comprises a single paradigm of complex transformations. The section is broadly divided in two over the bass B♭ (bars 12–17) and A (bars 18–20). This reference to the basic harmonic movement clarifies and establishes the processive transformations in melodic structure. Unit 2 is analysed as a complex transformation of unit 1 (bar 13): here the function of the repetition in bars 14–15 is revealed as an expansion of bar 13, explaining the elaborative function of the C♯–B♭ in bar 14, and in bar 15, explaining its transformation by inversion of the G–B♭ of unit 1. The bracketed unit 2a (like units 5a and 8a) shows alternative transformations which are metaphoric (that is, potentially identical), defined only by transposition or interval expansion. Metonymic transformations, on the other hand, rely on a Schoenbergian *Grundgestalt* in which the large shapes described by units 1 and 2 are contracted into melodic units of smaller duration.[47] Inversion, the primary process evident in units 1–10, is a metonymic phenomenon here because it inaugurates a process begun in unit 3 (bar 16) – that is, the A♭–F inversion of the G–B♭ of bar 13 – ending in unit 10. This inversion of the inversion (as I prefer to describe it) produces a transposition of the initial G–B♭ as a metonymic, processive event, and is structurally significant because the underlying bass B♭ allows unit 10 to function as a melodic cadence, returning the melodic rising third to its original shape (see bar 13) before the bass A in bar 18. Thus unit 10 indicates a return to stasis, a condition which has now emerged as a secondary feature of positional similarity: the unit is therefore metaphoric. The new pitch level of unit 10 also relates it to unit 3, so that the section (units 3–10) is

---

47 Such oppositional erasures are exemplified classically in the processes of developing variation and suggest that the organicist metaphor in Schoenberg asserts a preference for metonymy.

Example 7.3

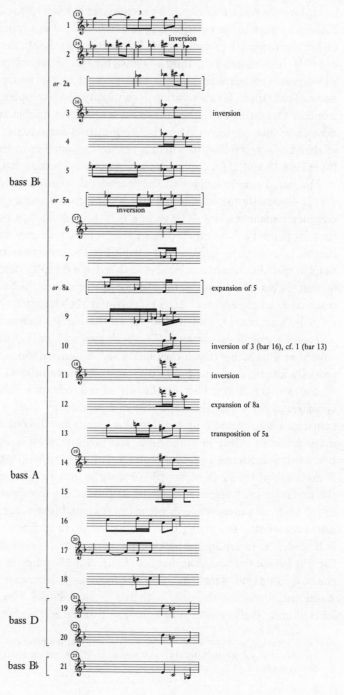

bounded by the minor third, confirming Ruwet's view that these two bars (16–17) are a single large unit – or, as should now be clear, a processive structure in which metaphorical relations of positional similarity are subsumed under metonymic processes of positional contiguity.

Units 11–18 (bars 18–20), on the other hand, begin a new phase of development expanding the minor third of unit 2 to a major third (E–C), and play on the alternative transformations of units 5a and 8a. Unit 12 is a transformation of 8a, and unit 13 is a transformation of 5a (because it returns to the pitch level of the neighbouring-note figure of unit 1). Unit 16 continues this process, but is also positionally contiguous with unit 17 (the modified return to unit 1) since the bass remains on A and the neighbouring-note figure is explicitly retained. Furthermore, the metaphoric function of units 19–20 is obvious: the descending triad has its origin in unit 12, uniting the dominant and tonic functions of the bass A– D, while the augmented triad in unit 21 (over B♭) is transitional to the first scene of the opera. In summary, then, the metonymic processes of the second section (bars 12–23) are uninterrupted, except for the points of articulation coinciding with the movement of the bass. This contrasts markedly with the Ruwet/Nattiez analysis in which points of articulation are emphasised as paradigmatic shifts, emphasising positional similarity over contiguity. In my analysis, though, the latter is emphasised by reference to the simplest aspect of harmonic structure (the bass note) so that metonymic processes are clarified.

Nevertheless, metaphoric correspondences are present in the second section. Ex. 7.4 shows the large-scale relation of bar 13 and bars 18–20 (units 1 and 11–18). The ascent to B♭ in bar 13, not regarded as significant in Ruwet, in fact describes a linear third span for the complete unit, ending on a B♭ triad as a point of articulation. Similarly, in bars 18–20 the linear third (E–F♯–G) over a stable bass as in bar 13 defines the large shape of this section and connects it to unit 17 of Ex. 7.3. In addition, the motion towards D (units 17–18 of Ex. 7.3) is achieved by contrary motion: this transfers the previously contiguous, metonymic principle of inversion, predominant in Ex. 7.3, to the movement of the bass. Since there is no clear dominant chord, functional tonal harmony yields here to the connection of positionally similar, metaphoric units. The insistent 'necessity' of these correspondences is an example of the way in which metaphor controls metonymy, in that the mobility of the signifiers in Ex. 7.3 is held in check by the large-scale melodic shape which acts as a signified both in itself and by its motion towards cadential goals: the new, metaphoric use of inversion in bars 20–1, leading to the final ca-

Example 7.4

dence, reinforces this domination of metaphor whose function is to define closure.

Connections/correspondences

My exploration of metaphor and metonymy in melodic structure scratches only the surface potential of the tropes. Reference to the role of the bass in defining the relations of melodic units opens up the question of harmonic organisation, which exhibits similar discursive functions. As the commentary to Ruwet's analysis demonstrates, harmony either confirms or challenges the organisation of melodic structure, and this suggests that there is a complex and mobile relation of congruence and opposition between the two parameters. Such opposition is *de facto* the most productive relation, involving tension between 'vertical' (inter-parametrical) rather than 'horizontal' (intra-parametrical) terms. Melody and harmony are not necessarily homogeneous in the Prelude, because both dimensions are quite systematic and contain models and structural routines: it seems reasonable to suppose, then, that complexity and ambiguity are created by inter-parametrical discontinuity, mirroring the clear intra-parametrical melodic discontinuities analysed by Ruwet (see Ex. 7.1). (For an example of harmonic discontinuity, see the opposition of diatonic and whole-tone chords in bars 1–4 and bars 5–6 respectively.)

However, I will limit the discussion here to an example of congruence that reinforces a metonymic relation of contiguity within paradigm I of Ex. 7.2. Recall that the relations based on G–A in Ex. 7.2 are primarily metonymic, even though the opposed units in bars 12–13 and 20–21 are

Example 7.5

presented as metaphoric (positionally similar). Ex. 7.5 shows that these two units and their repetitions are related metonymically through harmony: both segments begin with set-class 4–26 (the added sixth chord) and end with the triad (set-class 3–11); they are therefore positionally similar and paradigmatically related. Set-class 4–26, though, is derived initially from the combination of triads in bars 2 and 4. These bars can be regarded as containing single harmonic complexes, since there is no unequivocal indication of cadential priority for the first or second chord of each bar. (Debussy exploits this type of ambiguity, almost routinely, throughout the Prelude.) And because this derivation is only implicit in bars 2 and 4, its explicit realisation must be regarded as deferred until bar 12. In a case such as this, *différance* comes into play: the double operation of differing and deferring is present in the trope since the triadic units (bars 2 and 4) are distinctly different from their latent referent (the explicit 4–26 in bar 12ff.) and could be deferred almost indefinitely. The common pitches G–A define a metonymy, not a metaphor, because the genitive relation between the units is present in the deferred function of the triads in bars 2 and 4 as the possibility of combination in set 4–26. Furthermore, this function is not one of 'necessity' (which de Man ascribes to metaphor) because there is no harmonic or tonal role that demands the relation of 4–26 with the pitch classes G–A: that this relation is constant, however, reveals that a 'chance' metonymic relation of note and chord in bars 2–4 masquerades as a figure of necessity established by its repetition in later units.[48] Thus, what is established initially as a metonymy later appears to be a necessary, metaphoric inter-parametrical relation, a process that resembles the rhetoric of Proust's *A la recherche du temps perdu*: in de Man's interpretation, metaphoric structures purport to dominate metonymy but are in fact dependent on it.[49] Just as Proust frequently asserts the mastery of metaphor over metonymy, so Debussy asserts the predominance of metaphorical paradigmatic structures (demonstrated by Ruwet) over metonymic processes, as my analyses in Exx. 7.2 and 7.3 attempt to make clear.

There is of course a question of style here. Debussy's melodic structures are typically self-reflexive, so that even when clear oppositions are present the possibility exists of an analysis containing only transformations of the initial material. This stylistic fingerprint points to Debussy's particular mode of 'free play' in melodic structure which is captured only partially by the more familiar term 'arabesque': melodic units develop both progressively and retrogressively, supported or contradicted by harmonic processes, as musical analogues with the potentially limitless 'correspondences' in Symbolist literature. The strategies of de Man's analysis of rhetorical structure in Proust therefore present a stylistically congruent model for similar structures in Debussy. Genette's 'Métonymie chez Proust', the catalyst for de Man's study, relies on the operation of memory as the prime mover of Proust's novelistic discourse which turns on the axes of metaphor and metonymy: 'without metaphor, Proust says,

---

48 A similar function for repetition in the construction of metaphor in Proust is elaborated in Margaret E. Gray, *Postmodern Proust* (Philadelphia: University of Pennsylvania Press, 1992), pp. 67–94.

49 de Man, 'Semiology and Rhetoric', p. 15.

more or less, no true memories: we add . . . without metonymy, no linking of memories, no story, no novel'.[50] The trigger of memory is metaphor, but the expansion and exploration of a particular memory is metonymic, achieved by Proust's tendency toward 'assimilation by proximity', the projection of analogical affinity (metaphor) upon relationships of contiguity (metonymy).[51] If Genette's 'memory' is read as 'melodic opposition' a concise description of the twin axes of Debussy's musical discourse begins to emerge; add to this de Man's identification of 'logical tensions'[52] inherent in these rhetorical figures and the temptation to accept relations of musical units as inevitable can be firmly resisted: the point of the tropes is precisely that relations are essentially accidental; they are merely *presented* as necessary. What is often regarded as unfathomable ambiguity in Debussy is produced by the tension of the accidental in the creation of tropes and the appearance, even illusion, of inevitability when they are elaborated by the analyst as 'structure'. The difficulty of discussing such free play is eased by the application of a more sophisticated model than the traditional opposition of paradigm and syntagm, although this remains the essential ground of the model. As Barthes writes:

Rhetoric as a whole will no doubt prove to be the domain . . . of creative transgressions; if we remember Jakobson's distinction, we shall understand that any metaphoric series is a syntagmised paradigm, and any metonymy a syntagm which is frozen and absorbed into a system [i. e. a paradigm]; in metaphor, selection becomes contiguity, and in metonymy, contiguity becomes a field to select from. It therefore seems that it is always on the frontiers of the two planes that creation has a chance to occur.[53]

Ruwet's analysis is neither incorrect nor valueless, but it is blinded (to use one term of de Man's famous opposition) by Debussy's assertively metaphoric musical discourse. Insight (de Man's complementary term) into Debussy's creative 'transgressions' begins with Nattiez's revisions which open up the domain of 'neither/nor', the domain of latent and multiple modes of connection that differentiate language from rhetoric and structure from discourse.

50 Gerard Genette, 'Métonymie chez Proust', in *Figures III* (Paris: Seuil, 1972), p. 63.
51 See ibid., pp. 59–61.
52 de Man, 'Semiology and Rhetoric', p. 7.
53 Barthes, *Elements of semiology*, pp. 87–8.

8

Music as text: Mahler, Schumann and issues in analysis

ROBERT SAMUELS

There is a sense in which the claim that pieces of music are texts risks seeming trivial or silly. No-one has ever doubted that works of music are written-down artistic creations. In some ways they are obviously analogous to works of literature: both have authors and audiences; both are transmitted in printed media. We can talk equally well about the 'Eroica' Symphony or *Pride and Prejudice* with other people, or enjoy a performance (even if read silently) ourselves. There is no difficulty colloquially in referring to 'the text of Beethoven's symphony', or in the idea that this text is an important aspect of the work's transmission. And indeed, the prospect of a foray into the often dense world of contemporary textual theory merely in the service of musicological discourse is one which legitimately demands an explanation.

It is my contention that the invocation of both the term, 'text', and the concomitant theory is justifiable, and indeed that the exploration of the nature and limits of textuality in music is one of the most important currents in music analysis, and one which may reorient much critical endeavour. Questions of musical textuality have been raised by Carolyn Abbate's and Jean-Jacques Nattiez's discussions of narrativity,[1] in which the relation of music to narrative, to the possibility of narrating, has been wrested from nineteenth-century programme music and carefully redefined. Rather than rehearsing the issue of narrativity here,[2] I wish to examine the concept which is a necessary assumption of musical narrativity: that music is *textual*, in the sense of defining relations and articulating codes in a genuinely semiotic fashion. Thus I begin with an inspection of the concept of 'text' in recent critical theory.

---

1 Carolyn Abbate, *Unsung Voices: Opera and Musical Narrative in the Nineteenth Century* (Princeton: Princeton University Press, 1991); Jean-Jacques Nattiez, 'Can One Speak of Narrativity in Music?', trans. K. Ellis, *Journal of the Royal Musical Association*, 115/ii (1990), pp. 240–57.

2 I have addressed this in 'The Suicide of the Symphony: Musical Narrative and Mahler's Sixth', paper delivered at King's College, London, 1992. See also Alan Street's chapter in this volume, pp. 164–83.

Derrida and the 'general text'

When Jacques Derrida asserted that 'there is nothing outside the text', he produced a rallying-cry that has since had profound consequences in the human sciences. In one sense, this claim is among those made by the semiotic thought that Derrida might be seen to oppose: all human communication is effected by means of systems of signs, articulated in groups of occurrences that can be called texts. Indeed, it is by extending this understanding of sign system from manufactured artefacts such as books, clothes or television programmes to all aspects of human activity whatever that the texts studied by structuralist theory are displaced and decentred. If I am merely the confluence of texts without origins and without comfortingly reliable referents, then the text is simply where I find myself.

This concept of text leads to a much loftier self-image for theorists than that of the muse's handmaid: far from the mandarin inspection of esoteric examples of artistic creation, the engagement with texts, the study of textuality itself is, if not the essence of life, at least that which must now replace essentialist thinking. This replaces the concept of ontological essence with that of intertextual difference; and, as John Frow has pointed out, it is in this specific sense of the differences between texts, the identification of what is 'outside' a given text, and therefore 'nontextual', that Derrida develops the notion of the 'general text':

A 'text' that is henceforth no longer a finished corpus of writing, some content enclosed in a book or its margins, but a differential network, a fabric of traces referring endlessly to something other than itself, to other differential traces. Thus the text overruns all the limits assigned to it so far . . . everything that was to be set up in opposition to writing (speech, life, the world, the real, history, and what not).[3]

This assertion does not, as some seem to have thought, mean that everything is text and there are no longer any boundaries or differences in our experience. The text is precisely that which designates things as outside itself; simply, these margins and boundaries turn out ceaselessly to be complex and problematic. Frow quotes Gasché's description of this 'general text' as:

3 Jacques Derrida, 'Living on/*Border Lines*', trans. J. Hulbert, in Harold Bloom et al., *Deconstruction and Criticism* (New York: Seabury, 1979), pp. 83–4; quoted in John Frow, 'Intertextuality and Ontology', in M. Worton & J. Still (eds.), *Intertextuality: Theories and Practices* (Manchester: Manchester University Press, 1990), p. 49.

[the] border itself, from which the assignment of insides and outsides takes place, as well as where this distinction ultimately collapses.[4]

If the text is to be generalised, then, Derrida wishes to avoid its being totalised: the text, it turns out, is not where I find myself, but where I am lost, unable to discover an 'out there' which is not another text, and unable to construct a text except by positing an 'out there'.

This slippery and ultimately somewhat pessimistic discussion of the 'general text' ought to suggest that if we now turn to the nature of musical texts, it is in this context of a textuality that allows us to locate music within all other discourses, whilst insisting on its self-demarcation. In other words, there is an attractive prospect in being able to introduce musical discourse into other realms, and maybe elucidate it with new theoretical techniques; but at the same time, the apparent autonomy of the musical artwork, its methods of designating other music and indeed other forms of articulation as 'outside', as 'non-textual', must be interrogated. It is in this sense that Derrida makes an opposition between the concept of 'general text', of unclosure, to that of 'ideology', which is the attempt to close off the text.[5]

A musical text, then, is not a mere sequence of sounds any more than a literary text is a sequence of words.

Music in the past tense

To illustrate this point, I should like flatly to contradict one of Carolyn Abbate's best-known and most productive observations, that music 'seems not to have a past tense'.[6] The choice of a piece which does appear to possess this quality, however, is, fortunately for the purposes of this study, one made by Theodor Adorno. He hears the whole first movement of Mahler's Fourth Symphony as 'in the past tense': 'Once upon a time, there was a sonata' is the narrative he ascribes to it.[7] And it is clear that this textual gesture, this 'composing within quotation marks', leaves as its trace the boundary between first and second subjects. Adorno's disquiet stems from what he describes as the 'far too self-contained' second subject. It is, he claims, a theme from an instrumental song unable to be assimilated into the sonata form.

---

4 Rodolphe Gasché, *The Tain of the Mirror: Derrida and the Philosophy of Reflection* (Cambridge, Mass.: Harvard University Press, 1986), pp. 279–80; quoted in Frow, 'Intertextuality and Ontology', p. 50.
5 See Frow, 'Intertextuality and Ontology', p. 48.
6 Abbate, *Unsung Voices*, p. 52.
7 Theodor W. Adorno, *Mahler: Ein Musikalische Physiognomik* (Frankfurt, 1960), p. 86.

Example 8.1   Mahler, Symphony No. 4, first movement, bars 34–7

These brief comments can be elaborated by focusing on the general pause before the double bar line. The preparation of the dominant is pedantically emphatic, with the imitative texture giving semiquaver scales that are quite unusual for Mahler, evoking (for example) the end of a first subject group in Mozart (see Ex. 8.1). In fact, the scalic rush to the dominant degree clearly signals a 'bifocal close' to the first subject.[8] What makes the passage different from Mozart or Haydn is the imitation: what would be a unison emphasis of the tonal structure in a classical period form is divided between violins and cellos and basses, emphasising not the tonal function, but the fact that it *is* tonally functional. The music has brought us to what must be the threshold of the second subject, and the hesitation is a mark of a genuine aporia, a slippage; no theme whatsoever can satisfy the stylistic demands that such a preparation lays on it: neither continuing the Mahlerian 'modernism' of features such as the sleigh-bells, nor the 'archaism' of the tonal structure, will do.

Now it has to be admitted that Adorno can only manage this textual reading by mapping the dialectic of the historical development of musical form onto the social realities of Mahler's own time. But it is noticeable that this reading is both analytical (in the narrow sense) and critical (also in the narrow sense). It attempts to account for the presence of notes on the page, and its justification is in the history of sonata form and tonal

8 On the eighteenth-century origins of this feature, see Robert Winter, 'The Bifocal Close and the Evolution of the Viennese Classical Style', *Journal of the American Musicological Society*, 42 (1989), pp. 275–337.

process – not so far from the sort of assertion represented by a Schenkerian reduction of these bars. But where a Schenkerian reduction would find no problem at all, Adorno hears an intertextual problem: in fact, the problem of the unproblematic nature of this transition. And this understanding, again to expand on Adorno, leads us to be able to account for the most enigmatic and magical episode of the movement, the end of the development (bars 221–38).

Again, a traditional form of analysis would have no problems with this passage: the motivic material has almost all been derived from the first subject group in step-by-step fashion during the development, and the dissonant climax over a tonic G pedal is resolved by a detour to F♯ minor and some aurally explicit voice-leading (generally altering one note of each triad at a time by semitone step) to the dominant–tonic cadence after the double bar. But once more, disquiet is signalled by a pause, this time a pause not even within the bounds of metre, but simply introduced at the double bar-line. The recapitulation begins in the middle of a phrase, with the developmental outcome of the first and second subjects. Harmonically, this is a perfectly understandable completion of the passage before the double bar; motivically, its credentials are impeccable. One way of accounting for this moment is to say that thematic and harmonic schemes have got out of synchronisation, since the first subject begins before the double bar-line, disguised by the pause, the change of instrumentation and texture, and the voice-leading. But formally, and at the level of textual discourse, this moment is the outcome of aporia, presenting the continuity of formal units as a fiction. Mahler simultaneously meets the needs of presented continuity – in the thematic recapitulation and voice-leading – and presents this formal return as a disjunction, the harmonic grammaticality as an alienating, 'quotation-mark' device.

In semiotic terms, several codes of listening are required at this point. Codes of thematic continuity, motivic development and formal scheme conflict in a way which leaves as the only way of 'making sense' – or of 'producing the text', to use Michael Riffaterre's phrase – the resort to a code of 'musical narration', referring exclusively intertextually within the institution of symphonic composition. Two further features reinforce this reading of the semiotic situation. Firstly, Adorno notes that the coda, after a deliberately functional recapitulation, gives us what had been missed out at this general pause, following on the soulful and enigmatic lament by the solo horn (bars 333–9).[9] To use Barthes' terms from *S/Z*,

9 Adorno, *Mahler*, p. 78.

here a 'directional' code, that of thematic development, is deliberately made 'reversible', as if it were a form of motivic reference. Secondly, the most blindingly obvious feature of these bars is that they contain the opening motif, at pitch, of Mahler's Fifth Symphony on the trumpets. No motivic analysis can account for this interruption except as a gesture beyond the work, and most remarkably, forward to the as yet unwritten work, since the myth of compositional succession is part of the textuality of Mahler's symphonies. No matter whether this trumpet-call was inserted in a revision or not; here we have music not only in the past tense, but in the future tense too.

These are interesting moments, and well worth a much more extended analysis; but their usefulness for present purposes is as examples to illustrate how accepting the musical work as a textual field can lead beyond consideration of its autonomous organisation. Mahler is an unfair example, in that his compositional technique is constantly self-aware and overtly intertextual; but situations like those just described are exemplary of more general features of the musical text.

The text and the body

So far, the particular notion of text invoked here has been philosophical, literary and cerebral. However, no modern theorist could remain silent on the subject of the body in the text and the new corporeality that has invaded texts of all sorts. So it is to the body that we now turn.

Terry Eagleton has remarked that 'few literary texts are likely to make it nowadays into the new historicist canon unless they contain at least one mutilated body',[10] and he sees the entire history of aesthetics from the Enlightenment as the uniting of the body with the intellectual sphere. As the concern with the claims that texts make to systematic status has extended to the study of more obviously systematic and political institutions as textual, so the body has suffered. In Michel Foucault's *History of Sexuality*, the torturing of the body which is the result of oppressive regimes is chronicled with dispassionate clarity;[11] and the potential for the actualisation of the violence mimed by modernist texts in their dealings with language has featured in several recent literary studies.

Before turning to the treatment of the body by theorists, however, it would seem worthwhile to consider the field within musicology which

10 Terry Eagleton, *The Ideology of the Aesthetic* (Oxford: Blackwell, 1990), p. 7.
11 Michel Foucault, *History of Sexuality*, trans. R. Hurley, 3 vols. (New York: Allen Lane, 1979–88).

quite unequivocally equates musical meaning with the body's perceptions: the study of cognition. Of course, the theorist's body and the psychologist's subject are not quite the same; but some justification for the following discussion is found in Roland Barthes' use of the question, 'What does my body know?' to designate non-conscious, intuitive knowledge.[12] Further support is offered by the findings of Buck and others that emotional responses to artificial stimuli are dependent on cognitive criteria – in other words, that the definition of the emotion carried by a musical work rests on criteria that are culturally determined.[13] Thus the body's relation to a musical stimulus is bound up with music's textual status even at the level of cognition.[14]

Empirical studies have coexisted uneasily with music analysis; for present purposes, the discussion will centre on the theory of Lerdahl and Jackendoff, which has provoked a great deal of discussion within and outside the discipline of music analysis.[15] Their now famous claim to 'describe the intuitions of the musically experienced listener' is sustained by appeal to four musical structures, which they term metre, grouping, time-span and prolongation. In many ways, this theory is already textual; the presence of preference rules means that a variety of interpretations of a given musical surface is deemed cognitively admissible, and many interesting moments are explained as conflicts between alternative readings. Musical cognition is presented as an interaction between distinct but interrelated structures – which is also a claim made by semiotics.

There are several obvious differences between the sort of analysis of Mahler's Fourth Symphony that was sketched above, and the information represented by Lerdahl and Jackendoff's reductive trees. These differences have been represented in common criticisms of *A Generative Theory of Tonal Music*: for instance, that rhetorically important events are often subsumed into unimportant positions in reductions; or that the theory of tensing and relaxing that governs prolongational reduction is too general to capture musical expression. But what is of real interest for present purposes is the way in which the theory claims to arrive at cognitive description.

---

12 Roland Barthes, *Camera Lucida: Reflections on Photography*, trans. R. Howard (New York: Hill & Wang, 1981), p. 504.
13 Ross Buck, *The Communication of Emotion* [Guilford Social Psychology Series] (New York: Guilford, 1984).
14 Robert Hatten, 'Semiotic Perspectives on Issues in Music Cognition', *In Theory Only*, 11/iii (1989), pp. 1–11.
15 Fred Lerdahl & Ray Jackendoff, *A Generative Theory of Tonal Music* (Cambridge, Mass.: MIT Press, 1983).

The flow of musical information is represented in Lerdahl and Jackendoff's first three structures as resolutely 'bottom-up': the listener relates local phenomena to each other, and then subsumes these relations hierarchically until the whole piece is heard as a single, closed group. This is seen most clearly in their discussion of the Bach chorale, *O Haupt Voll Blut und Wunden*, in which each level is built up step by step (pp. 129–32). This of course represents a *narrative* of musical cognition: the unfolding of the piece is made intelligible through time, so that the final tree explains why it sounds finished at the point at which it ends. Lerdahl and Jackendoff acknowledge the influence of Leonard B. Meyer's implication-realisation model whilst greatly improving on it in both rigour and subtlety. However, there are moments when this process seems only able to proceed by means of information flowing in the opposite direction, 'top-down'. One such is their discussion of the opening of Beethoven's 'Tempest' Sonata (pp. 254–6). This analysis chooses the opening V^6 sonority as the 'head', instead of the tonic chord in the third bar, or, more surprisingly, the arrival of the tonic at the end of the introduction in bar 21. The reason for the first is straightforward, but the reason for the second is given as 'parallelism, since any equivalent to measure 21 is omitted in the recapitulation (in large part because its motivic material is exhausted in the development section)'. The listener, then, apparently re-evaluates the opening of the sonata when the introduction fails to lead to the first subject in the recapitulation. In other words the cognition of the opening is dependent on future, 'already heard' events (and it is on this quality of being 'already heard' that I wish to focus). But what is more interesting than this large-scale determination of local feature is the parenthesis, '(in large part because its motivic material is exhausted in the development section)'. Does this observation – which appeals to a process (motivic development) explicitly made secondary within the preference rules – refer to the cognition of the piece, or account for its organisation beyond its cognitive impact? Lerdahl and Jackendoff are at pains not to deny the importance of motivic development, but to consign it to a subordinate cognitive position: the comment that it is 'exhausted' in Beethoven's Sonata has to be a conscious, non-intuitive observation. Yet the parenthesis here is adduced precisely as an intuition about the feature that the parallelism rule invokes. Neither explanation is really possible, for each relies on the other: the parenthesis exposes the margin of cognition, identifying it as text.

This is not for a moment to imply that my observation identifies a weakness in the theory, or levels criticism at the concepts of structure which compose it. On the contrary: my purpose in drawing attention to this reliance of 'bottom-up' processing on 'top-down' information is to show that Lerdahl and Jackendoff cannot account for music as a single listening experience. The music has to be 'already heard' for cognition to operate, just as the past tense of a novel refers to the 'already read'. Lerdahl and Jackendoff are quite clear that their analyses are 'final state' descriptions, the outcome of temporally present intuitions. But these intuitions are at the same time the outcome of the non-temporal hierarchies. This is not a criticism of the theory, but an observation of its textual limits. As Lerdahl has more recently observed, the theory both 'assigns' and 'generates' structure.[16] This theory of cognition seems to uncover the fact that we can never hear music for the first time: our perception of it is always reliant on having heard it before, having constructed it from information outside itself; and this must be true even of first performances.

The literal investigation of the body's perception of music throws us back on textual concerns. The final stage of this study, then, is to ask how the body makes its presence felt within the musical text.

Barthes and the body

The body has come to be indispensable as the location of the text's operations. If the author is dead, and the reader an intertextual construct, at least the body remains as an outpost of the phenomenal in the realm of discourse. And it is in just this way that the doyen of French structuralists, Roland Barthes, unites the body with his meditations on music.

Barthes invokes the body as a means of identifying knowledge which is not conscious: 'What does my body know of photography?' he asks in *Camera Lucida*.[17] Thus far, the body seems the natural site of musical meaning: after all, listeners will attest their reactions to a piece of music more readily than any other art form, and claims have frequently been made for the meaning of music to reside in immediate emotional impact. However, Barthes takes his observations a little further, especially in his comments on his favourite composer, Schumann.

A detailed study of Barthes' love for Schumann is beyond the scope of this paper, and has in any case been attempted elsewhere.[18] But his most

16 Lerdahl, 'Analyse de "La terrasse des audiences du clair de lune" de Debussy', *Analyse Musicale*, 16 (1989), pp. 54–60.
17 Barthes, *Camera Lucida*, p. 504.
18 Andrew Brown, 'Music's Body: Some Notes on Barthes and Schumann', paper delivered at Cambridge University, 1991.

intriguing comments come in 'Rasch', an essay on the *Kreisleriana* printed in *The Responsibility of Forms*. Barthes opens with a paragraph as disconcerting for its violence as for its obscurity:

In Schumann's *Kreisleriana* (Opus 16; 1838), I actually hear no note, no theme, no contour, no grammar, no meaning, nothing which would permit me to reconstruct an intelligible structure of the work. No, what I hear are blows: I hear what beats in the body, what beats the body, or better: I hear this body that beats.[19]

The transitive and intransitive forms of the verb 'to beat' here mark what Barthes hears as the Schumannian body: an irreducible corporeality which protests against its imprisonment in the codes of tonality and rhythm. Barthes hears this body in several ways: the opening of the second piece, for instance, is 'the body stretching', a gesture derived simply from the musical contour. The seventh variation, however, is the beating of rage and panic within the 'docile language' of tonality; here Barthes is making a more analytical comment about the *sforzando* dynamics of the melody and the insistent rhythm coupled with repeated harmonic progressions.

Barthes is aware that such extravagant metaphors leave him open to the charge of solipsism, and indeed this is part of the point: musical meaning of this sort, he contends, is a 'third meaning' beyond straightforward reference and symbolic interpretation. It is this 'third meaning', which he names 'signifying', that Barthes claims to be the entire province of musical meaning:

[In] music, a field of *signifying* and not a system of signs, the referent is unforgettable, for here the referent is the body. The body passes into music without any relay but the signifier. This passage – this transgression – makes music a madness: not only Schumann's music, but all music. In relation to the writer, the composer is always mad (and the writer can never be so, for he is condemned to meaning).[20]

So music contains the gestures of meaning, but these can only ever refer to the body that produces them. This is remarkably close to Adorno's comment on Mahler's music, 'it is not that the music narrates, but the composer wishes to make music the way that other people narrate'.[21] For Barthes, the body is crucially *inside* the music, 'beating' like a heart,

19 Barthes, *The Responsibility of Forms*, trans. R. Howard (Oxford: Blackwell, 1986), p. 299.
20 Ibid., p. 308.
21 Adorno, *Mahler*, p. 86.

Example 8.2   Schumann, *Kreisleriana*, Op. 16, No. 2, bars 17–20

letting the music beat within it like desire, 'beating' against its imprison-ment.

For our purposes, Barthes' comments are suggestive; but his musical observations are only at the most informal level. If this metaphorical writing seems to capture something of music's specificity, can we take the investigation of the body and musical meaning any further? What is it that Barthes hears in the *Kreisleriana*?

If we take one of the less casual comments, on the second variation, we may be able to approach an answer. As remarked above, Barthes hears the opening as 'stretching', and then he equates the 'contraction' or 'curling up' with the approach to the repeat of this material, commenting, 'Here everything converges: the melodic form, the harmonic suspension'. These bars are remarkable in several ways (Ex. 8.2): the scalic movement is given in contrary motion, creating a wide-spread texture which gives the impression of voices in between the two hands (because of the cre-scendo). Chromatic elaboration of the dominant seventh on C then dis-guises the swift transition through a ⁴₂ chord resolving by step. As with the Mahler, the relatively straightforward voice-leading and the com-pletely transparent form hint at an unease: the elaboration of the opening figure is a moment of excess in this piece; the chromaticism runs ahead of the harmony, until the ritardando and semiquavers are needed because the music 'runs out of time'. This feature requires a code of intertextual reference which Barthes locates in the body. Perhaps the distinction that he makes in *Le plaisir du texte* is appropriate here, between the ordinary 'pleasure' of fulfilled expectations (such as would be the moments of tensing and relaxing in Lerdahl and Jackendoff's prolongational reduc-tions, including the relaxation of the harmonic resolution *via* the ⁴₂ chord here), and the much more erotic, unpredictable '*jouissance*' represented by unpredictable moments of excess.[22]

---

22 Barthes, *The Pleasure of the Text*, trans R. Miller (London: Jonathan Cape, 1976), p. 19.

These brief examples should indicate, however partially, that analysis of music that attempts to take account of its textuality finds a musical body that, like Barthes' Schumannian one, will not stay still: it is pulsional, constantly opening up fields of reference that it is powerless to close; it indicates that 'here is the trace of another text', whilst leaving the listener to supply that text herself. If our analytical voyages through this text have barely started, the indications are that they will be fruitful.

9

The obbligato recitative: narrative and Schoenberg's Five Orchestral Pieces, Op. 16

ALAN STREET

Schoenberg's Five Orchestral Pieces, Op. 16, were composed in a little over two months, between late June and early August of 1909. As such they represent a cardinal product from that phase of revolutionary creativity which saw the completion of the *Hanging Gardens* song cycle, the Piano Pieces, Op. 11 and the monodrama, *Erwartung*, all within the same calendar year. The pieces were originally left untitled; indeed it was not until 1912, in response to an enquiry from the publishers, C. F. Peters, that the composer appended the title headings by which they have subsequently become familiar. Though he eventually felt able to comply with Peters's request, Schoenberg remained far from enthusiastic about the proposal. A diary entry for 28 January[1] gives a clear insight into the reasons for his reluctance: in short, a belief that titles were redundant, since 'whatever was to be said has been said by the music'. Schoenberg was prepared to go further on this point, however, adding that the beauty of music 'is that one can say everything in it, so that he who knows understands everything; and yet one hasn't given away one's secrets – the things one doesn't admit even to oneself'. Titles, by contrast, might be all too explicit. Hence, to counter the risk of unwanted exposure, Schoenberg settled on epigraphs which juxtaposed the enigmatic with the technical. Evasive in their personal derivation, these were described as follows:

I.   Premonitions (everybody has those)
II. The Past (everybody has that too)
III. Chord-Colours (technical)
IV. Peripeteia (general enough, I think)
V.   The Obbligato (perhaps better the 'fully developed' or the 'endless') Recitative

Writing on the final piece from this sequence, Carl Dahlhaus draws attention to the way in which its seemingly self-contradictory title nonetheless defines the essential tension inherent in its musical substance. In this respect the combination of fixed obbligato and free recitative ele-

---

1 Quoted in Walter B. Bailey, *Programmatic Elements in the Works of Schoenberg* (Ann Arbor: UMI Research Press, 1984), p. 131.

ments represents a logical consequence of the composer's stated aesthetic intention: to express 'the inexpressible in free form'.[2] Moreover, as Dahlhaus goes on to explain: 'that he took the musically binding statement as an expression of the "inexpressible" is to be understood in the light of Schopenhauer's metaphysics of music to which Schoenberg subscribed'.[3] The key exposition of Schoenberg's attachment to Schopenhauerian principles is to be found in his essay 'The Relationship to the Text', also of 1912. There, Schoenberg lamented the contrast between the composer who 'reveals the innermost essence of the world and utters the most profound wisdom in a language which his reason does not understand',[4] and the naive listener who seeks to reduce this truth to a banal succession of images. Furthermore, verbal explanation, however sublimated, could only give rise to distorted comprehension. For as Schoenberg interpreted Schopenhauer's credo, the purpose of music was to become a language in its own right: to develop an eloquence and attain a plenitude of meaning which might thereby render poetic analysis obsolete.

Of course, by 1912 a composer's espousal of Schopenhauerian doctrine was hardly anything new; a similarly dedicated lineage could be traced back through Mahler to Wagner at least as far as 1854. To this end, the trenchancy of Schoenberg's adherence perhaps argues most forcefully for a perspective of aesthetic continuity linking music either side of the break with tonality. But in spite of the change in substantive conditions, it is also as well not to underestimate the oblique theoretical support which the composer drew for his technical revolution from Schopenhauer's message. Undoubtedly, Schoenberg was attracted in large part by the tenor of a metaphysical system which gave primacy not merely to aesthetic contemplation, but to the Utopian power of music as its highest fulfilment. As Peter Franklin summarises the issue, there was every reason to empathise with a vision in which music was 'potentially the most intimate and direct representation of an individual consciousness on the level of its most essential reality and in the very element of that consciousness, namely Time'.[5] However, the emancipation of the dissonance, as its name implies, also opened up a new and palpable freedom in the

2 Quoted in Carl Dahlhaus, *Schoenberg and the New Music*, trans. D. Puffett and A. Clayton (Cambridge: Cambridge University Press, 1987), p. 144.
3 Ibid., p. 144.
4 Arnold Schoenberg, 'The Relationship to the Text', in *Style and Idea: Selected Writings of Arnold Schoenberg*, ed. L. Stein, trans. L. Black (London: Faber, 1975), p. 142.
5 Peter Franklin, *The Idea of Music: Schoenberg and Others* (London: Macmillan, 1985), p. 15.

realm of structure: a universe of untied and untried possibility through which to map and perhaps ultimately transcend the dynamic of the Will. Tonal logic might well be exhausted. Yet this need no longer matter if the new phonic resource could be made to articulate to its anticipated capacity. Expressing 'the innermost essence of the world' therefore became a question of fashioning, even unconsciously, the appropriate fusion of grammar with rhetoric. And this, as Dahlhaus observes, is 'the essence of the obbligato – musically binding – recitative as realised in Schoenberg's Op. 16, No. 5: . . . a question of eloquent music, music that "speaks", without the *Hauptstimme* of the piece bearing the least resemblance to recitative in the usual sense of the word'.[6]

To all intents and purposes, Dahlhaus might be taken to have closed the matter. In other words, the 'Obbligato Recitative' stands revealed as an example of the purest musical formalism. Nonetheless, as he relates in his book, the *Idea of Absolute Music*, even the most committed of Schopenhauer's disciples might be forced into an awkward compromise if they chose also to defend the aesthetic of programme music. Schopenhauer himself had set the judgemental terms on this issue, treating both programme and song text alike as standing 'in the same relation to [music] . . . as an arbitrary example does to a general concept'.[7] Wagner, by contrast, chose to vacillate over the point, even going so far as to read Beethoven's C♯ Minor Quartet, Op. 131, as a hermeneutic parable, depicting the 'inner biography' of an 'ideal subject'.[8] Genius might be allowed this degree of latitude within Schopenhauer's metaphysical scheme; even so, abnegation remained fundamental and could not be permitted to degenerate into straightforward psychology. Thus Mahler likewise was careful to avoid any impression of psychobiographical reduction, distinguishing between the function of an external programme (acting both poietically and aesthesically as compositional catalyst and narrative signposting), and an internal programme (depicting the unbounded sensation of an authentically aesthetic subject).

Whatever the tone of his theoretical pronouncements, Schoenberg too was not averse to programmatic composition in practice. As Walter Bailey notes, though his exposure to programme music came relatively late (around 1898), Schoenberg remained faithful to programmatic inspiration throughout the rest of his composing life. Within this span, Bailey

6 Dahlhaus, *Schoenberg and the New Music*, p. 144.
7 Quoted in Dahlhaus, *The Idea of Absolute Music*, trans. R. Lustig (Chicago: University of Chicago Press, 1989), p. 131.
8 Quoted in ibid., p. 133.

detects three main categories of approach: the first two are primarily historical, dividing around the approximate date of 1914 when Schoenberg turned from an essentially poetic inspiration, determining both form and content, to thematic subjects supported by verbal texts; the third, however, is qualitative, and comprises those pieces with secret programmes, a class which includes, among other works, the first three String Quartets and the Piano Concerto. In all of these compositions, Bailey asserts, the programme occupies an ancillary position. In summary, it functions as an initial symbolic release of creative spirit, eventually becoming subsumed – to a greater or lesser degree – under the dictates of an abstract structure.[9]

Overall, Schoenberg's attitude towards programme music appears close to that of Mahler. Yet his insistence on the marginalisation of external influence is certainly more vehement, a fact explained, at least in part, by the heightened anxiety endemic to early Expressionism. However coherent the movement may have been in the earlier part of this century, Schoenberg's sympathies were firm to the extent that the essay 'The Relationship to the Text', together with a manuscript facsimile of his Op. 20, *Herzgewächse*, was included in the almanac, *Der Blaue Reiter*, of 1912. The emphasis on distortion, fragmentation and the direct communication of intense emotion perhaps finds its sharpest definition for the composer in Adorno's statement that

the essential, disrupting moment is . . . the function of musical expression. Passions are no longer simulated; rather does [Schoenberg's] . . . music record, untransposed, the impulses of the unconscious, its shocks and traumas. The seismographic registration of traumatic shocks becomes, at the same time, the law of the form of the music.[10]

Such a turn towards emotive immediacy must have jibed rather awkwardly with the contemporary dependence on text setting which Schoenberg describes in his essay on the Op. 22 Songs and the first version of 'Composition with Twelve Tones'. Yet it is to be remembered that these writings date from 1932 and 1941 respectively; in 1912, as Alan Lessem observes, the composer admitted only to seeking the inner meaning of his poetic sources.[11] Indeed 'The Relationship to the Text' declares how

9 See Bailey, *Programmatic Elements in the Works of Schoenberg*, p. 5, and especially pp. 159–63.

10 Quoted in Alan Lessem, 'Schoenberg and the Crisis of Expressionism', *Music and Letters*, 55 (1974), p. 434.

11 Lessem, *Music and Text in the Works of Arnold Schoenberg* (Ann Arbor: UMI Research Press, 1979), p. 3.

Schoenberg, inspired by the first words of a text, had written many of his songs 'straight through to the end without troubling . . . in the slightest about the continuation of the poetic events, without even grasping them in the ecstasy of composing'.[12] Even Schopenhauer himself could be said to have held a higher regard for verbal art, identifying tragic drama as the highest representational form through the depiction of Will in conflict with itself. By comparison, Schoenberg, in the years between 1908 and the beginning of the First World War, felt compelled to minimise all forms of linguistic mediation within his music. And in this respect, as Dahlhaus comments, the Fifth Orchestral Piece manifests its nature as musical prose in a doubly emphatic sense: firstly in that 'it demonstrates that music can be fashioned in a binding manner without the support of a text, even when it assumes the consequences of atonality', and secondly as 'a commentary on *Erwartung*, [whereby] . . . it shows that the atonal, asymmetrical and athematic structure of the opera does not force one to see the text as the primary aesthetic factor'.[13]

The rhetoric of Romanticism

Once again the issue appears conclusively resolved in favour of a formalist conception. On this count, any attempt at a narrative analysis of the Orchestral Pieces might seem not to enhance but merely to diminish the magnitude of Schoenberg's achievement. Nor, for that matter, does the substantive evidence really offer much encouragement to a discursive reading. For after all, each of the pieces is genuinely instrumental in kind; moreover their relative brevity militates strongly against an impression of fictive continuity. Rather, with due acknowedgement of the *a posteriori* judgement involved, the pieces of the set appear to relate to their titles according to Hanslick's paradigm of either distilling a basic mood or presenting an illusion, 'if not a graphic representation'.[14] In fact, were a specimen to be required for narratological analysis, it might be better sought, at least with reference to current thought on nineteenth-century musico-poetics, in the more intimate medium of the Op. 11 Piano Pieces.[15] Yet whatever the apparent prospects, the matter must come down, in Dahlhaus's view, to a fundamental question of aesthetics.

12 Schoenberg, 'The Relationship to the Text', p. 144.
13 Dahlhaus, *Schoenberg and the New Music*, p. 147.
14 Quoted in Bailey, *Programmatic Elements in the Works of Schoenberg*, p. 8.
15 See Lawrence Kramer, *Music as Cultural Practice, 1800–1900* (Berkeley: University of California Press, 1990), especially chapters 2, 3 and 6.

For instance, the addition in 1925 of a revised title – 'Summer Morning by a Lake (Colours)' – to the third piece (already reheaded 'Farben' in the second edition of 1922) clearly invites some programmatic interpretation. Even so, Dahlhaus argues, while the supplement did not form part of Schoenberg's original conception, its function must be understood as illustrative rather than intrinsic.[16] Against Dahlhaus's sober conclusion, however, must be placed the comment of Richard Hoffman, a Schoenberg pupil, that the composer assented to a poetic elaboration on the grounds that by then he felt old enough to withstand being dubbed a romantic.[17] Dahlhaus too notes this admission, but interprets it more as a psychological reaction to the anti-romantic polemics of the New Objectivity during the 1920s.[18] Dahlhaus's reasoning here is characteristically scrupulous; nonetheless it forcibly diminishes the dimension of poietics to the problematic level of authorial intent. Hence, not only does his strategy deprive analysis of a qualifying ground by all but disregarding inspirational stimulus as an element of the creative process, but it also places excessive emphasis on a category which, if only because of the unreliable effects of irony, can never be taken simply at face value.

Reading for the plot: three allegories

Granted these difficulties, and in light of Schoenberg's occasional reorientation on aesthetic questions, it is perhaps worth reopening the poietic perspective by asking whether the Op. 16 Pieces might be persuaded, if only through their titles, to yield up something more. It is important to register, however, that the interpretive aim is not simply one of wilful manipulation in the interests of forming a narrative link; for in fact Mahler's Schopenhauerian example indicates that a vestigial discursive sequence might indeed be compatible with an underlying stream of musical sensation. In this regard, then, the Fifth Orchestral Piece also represents the most suggestive element of the set – imparting, through the recitative, a resonance which is not only inherently narrative in type, but also, by association, dramatic in function. By comparison, the first and third pieces, 'Premonitions' and (formerly) 'Colours', describe experiential, even affective states. Yet 'Premonitions' also implies a future time to which the second piece, 'The Past', adds an unambiguously ret-

---

16 Dahlhaus, *Schoenberg and the New Music*, p. 100.
17 Cited in Bailey, *Programmatic Elements in the Works of Schoenberg*, p. 132.
18 Dahlhaus, *Schoenberg and the New Music*, pp. 100–1.

rospective dimension. As what Aristotle, in the *Poetics*, terms 'a change from one state of affairs to its opposite',[19] 'Peripeteia' fulfils the expectancy of 'Premonitions'. More importantly, though, its specific purpose as a reversal in the context of Greek drama joins the temporality of the first two pieces to the potentially dramatic recitative of the last, a relationship made more binding by Aristotle's insistence on a basis in probability or necessity. Conversely, the third piece, understood as 'Colours', seems to insert an element of contingency into this scheme. But reinterpreted as 'Summer Morning by a Lake', the relationship of time to place, or rather space, becomes far more vivid: in effect a symbolic element of *mise en scène*.

Albeit a modest beginning – no more perhaps than 'once upon a time' – this fabular construction nonetheless exemplifies Frank Kermode's belief that 'stories as we know them begin as interpretations'.[20] In other words, to quote Peter Brooks, 'any narrative from the very simplest, is hermeneutic in intention, claiming to retrace an event in order to make it available to consciousness'.[21] Narrative, therefore, is a form of understanding; an explanation, whose logic and dynamic is determined by plot. So far, my reading of the Orchestral Pieces contains only a few undefined stages within its discursive shell; a compelling narrative analysis would need to proceed much further with the definition of actors and events. For example, to take only the most obvious questions, if the premonitions of the first piece presuppose an experiencing subject, who might it be? And what are the objects of this individual's anticipation? Similarly, who is/are the victim(s) of the reversal of fortune in 'Peripeteia'? How and why?

1 'New Music: My Music'

One solution to these questions has been supplied by Philip Friedheim, who neutralises psychodramatic connotations in favour of a technical allegory representing the compositional passage towards atonality.[22] Friedheim's programmatic outline is relatively modest. Yet it might be profitably expanded with structural and aesthetic observations as follows.

19 Aristotle, 'On the Art of Poetry', in *Classical Literary Criticism*, trans. T. S. Dorsch (Harmondsworth: Penguin, 1965), p. 46.
20 Frank Kermode, 'Secrets and Narrative Sequence', in W. J. T. Mitchell (ed.), *On Narrative* (Chicago: University of Chicago Press, 1981), p. 81.
21 Peter Brooks, *Reading for the Plot* (Oxford: Oxford University Press, 1984), p. 34.
22 Philip Friedheim, 'Tonality and Structure in the Early Works of Schoenberg' (PhD dissertation, New York University, 1963), pp. 480–5.

Firstly, 'Premonitions', a stylistic transition exemplified by a diatonically conceived yet tonally destructive D–A–C♯ [0, 1, 5] trichordal pedal. Secondly, 'The Past', a traditional form supported by a recurrent pure fifth pedal on D and A, itself the focal point of a distorted tonal construction. Thirdly, 'Summer Morning by a Lake (Colours)', representing reflections of past practice through chordal as well as motivic connection, and an additional descending stratum again based on fifths. Fourthly, 'Peripeteia', linked to 'Premonitions' through a number of shared pitch-class sets. And lastly the 'Obbligato Recitative', an exploration of post-tonal possibility bringing to consummation Schopenhauer's vision of 'a principal voice . . . progressing with unrestrained freedom, in the uninterrupted significant connection of one thought from beginning to end and expressing a whole: the highest grade of the Will's objectification'.[23]

2 'Turn of Time'

Though relatively general, Friedheim's account succeeds in dramatising the allegorical significance of the Op. 16 set. A more figurative though no less culturally valid interpretation, however, may be drawn from Paul Ricoeur's *Time and Narrative*. Referring to the work of Frank Kermode, Ricoeur notes how the intellectual invalidation of the Judeo-Christian Apocalypse myth and the consequent demise of a Biblical master plot has resulted in a sense of an ending forever postponed within the common consciousness. Yet this ruin of the fiction of the imminent end is far from emancipatory; rather it brings about enslavement to an immanent myth of crisis: in short, 'an indefinitely extended peripeteia'.[24] At the same time, Ricoeur argues, it is significant from an aesthetic point of view that the myth of the end, though repeatedly invalidated, has never been fully discredited. Likewise the notion of peripeteia, though continually extended, has so far stopped short of a descent into meaninglessness. On this count the authorial contract, what Tzvetan Todorov, following Hans Robert Jauss, calls the 'horizon of expectation',[25] remains intact. Correspondingly, artists and public are still bound together by the institutional conditions of production and reception.

23 Quoted in Franklin, *The Idea of Music*, p. 12.
24 Paul Ricoeur, *Time and Narrative*, vol. 2, trans. K. McLaughlin and D. Pellauer (Chicago: University of Chicago Press, 1985), p. 23.
25 Tzvetan Todorov, *Genres in Discourse*, trans. C. Porter (Cambridge: Cambridge University Press, 1990), p. 18.

To interpret the relevance of Ricoeur's thesis for Schoenberg's Op. 16, one must again turn to the fifth piece, but this time under its alternative guise as the 'endless Recitative'. The fourth piece, 'Peripeteia', too is eminently suggestive. For while this pair together demonstrate the superabundance of a new musical sense, they also hint at the slide into lawlessness threatened by the crisis of modernism. In this regard, the ländler elements which characterise the 'Obbligato Recitative' mark a continued adherence to the authorial contract – that is, to the socially conditioned confines of genre. Admittedly, the piece breaks almost every rule of a traditional ländler form. Yet as Maurice Blanchot observes, 'one has to think that every time, in exceptional works where a limit is reached, the exception alone is what reveals to us that "law" of which it also constitutes the unexpected and necessary deviation'.[26]

Genres, by extension, always come into being through the transformation of earlier genres. And the multiple meanings generated by the genre of ländler within the 'Obbligato Recitative' echo in many directions. For instance, they reverberate not only along the dramatic symphonies of the nineteenth century (a resonance further amplified by the explicit reference to a final-movement instrumental recitative), but also, in the guise of the dance form, through to the origins of the instrumental suite. On an extra-musical plane, the folk context of the ländler recalls the oral tradition of story telling evoked by Walter Benjamin.[27] And carrying this linguistic association on into the sphere of textual erotics, the ländler also acts as an inscription of the body in discourse, *via* the figure of the dance: what Paul de Man, writing on Yeat's poem 'Among School Children', refers to as the convergence of desire with musical form.[28]

3 'How One Becomes Lonely'

The idea of a language infused with the passion of and for meaning is familiar from the work of both Roland Barthes and Julia Kristeva. With respect to fictive discourse, this entails the belief, in Peter Brooks's

26 Quoted in ibid., p. 14.
27 Walter Benjamin, 'The Storyteller: Reflections on the Work of Nikolai Leskov', in *Illuminations: Essays and Reflections*, ed. H. Arendt, trans. H. Zohn (New York: Schocken, 1969), pp. 83–109. According to Mosco Carner, few ländler melodies were ever written down, except in abbreviated form ('Ländler', in Stanley Sadie (ed.), *The New Grove Dictionary of Music and Musicians* (London: Macmillan, 1980), vol. 10, pp. 435–6).
28 Paul de Man, *Allegories of Reading: Figural Language in Rousseau, Nietzsche, Rilke and Proust* (New Haven: Yale University Press, 1979), p. 11.

words, that 'narratives both tell of desire – typically present some story of desire – and arouse and make us use desire as a dynamic of signification'.[29] Desire in these terms embraces sexual longing; more importantly, however, it signifies a force both larger and more polymorphous: in sum, a power denoted by Freud's concept of Eros. Although the analysis of aesthetic desire takes its inspiration from a spectrum of sources, Freud's formulation nonetheless remains signal, not only for its historical prominence, but also the manner of its discursive realisation. As Malcolm Bowie has suggested, Freud's consulting-room and clinical meta-narratives would seem remarkable for their hermeneutic performance alone. On the one hand they may be presented as the theoretically validated product of scientific resolve. Yet on the other, they may be read as a virtuoso feat of inspired interpretation suspended above the daemonic primary stuff of experience. As a consequence, Bowie argues, Freud's confrontation and mapping of the unconscious holds strong contemporary parallels with Schoenberg's manipulation and regulation of the dissonance. For Bowie, echoing Adorno, Schoenberg's composition too 'throws into relief an antithetical quality of the mental life: the unthinkable continuum of human thought and the unrelenting propulsive force that passion gives it'.[30] And this testament to a 'mute, blind, intractable and unsubduable impetus'[31] fashions an even firmer connective link in light of Freud's later identification of the unconscious with the ceaseless movement of Schopenhauerian Will.

As Terry Eagleton notes, Schopenhauer's reification of the Will effectively turns desire into a metaphysical force.[32] Such a metamorphosis stands far removed from simple psychologism. Nonetheless, the capacity of aesthetics to commune with the Will at least enables genius to pass from a world of empirical corruption into the sphere of transcendent contemplation. Music, of course, instantiates the most direct medium of transformation. Yet as I have also mentioned, Schopenhauer placed considerable value on drama as the representation of conflicting individual wills. Bowie specifically references Zemlinsky's *The Mermaid* and Schoenberg's *Pelleas und Melisande* as examples of triangular love dramas depicting – in the wake of *Tristan* – a three-way circuit of desire leading

29 Brooks, *Reading for the Plot*, p. 37.
30 Malcolm Bowie, 'A Message From Kakania: Freud, Music, Criticism', in P. Collier and J. Davies (eds.), *Modernism and the European Unconscious* (Cambridge: Polity Press, 1990), p. 9.
31 Ibid., p. 12.
32 Terry Eagleton, *The Ideology of the Aesthetic* (Oxford: Blackwell, 1990), p. 159.

to a long-deferred amorous expiration. But as Edward Timms observes, more literal currents 'of attraction and rivalry also played their part in that explosion of creativity in [pre-war] . . . Vienna. In this sense the erotic subculture was not really a separate dimension. Erotic energies interfused the whole network of intellectual and artistic endeavour.'[33]

This quotation is taken from an account of the erotic triangle formed in 1907 between Karl Kraus, Fritz Wittels (Freud's first biographer) and Irma Karczewska. However, in the present context, it also evokes events from the following year when Schoenberg's wife, Mathilde, eloped with the painter Richard Gerstl. Around this event, the extra-musical and textual elements of *Verklärte Nacht*, *Pelleas und Melisande*, the *Hanging Gardens* song cycle, *Erwartung* and *Die glückliche Hand* appear to converge in a dual motion of prophecy and retrospection. The event itself is commonly held to be represented through the 'Ach du lieber Augustin' tune – particularly its refrain of 'everything's lost' – included in the scherzo of the Second String Quartet. Yet it is reasonable to ask, in view of the continuity of Schoenberg's extra-musical inspiration, whether this really tells the whole of the story. Even if the essential plot-line is understood, any supplementary interpretation would need to find evidence for the inscription of character. So familiar are we with the composer's creative evolution, however, that the proliferation of set-classes 6–Z44 and 8–14 has come to add a signatory conviction to most forms of Schoenbergian harmonic analysis. Moreover, the obsessive reproduction of these collections has its visual analogue in the composer's self-portraits of the period: a sequence of confrontations reminiscent of Lacan's 'mirror stage', whereby self-recognition declines into radical self-alienation and a narcissistic desire to recapture the paradise of authentic self-presence.

What I am suggesting, therefore, is that Schoenberg's Five Orchestral Pieces be read as a form of autobiographical narrative. In the first instance, this assumes, as Todorov observes, a bipartite version of the authorial contract which identifies author with narrator and narrator with chief protagonist.[34] In the second instance it entails an identification of technique: in this case a version of Edouard Dujardin's interior monologue, a discourse neither heard nor pronounced, yet in which, as Dujardin states, 'a character expresses his most intimate thought, the one closest to [the] unconscious, previous to any logical organisation, that is, a discourse in the state of coming into being, and in which he uses direct

33 Edward Timms, 'The "Child-Woman": Kraus, Freud, Wittels, and Irma Karczewska', *Austrian Studies*, 1 (1990), p. 105.
34 Todorov, *Genres in Discourse*, p. 25.

phrases reduced to a syntactic minimum'.[35] Dujardin's definition goes well with Dahlhaus's characterisation of 'an atectonic, caesura-less, asymmetrical style' for the ' Obbligato Recitative'.[36] But it addresses only the stylistic aspect of manner, leaving the issue of matter so far untouched. On this count, my third narrative qualification is analytical, yet of a Freudian, rather than, say, Fortean kind. In his essay, 'Mourning and Melancholia' of 1914, Freud reflects on the topic of object loss, describing its manifestations under each condition. Mourning he interprets as a response to palpable loss; a process of ego inhibition and cathectic expenditure gradually ameliorated over the passage of time. Melancholia, similarly, may be a reaction to the loss of a loved object. Yet where the exciting causes are different, Freud notes, 'one can recognise that there is a loss of a more ideal kind. The object has not perhaps actually died, but has been lost as an object of love.'[37] In consequence, the ego may be subject to impoverishment on a grand scale. For 'in mourning it is the world which has become poor and empty, in melancholia, it is the ego itself'.[38] However, the picture is actually more complex than a simple diminishing of ego. Instead, the ego, having sanctioned an attachment of the libido, finds itself forced to reabsorb the libido, an act which causes it to become self-divided. And this, for Freud, exposes the true nature of melancholia as a product of narcissism, in particular its ambivalent and regressive tendencies.

From this background, then, an autobiographical, or perhaps better psychobiographical reading of Schoenberg's Op. 16 begins in the realm of expectation. In this respect, 'Premonitions' perhaps signifies a play of negative anticipation, even an unconscious evasion of the present determined by a libidinal ambivalence. In discussing the causes of melancholia, Freud mentions that object-identification also arises in the context of transference neuroses. Correspondingly, the second piece follows a transferential realisation of past structural effects within the present – what Freud in the Dora case history calls 'new impressions . . . reprints' or 'revised editions' of old texts.[39] Remembrance of this kind is brought into

35 Quoted in K. M. McKilligan, *Edouard Dujardin: 'Les Lauriers sont coupés' and the Interior Monologue* (Hull: University of Hull Publications, 1977), p. 60. My thanks to Dr Alison Sinclair of Clare College, Cambridge for advice on translating this passage.
36 Dahlhaus, *Schoenberg and the New Music*, p. 145.
37 Sigmund Freud, 'Mourning and Melancholia', in *On Metapsychology: the Theory of Psychoanalysis* (Harmondsworth: Penguin, 1984), p. 253.
38 Ibid., p. 254.
39 Quoted in Brooks, 'The Idea of a Psychoanalytic Literary Criticism', *Critical Inquiry*, 13/ii (1987), p. 342.

Example 9.1   Schoenberg, String Quartet No. 2,
Op. 10, second movement, bars 165–80

Example 9.2   Schoenberg, 'Vergangenes', Op. 16/ii, bars 82–92 [210–20]
(1922 version, texture simplified)

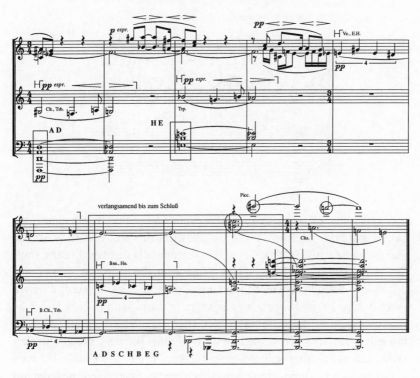

play when recollection in the intellectual sense is blocked by either repression or resistance: a comparison of signature collections from the 'Augustin' passage of the Second Quartet (Ex. 9.1) and the close of the Second Orchestral Piece (Ex. 9.2) retrieves a shadowy emotive relationship between characters from its discursive setting.[40]

That the above association should be inscribed through Schoenberg's customary D-centred harmony seems ironically fortuitous in this joint context. Referring back to the 'Augustin' setting, however, it is also relevant to note how the tune's bluff diatonicism is clouded by chromatic descant and bass lines derived from the section beginning at bar 65 of the scherzo (Ex. 9.3). The correspondence is pitch specific, allowing for enharmonic equivalence. And this latter property in turn exposes a fur-

40 Ciphers have been interpreted in the Op. 10 String Quartet by Michael Graubart
(review of H. H. Stuckenschmidt, *Schönberg: Leben, Umwelt, Werk* (Zurich: Atlantis,
1974), in *Tempo*, 111 (1974), pp. 47–8). [Ed.]

ALAN STREET

Example 9.3   Schoenberg, String Quartet No. 2,
Op. 10, second movement, bars 65–7

ther symbolic nexus through a dyadic projection of the *Tristan* chord (see circled pitches). As Allen Forte has shown in his study of the *Hanging Gardens* cycle, this collection (4–27) is prominently displayed in the vocal line at the end of the first song as a figure for the composer's emotional dilemma.[41] Already inherent in the initial passage from the second movement of Op. 10, its Wagnerian resonance is made plain in bars 167–8 by the renotation of the cello line which then completes (as well as a turn towards E major) a literal spelling of the *Tristan* sonority along with first violin and viola. Although the quasi-canonic/stretto association between viola and second violin strengthens this allusion, Schoenberg never states the chord as a single simultaneity. Hence the disjunct re-emergence of the collection over the final three bars of the Second Orchestral Piece discloses a comparably fatalistic uncertainty: a connection made explicit with Op. 15 via the high G♯/A♭–F dyad[42] and prepared more obliquely with reference to the 'Augustin' passage by virtue of the distorted quadruplet echoes of its head motif (Ex. 9.4).

The third piece, 'Summer Morning by a Lake (Colours)', has so far been understood as an element of spatial stage-setting. As described by Egon Wellesz, its effect is entirely benign: a portrait of dawn on the Traunsee.[43] Conversely, it is also possible to imagine this point of repose as part of a more portentous scenario: in effect, a moment of impending

41 Allen Forte, 'Concepts of Linearity in Schoenberg's Atonal Music: A Study of the Opus 15 Song Cycle', *Journal of Music Theory*, 36/ii (1992), pp. 374–6.
42 See ibid., p. 374.
43 Egon Wellesz, *Arnold Schoenberg*, trans. W. H. Kerridge (London: Galliard, 1971), p. 123.

Example 9.4   (a) Schoenberg, Op. 10/ii, bars 165–6;
(b) Schoenberg, Op. 16/ii, bars 86–7 [214–15]

(a)

(b)

revelation finally confirmed during a family holiday in Gmunden in 1908.[44] The supposition is made more plausible still by Aristotle's linking of peripeteia to anagnorisis or recognition as the essential turn from ignorance to knowledge within the plot of tragic drama. Yet the key words of Schoenberg's title revision perhaps convey more than this: not only a reference to the time of Mathilde's elopement, but also an allusion to the figuration of desire through liquid tropes. For as Lawrence Kramer has recently pointed out with reference to *Tristan*, the mobility of desire, in particular as a province of femininity, was habitually associated throughout the nineteenth century with such images of fluidity.[45]

Following this scene by the brook, the storm-laden significance of 'Peripeteia' appears all too obvious: it is the reversal of fortune which forms the root cause of Schoenberg's melancholia. Here too, however, events are possibly not all that they seem. Although Schoenberg's marriage collapsed, the break was in fact only temporary: Mathilde was eventually persuaded – by Webern, among others – to return to her husband. As a consequence, Richard Gerstl committed suicide on 4 November 1908. At some level, Schoenberg must have felt this tragedy: at least until his departure from the Schoenberg circle, Gerstl had been a close family friend. Hence in this regard, the Op. 16 Pieces come to register a double trauma: mourning and melancholia. As the apotheosis of this narrative sequence, the 'Obbligato' or endless 'Recitative' transmits meaning across possibly two discursive fields. Most vitally it represents the cathartic refusal of ending as extinction: in Schoenberg's own words, 'if death does mark the end of tragedy, it is still not the end of everything'.[46] On this count, Freud's description of a melancholic struggle between preservation of the life force and suicide again finds an analogue in the character

---

44 See Jane Kallir, *Arnold Schoenberg's Vienna* (New York: Galerie St. Etienne and Rizzoli, 1984), pp. 28, 90 (n. 26).
45 Kramer, *Music as Cultural Practice*, p. 141.
46 Schoenberg, *Theory of Harmony*, trans. R. E. Carter (London: Faber, 1978), p. 126.

Example 9.5   Schoenberg, 'Das obligate Rezitativ',
Op. 16/v, bars 5–9 [336–40] (1922 version)

association depicted over the opening bars of Schoenberg's piece (see Ex. 9.5). In one respect this gesture seals the case for narrative, because, as Walter Benjamin observes, the ground of death is in fact the ultimate 'sanction of everything that the storyteller can tell'.[47] But perhaps the endlessness of the Fifth Orchestral Piece, a seeming rebirth of music from the spirit of tragedy, also reserves a final testament to the positive power of narration: in sum, its unending capacity to reinscribe the necessary fictions through which the human subject itself is constituted and thereby enabled to map its symbolic place in existence.

Blindness and insight

All this and yet. So far, narrativising drives have been given free rein within the present paper. Sceptical of their seductive power, however, I want to close this study with a capsule critique of the objections which might be employed to deconstruct the mystified desire for meaning. Firstly, as Jonathan Culler writes, narrative theory in virtually all its forms establishes an essential distinction within fictive construction between story (a series of actions or events) and discourse (their narrative presentation).[48] Story is anterior to the extent that it functions as a non-textual given – an ideal sequence whose identity the reader must attempt to retrieve from the partial (that is, selective) representation of discourse. Discourse, by these terms, is coercive. In other words, it develops semantic connections which the reader may find almost impossible to resist. The Oedipus myth, for example, establishes a classic thematic compul-

47 Benjamin, 'The Storyteller', p. 94.
48 Jonathan Culler, *The Pursuit of Signs: Semiotics, Literature, Deconstruction* (London: Routledge, 1981), p. 169.

sion which can only be satisfied by Oedipus's death. Yet, as Culler observes, in terms of an event sequence Oedipus's innocence is never conclusively eliminated: in Sophocles' play, Laius' murder is publicly reported by a witness as having been committed by a number of robbers, rather than the single man with whom Oedipus is identified.[49] The propulsive effect of a signifying structure may not seem to matter in the context of literature. But as Freud well knew, the thought of effects either excising or supplementing causes might have deep ethical implications for the reliability of consulting room narratives. In the last analysis, the logic of story and discourse may coincide to the degree that priority is undecidable. But certainly either the flaw of a loose thread, or the sheen of an excessive neatness, gives reason for close scrutiny.

Taking my third reading of the Orchestral Pieces as a model, then, its thematic conditioning of actors and events gives a singular version of historical circumstances. Writing on the configurative menage between Kraus, Wittels and Karczewska, Edward Timms notes that the association was determined not, as might be thought at first blush, by Kraus's possessiveness, but rather by his wish actually to abandon Irma to Wittels.[50] Similarly, one cannot uncritically picture Schoenberg as a cuckold: to take only Stuckenschmidt's testament on the matter, the composer's marriage was already under strain – independently of Gerstl's influence – as early as 1907 or even 1906.[51] Historical resistance to the prevailing semantic drift can also be adduced from Schoenberg's compositional canon, because, if other works of the period to 1920 adopt erotic betrayal as a figure for the degraded spirituality held to be characteristic of the time, then it must be questioned whether personal experience can be taken as paramount in any legitimate way. Indeed, it may be wondered whether my reading does anything more than over-indulge what Italo Calvino called 'a British genius for biography'.[52] If not, then motives must be re-examined. For there can be little value in an interpretation which blindly treats any work as a superficial surface trace for a more 'significant' authorial neurosis.

Yet there are larger issues at work here too. As Peter Brooks admits, much psychoanalytic criticism stands discredited not only for its shallow-

49 Ibid., pp. 173–5.
50 Timms, 'The "Child-Woman"', p. 90.
51 H. H. Stuckenschmidt, *Schoenberg: His Life, World and Work*, trans. H. Searle (London: Calder, 1977), p. 94.
52 Quoted in R. Winder, 'For Literature, Read Real Life', *The Independent*, 30 March 1991, p. 25.

ness, but also for its naivety towards the consequences of literary – and particularly deconstructive – theory.[53] For example: on the one hand, the collapse of intention cuts off any direct route to the notion of an authorial subject, while on the other, the failure of reference to redeem rhetorical reflexivity questions whether language can ever be relied upon to articulate phenomenal experience. To this end, Brooks proposes that psychoanalysis be redeployed to chart the interplay of form and desire which passes reciprocally between text and reader. In essence his suggestion amounts to a formalist erotics: above all, a study of the temporal delay and advance figured by the text and encouraged by the reader. The sense of an ending determined by temporality thus once again evokes the condition of music, and in particular the 'Obbligato' or endless 'Recitative'. However, what was earlier understood as a tragic psychodrama might now be rethought as a self-reflexive instantiation of Brooks's polymorphous perversities of form – what he calls the process of 'clock-teasing' through which meaning is created.[54]

Brooks's thesis suggests one direction in which a psychoanalytics of music might progress. Nonetheless, while it acknowledges the unreliability of language it also casts doubt on the intrinsic nature of narrative. So far, of course, this essay has evaded one obvious yet fundamental issue: how far can one speak of narrativity in music? Here the work of Jean-Jacques Nattiez and Carolyn Abbate gives cause for thought. In truth, my readings of the Five Orchestral Pieces are a multiple yet deliberate illustration of the wrong turns by which, as Nattiez argues, the case for musical narrative declines from metaphor into ontological illusion.[55] The absence of a subject/predicate association in music; the necessity for verbal supplements to engender narrative disposition at the aesthesic level; the turn towards poietic reconstruction based on what Nattiez terms the 'reservoir of philosophical, ideological and cultural traits characteristic of a particular epoch':[56] all of these conditions have been exploited in the interests of prolonging a discursive continuity. By contrast, such formulations are not, as Nattiez remarks, 'strictly speaking . . . in the music, but in the plot imagined and constructed . . . from functional objects'.[57] And if these reflective artefacts retain some analyti-

---

53 Brooks, 'The Idea of a Psychoanalytic Literary Criticism', pp. 334–5.
54 Ibid., p. 340.
55 Jean-Jacques Nattiez, 'Can One Speak of Narrativity in Music?', trans. K. Ellis, *Journal of the Royal Musical Association*, 115/ii (1990), p. 245.
56 Ibid., p. 250.
57 Ibid., p. 249.

cal insight, it is in the guise of a formal template conjoined with an abstract schema of behaviour, or way of being, characteristic of an early Viennese *Zeitgeist*.

Abbate too follows out this logic of music as a discursive style rather than narrative substance. Consequently, any attempt to read music as a speaking sequence amounts to nothing more than an act of ventriloquism: a manipulation of the figure of prosopopoeia for the sake of jumping the abysmal gap between word and work. For Abbate, there is every reason to resist the trope of music as language – indeed, to reverse the current polarity in order to reconsider the tropological structure of writing about music.[58] Under these terms, then, musical criticism returns to the question of its allegorical condition; to the inevitable divide which separates all modes of commentary from composition. In the event, this move is perhaps no more remarkable at base than an encounter with the limits of representation – that force, in W. J. T. Mitchell's words 'by which we make our will known and, simultaneously, that which alienates our will from ourselves'.[59] No representation can escape this predicament, because, as Mitchell observes, 'every representation exacts some cost, in the form of lost immediacy, presence or truth, in the form of a gap between intention and realisation, original and copy'. Sometimes this difference is slight; at others, in a last echo of Schoenberg's Op. 16, it may seem as ample as the gap between life and death. But representation does provide something in the way of compensation for the charge it levies, for the divorce it opens. One of the things it gives us is music.

---

58 Carolyn Abbate, *Unsung Voices: Opera and Musical Narrative in the Nineteenth Century* (Princeton: Princeton University Press, 1991), p. 18.
59 W. J. T. Mitchell, 'Representation', in F. Lentricchia and T. McLaughlin (eds.), *Critical Terms for Literary Study* (Chicago: University of Chicago Press, 1990), p. 21.

10

Music theory and the challenge of modern music: Birtwistle's 'Refrains and Choruses'

JONATHAN CROSS

The work of Harrison Birtwistle is just one contemporary example among many of a music which is apparently consistent and coherent yet whose method or system is virtually impossible to unravel.

> I've only once been able to explain my method and that was when my son Silas asked me what I did with all those numbers and I felt it my duty to tell him. It was some time ago and I've forgotten what I said but I couldn't do it again. I've certainly created a vocabulary for doing things but some items get thrown out, some forgotten. . . . In any case it never seems to help me when composers talk about what they do. All that matters is that the composer has a responsibility to his material. But that's obvious.[1]

Neither is this the case only with the newest of music. Jonathan Bernard's theoretical study of the music of Varèse, for instance, begins by pointing out that in such circumstances the theorist really is groping in the dark:

> The actual devising of a theory, and from it an analytical method, must remain an exercise based largely on conjecture. The available hard evidence of Varèse's compositional procedures is very skimpy, principally because Varèse did not think that it was anyone else's business how he composed.[2]

Bernard's monograph makes no claim to completeness. There is still no exhaustive study of the music of Varèse, despite his being cited by figures as diverse as Birtwistle, Boulez and Feldman as an important influence on their thinking. The work of many other major figures in the history of twentieth-century Western music similarly remains incompletely treated by music theorists and analysts. Furthermore, the lack of consensus about how to approach modern music is not restricted to the work of individualistic composers. Writers cannot even agree on how to deal with

---

1 Harrison Birtwistle in conversation, December 1983, quoted in Michael Hall, *Harrison Birtwistle* (London: Robson, 1984), p. 149.
2 Jonathan Bernard, *The Music of Edgard Varèse* (New Haven: Yale University Press, 1987), p. xviii.

the so-called classical atonal repertory of the earlier years of the century, as was illustrated by a celebrated exchange in the pages of *Music Analysis* between Richard Taruskin and Allen Forte over the tonal or non-tonal nature of Stravinsky's *The Rite of Spring*.[3]

The challenge of modern music

Why, then, when theorists and analysts have agreed, to a large extent, on a body of 'truth' about the tonal practice of the seventeenth to nineteenth centuries, have they found it so difficult to agree about the 'meaning' of the music of our own century? The answer to this question might, at first, seem obvious in that it is quite clear what tonal music is, that there *is* a readily identifiable common practice, but that this is not so with twentieth-century music. The only fact theorists, analysts and critics alike have agreed on is that there is usually an absence of traditional tonal harmony and key relationships in the new repertory, though arguments still rage as to what the term for this music should be.[4]

But is the development of an all-embracing theory of atonality, along the lines of a theory of tonality, really possible or even desirable? Allen Forte's work, for instance, acknowledges that there *is* such a thing as an atonal canon and that this can be demonstrated in purely technical (i. e. set-theoretic) terms.[5] Undoubtedly, as I shall discuss below, the composers Forte discusses (Bartók, Berg, Ives, Schoenberg, etc.) are all, in their own ways, *modernists*, but whether this is enough to justify our looking for some procedure, implicit or explicit, which unites and unifies their music is quite another question. It is this quest after unity which seems to be the crux of the matter – and the stumbling block of much analysis of contemporary music. In a much-cited article, Joseph Kerman traced this essentially nineteenth-century view that the purpose of analysis (what he called its 'ruling ideology') is to demonstrate organicism.[6]

---

3 See *Music Analysis*, 5 (1986), pp. 313–37.
4 'Atonal', 'non-tonal', 'post-tonal' – not to mention Schoenberg's 'pantonality' and 'suspended tonality', Arthur Berger's 'antitonality' ('Problems of Pitch Organization in Stravinsky', in Benjamin Boretz and Edward T. Cone (eds.), *Perspectives on Schoenberg and Stravinsky* (New York: Norton, rev. 1972), p. 123) or Wallace Berry's 'irrelevant tonality' (*Structural Functions in Music* (Englewood Cliffs: Prentice Hall, 1976), p. 172).
5 Allen Forte, *The Structure of Atonal Music* (New Haven: Yale University Press, 1973).
6 Joseph Kerman, 'How We Got into Analysis, and How to Get Out', *Critical Inquiry*, 7 (1980), pp. 311–31. A number of writers have more recently addressed the issues surrounding organicism in music – see, in particular, Alan Street, 'Superior Myths, Dogmatic Allegories: The Resistance to Musical Unity', *Music Analysis*, 8 (1989), pp. 77–123, and David Montgomery, 'The Myth of Organicism: From Bad Science to

Whether it is by adapting Schenkerian theory, applying pitch-class set theory, adopting a motivic approach, or by whatever other means, many analysts of modern music have been more concerned with demonstrating the consistency of their own theories and with perpetuating the nineteenth-century belief that the only great music is that which is wholly unified, than with actually asking themselves whether or not their critical approach was fully appropriate to the music.

If it is true that the music of the twentieth century has been very different from the music of the preceding three centuries, we now need to consider the crucial questions of how and why this is so. In what ways does modern music demand a complete rethinking of our critical approach to it? In his collection of essays on 'Patterns and Predictions in Twentieth-Century Culture', Leonard B. Meyer wrote about the pluralism of the modern age (at least, how he viewed it in the 1960s) and argued a case for a move away from a belief in progress in the arts – in what he called a 'causal' or 'teleological' view of history – and towards a position of 'fluctuating stasis' which he defined as:

a steady-state in which an indefinite number of styles and idioms, techniques and movements, will coexist in each of the arts. There will be no central, common practice in the arts, no stylistic 'victory'.[7]

And the same, surely, is true of the individual modern work of art. If a form is built of many apparently contradictory components, this does not necessarily invalidate it as a legitimate aesthetic statement. It can nevertheless be perceived as coherent, and the 'relatedness' or connectedness of the parts is not seen to be achieved by subsuming them under some magical, all-encompassing law of unity imposed from outside of the work, but by viewing the form as a 'steady-state' whose constituent elements are contained by the form and are given meaning by their opposition to one another.

This is where an understanding of the nature of modernism as a common aesthetic becomes essential. There was in all the arts at the turn of the century a move away from the nineteenth-century ideal of the organically-coherent artwork. Fragmentary ideas (musical, visual, literary) could appear as and when they willed to form a non-directional, anti-

Great Art', *Musical Quarterly*, 76/i (1992), pp. 17–66. (See also Robert Snarrenberg, this volume, pp. 29–56 [Ed.])

7 Leonard B. Meyer, *Music, the Arts, and Ideas* (Chicago: University of Chicago Press, 1967), p. 172. I take 'stasis' here to imply something stable yet dynamic, rather than something which has ceased to develop or renew itself. The notion of cultural stasis, if taken literally to mean stagnation, is unsatisfactory.

teleological art. This is what has been termed the 'urge to fragmentation'[8] which characterises so much modern art – the need to let sounds or colours or shapes or words 'be themselves'. We now need to develop a critical language that can take account of such a situation.

Though early works of modernism may appear to have betrayed their nineteenth-century origins with vestiges of continuity, of narrative structures, of representationalism (the language of 'unity' and 'continuity' used by Schoenberg and Webern might be seen to support this – something which the post-World War II European avant-garde found particularly hard to take), such features occurred within a new context and it is *this* which must be the starting-point for any discussion of these works. It is the discontinuity of, for example, Stravinsky's neo-classical music, not its apparent closeness to functioning tonal works, that should be of primary interest.

This is what made modern art so different from the art that preceded it. Modernism has to be viewed in terms of crisis, the break-up of the old order, of the old aesthetic, and of old kinds of meaning.[9] The manifold means by which that crisis was expressed – whether in terms of abstraction, fragmentation, atonality, plurality or the barely perceptible motivations of the unconscious mind – matter less than the fact that that crisis was being self-consciously articulated. Modern art does not pretend to be about anything else other than itself. Therefore it needs to be understood in its own terms and, in order even to begin to be able to discuss it, one has of necessity to adopt the language of modernism, the language of opposition, of difference, of crisis.

It would seem possible, then, to be able to discuss modern music in terms of absolute oppositions, and to expect that such oppositions should not be subsumed into some background unifying scheme. A work of modern art can be intelligible, can be coherent, without necessarily being organically integrated. Some writers, most notably Arnold Whittall, have proposed that it *is* possible to find ways of acknowledging the relatedness of the constituent elements of a modern musical composition without denying the contradictions between those elements.[10] How, therefore,

---

8 See James McFarlane, 'The Mind of Modernism', in Malcolm Bradbury and James McFarlane (eds.), *Modernism 1890–1930* (Harmondsworth: Penguin, 1976), p. 81.

9 'I do think we can already discern a difference of kind in the contemporary revolution: it is not so much a revolution, which implies a turning-over, even a turning-back, but rather a break-up, a devolution, some would say a dissolution. Its character is catastrophic.' Herbert Read, *Art Now* (London: Faber, rev. 1960), p. 44.

10 See Arnold Whittall, 'Webern and Atonality: the Path from the Old Aesthetic', *Musical Times*, 124 (1983), pp. 733–7.

does one go about incorporating these general principles into a method of analytical investigation?

The identification of oppositions in a work is not necessarily problematical in itself: opposition is not unique to twentieth-century art. However, opposition, contradiction, fragmentation, would appear to be the *raison d'être* of much modern art. This might at first suggest a kind of two-dimensional music which has retained the surface oppositions of tonal music but has discarded its all-embracing functional tonality in favour of an artificially imposed scheme or form. These oppositions are, in fact, usually controlled or contained, but in a very different way. The difference between tonal and non-tonal oppositions is something akin to the difference between centripetal and centrifugal forces:[11] the one is synthetic, bringing opposing elements towards a centre, the other is antithetical, holding in some kind of balance or tension forces whose tendency is to move as far as possible away from one another and from the centre (the 'urge to fragmentation'). What is important to consider is the nature of that containment, the '"modernist" *balance* of discontinuities', as Whittall puts it.[12]

The problem for the analyst still remains, however: how are these rules of containment,[13] this balance or tension – or, in Stockhausen's words, this 'present' or 'all-permeating light'[14] – to be defined? Perhaps one can go only as far as saying that, in the light of what we know about the nature of modern art, it is *likely* that the disparate and opposed elements in any given composition, if it is a coherent utterance, are ordered or controlled in some way, but that any investigation of that ordering must proceed empirically. This means that methods of investigation might well be different for every piece – or at least different for every composer or 'style'. To proceed otherwise would be to deny the very plurality which Meyer identified as one of the features of twentieth-century culture. All

---

11 My use of an analogy from the natural sciences here should not be taken as an indication of organicist tendencies. Such 'scientific' language was, of necessity, used by such modernists as the Futurists: 'It is clear that in one and the same picture or work of art there may be more than one centrifugal and centripetal nucleus in simultaneous and dynamic competition' (Gino Severini, 'The Plastic Analogies of Dynamism: Futurist Manifestos', repr. in Umbro Apollonio, *Futurist Manifestos* (London: Thames & Hudson, 1973), p. 124).

12 Whittall, 'Webern and Atonality', p. 735.

13 An idea borrowed from Foucault's *The Order of Things*, via Alan Sheridan's *Michel Foucault: The Will to Truth*, via Whittall – see 'Music Analysis as Human Science?', *Music Analysis*, 1 (1982), p. 34.

14 Karlheinz Stockhausen, 'Concerning My Music' and on *Momente*, in Karl H. Wörner, *Stockhausen: Life and Work* (Berkeley: University of California Press, 1973), pp. 30, 47.

that remains in common from one work or composer or style to the next is just that general aesthetic notion of the containment of opposed elements. This is an entirely different state of affairs from assuming the *a priori* existence of an organic unity which binds together all aspects of a work, however seemingly opposed they may be on the surface, by a common *technical* procedure. It simply says that the oppositions of a modern work of art can be understood to take place within a context which gives those oppositions meaning but never negates their strength *as* oppositions. The following brief analysis of a section from a modernist work is an attempt to see how these general ideas might operate in practice.

Birtwistle's *Refrains and Choruses*

The music of Harrison Birtwistle represents a unique and individual response to the modernist debate. Despite frequent performances in the concert halls and opera houses of Europe, his output has, to date, remained relatively impervious to serious analytical inquiry.[15] It presents a fascinating challenge to music theory. *Refrains and Choruses* for wind quintet was his first published piece and dates from 1957. In many ways it introduces us to various compositional procedures which are to be found time and time again in his music – even his most recent – although in one important respect it is virtually unique among his output in that it is 'through composed': there are not to be found here any large-scale formal repetitions as in the majority of his later works. This could be one of the important reasons why, in a brief published note on the work,[16] Birtwistle chose to emphasise the linear or connecting processes in the music at the expense of whatever else might be discovered to contradict these. A suggestion of this long-term connectedness is given, for example, by the way in which a link is implied between the first and last gestures of the piece. The work begins with a middle C for solo horn and ends by picking out the Bb and D on horn and clarinet which surround the C symmetrically (Ex. 10.1). By stressing the importance of the manner in which one section is connected with its successor, Birtwistle is further pointing to this large-scale linear process, how the beginning is

15 A task which is not aided by Birtwistle's reluctance to discuss his own working methods: 'I wrote it [*Refrains and Choruses*] completely off the top of my head. I can't justify a single note. I didn't know why I was doing it or why it is like it is.' Quoted by Huib Emmer in a liner note for the CD recording of the work (Amsterdam: Etcetera, 1992) [KTC 1130].

16 Quoted in Hall, *Harrison Birtwistle*, p. 173.

Example 10.1

Example 10.2 Birtwistle, *Refrains and Choruses*, bars 131–54

190

Example 10.3

linked with the end. This is not to suggest for a moment that the work is directed in any tonal sense; connectedness on every level of structure is not to be found. But continuity *is* an important component of the work's structural identity. Like the work of many modernist composers before him, Birtwistle's understanding of form here has more to do with process than with any structural 'ready-mades'.

What, then, is the context for this apparent linear development? How is musical material generated in the first instance and how is it contained and shaped? First, it is important to identify the opposition established in each section of the work between two distinct elements which Birtwistle defines as *chorus* (the constant element) and *refrain* (the recurring element). In the final section of the work (Ex. 10.2), the refrain is represented as a recurring chord, a vertical sonority in all five voices, which undergoes a process of registral contraction from its widest possible arrangement (bar 131) to the closest cluster at the end of the work. In between these chords is to be found the chorus material, which is derived from a single twelve-note collection.

One of the major constructive principles in the work would appear to be that of symmetry which controls local pitch configurations, registral placement and longer-term processes. The chorus material in this final section has its origins in a simple symmetrical pattern. Beginning with a major seventh between flute and horn, a two-voice line emerges which presents all twelve notes of the chromatic scale only once and whose lines mirror one another (see Ex. 10.3). However, halfway through this symmetrical unfolding there is a statement of the refrain chord, after which the lines are transferred down an octave to clarinet and bassoon (Ex. 10.4). The symmetry is therefore exact in the abstract but its realisation in the music is distorted as a result of octave transfers. This particular ordering of the twelve notes then becomes the source for all the rest of the chorus material. The two-voice texture in rhythmic unison is maintained, as is the intervallic mirroring (but now only approximately – as contrary motion), until bar 145 when, in keeping with the process of contraction in the refrain, a single voice emerges. Up to this point the pitches are taken in linear fashion, though not always according to a strict ordering:

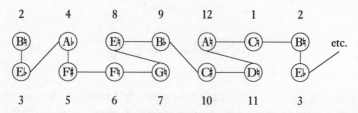

Occasionally, there seem to be 'wrong' notes: these may be printing errors, they may be inadvertencies on the part of the composer, or they may be deliberate compositional disruptions. Whatever their origins, they are allowed to stand.[17]

Example 10.4

The appearance of the single clarinet line initiates a disruption of the pattern: 'rogue' notes enter and are emphasised, principally the Ab in bars 149–50 and the final D of bars 152–4; and the pitch ordering is retrograded (Ex. 10.5). All this signals a 'closing in', a limiting of means, just as the refrain is contracting and the frequency of its statements are increasing to indicate the inevitable move towards the work's conclusion. There is no necessary connection between refrain and chorus here. Though both, in one sense, have 'static' pitch material which is being 'processed' (the chorus in terms of linear rotations, the refrain in terms of register), that material always remains quite clearly distinct: one restricted to five unchanging vertical pitch-classes, the other employing the entire chromatic horizontally. Yet, in one obvious way, the chorus is contained by the refrain – that is, it generally operates within the registral confines set by the extremes of the refrain: as the vertical space occupied by the refrain contracts, so does that of the chorus.

Thus, in the final 23 bars of the piece we are presented with a clear

17 Though Birtwistle claims he does *not* tolerate mistakes, he nevertheless seems to believe that such lacunae are a part of, rather than a distraction from, the end result – a decidedly modernist stance.

Example 10.5   Pitch sequence, bars 148–54

formal process which is articulated in more than one way simultaneously. This might be expressed as a move from a music which is widely spaced to one which is confined and contained; and it is variously achieved by the contraction of the refrain pentachord (which in fact appears to punctuate the overall process with the generally increasing frequency of its appearances), the corresponding contraction of the registral space of the chorus, the refining of the chorus from two-part counterpoint to a single voice, and the operation of the same kind of rotational process in both elements but on mutually exclusive pitch material. The music is thus 'directed' towards its conclusion, yet refrain and chorus remain opposed, held in a meaningful balance by this process. There might appear to be some kind of resolution or synthesis at the end by way of which the last chorus note on the clarinet is taken into the final statement of the refrain chord. But this is not the case: although the D is injected into the chorus line, it can be seen in Ex. 10.5 that it does not necessarily 'belong'. The opposition is controlled or suspended, not removed. The two kinds of music here are part of the same process but cannot ultimately be seen to be subsumed into some (non-existent) background unity.

Conclusion

Modernism has presented musical analysis with a fierce challenge. It is not just that analysis has never attempted to grapple fully with the problems raised by modern music; it is that modern works seem to have confronted the very ability of analysis to say anything pertinent or meaningful about them. Where formalist analysis has essentially been concerned with the explication of the structure of a musical work in terms of synthesis and connectedness, I have argued that, in accordance with developments in twentieth-century art, a new analytical awareness is necessary which acknowledges the validity of opposition as a central and positive constructive principle that challenges but does not necessarily undermine our understanding of what makes a musical utterance coherent.[18]

18 Cf. Craig Ayrey, this volume, p. 129 [Ed.]

My brief example from Birtwistle illustrates ways in which this might be possible.

Some have argued that analysis must change in order to provide a resistance to 'the use of convenient conceptual props';[19] my view is a more cautious one in which I suggest that analysis can be enlarged to encompass the challenges presented by modern music (we must take care not to throw away the analytical baby with the theoretical bathwater). Because the structure of a modern work of art is unlikely to be closed or organically unified (indeed, it is likely to point in more than one direction at once), any reading must be provisional. What is certain is that a broadly-based and flexible analytical outlook is required.

19 Street, 'Superior Myths, Dogmatic Allegories', p. 121.

11

'Répons': phantasmagoria or the articulation of space?

ALASTAIR WILLIAMS

Spatial configurations

Répons is primarily a spatial work, most obviously in its array of sound trajectories, but also in its fascination with surface intricacy. One positive feature of the postmodernist emphasis on place, locale and detail exerts itself in a renewed interest in surface configurations, demonstrated in literature, art and music on the planes of both production and reception. Scrutiny of *Répons* demands a response to the shifting mirages of its surfaces, at least as much as it suggests exploration of the techniques of chord transformation which underlie this profusion of sound.

The spatial dimension of aesthetic thought is fraught with difficulties. Lukács offers a piercing critique of the effect of industrialisation on our perception of time, arguing that when humankind is subordinated to the machine, 'time sheds its qualitative, variable, flowing nature; it freezes into an exactly delimited, quantifiable continuum filled with quantifiable "things" . . . in short, it becomes space'.[1] Following Lukács, one of the central tenets of Adorno's Stravinsky critique is that the latter collapses temporal development into empty space. Where development of material accedes to static sonority, Adorno locates the ravages of instrumental reason and detects an essentialism which posits an unchanging world order. The injustices of a particular political and economic situation are translated into the natural order of invariant material organisation. Certainly, the dangers of an uncritical mode of spatial thought should not be underestimated, but the experience of time-space compression is too strong in an age of global communication and travel for the spatial not to exert a hold on our imaginations. The possibility of related events happening simultaneously across large geographical spaces poses problems

I should like to thank Universal Edition (London) for the loan of a score of *Répons*.

1 Quoted in David Roberts, *Art and Enlightenment: Aesthetic Theory after Adorno* (Lincoln, Nebraska: University of Nebraska Press, 1991), pp. 84–5.

for the concept of coherent, successive events in time – a sense which underpins traditional narrative techniques and the positing of an unfolding temporal logic in music. As David Harvey points out, 'such structures were inconsistent with a reality in which two events in quite different spaces occurring at the same time could so intersect as to change how the world worked'.[2] Harvey's remark is made within the context of a cycle of time-space compression caused by industrial and economic organisation early this century which underlies much modernist experience; it is, however, highly applicable to the intensified cycle of time-space compression which we experience today as a result of moves away from central production to diversified techniques of flexible accumulation.

Awareness of the simultaneous existence of heterogenous social spaces rather blunts the modernist aesthetic of a single advanced historical material. Instead, we are confronted with a sense of multi-layered history; each layer pursuing its own course through time. Such a model provides an insight into the differentiation of modernist musical materials in both a geographical and social sense. In addition to this, it is possible to understand a renewed sensitivity to spatial configurations as taking place within musical material. The intersection of horizontal and vertical within serialist organisation suggests a sense of time-space compression but not really an interaction of spaces within the music. *Répons* takes on spatial organisation as a creative issue.

The profusion of surface phenomena in *Répons* and their relationships to structural material and methods of organisation raise issues which pertain to the interaction between unity and diversity, surface immediacy and structural coherence. Adorno's *Aesthetic Theory*[3] and his wider philosophical thought expand these matters, which touch upon the central tensions between modernism and postmodernism, into more general issues of identity and non-identity thinking, mimesis and construction. The dialectic of identity and non-identity is one which recognises the claims of both the universal and the particular, but which refuses to let unifying tendencies crush the particular. 'To change the direction of conceptuality, to give it a turn towards non-identity, is the hinge of negative dialectics.'[4] Related to this is the dialectic of mimesis and construction. The particular moment of a piece of music has a sensual beauty

2 David Harvey, *The Condition of Postmodernity* (Oxford: Blackwell, 1989), p. 265.
3 Theodor W. Adorno, *Aesthetic Theory*, trans. C. Lenhardt (London: Routledge, 1984).
4 Adorno, *Negative Dialectics*, trans. E. B. Ashton (London: Routledge and Kegan Paul, 1973), p. 12.

and immediacy which mimes nature and expression – using mimesis in a literal sense – and is divergent with and yet dependent on an organisational logic. The two sides cross over and are realised in terms of each other. Mimesis without construction is false affirmation; construction without mimesis is instrumental rationality or domination as an end in itself.

The latter tendency is the target of Adorno's attack on the high modernist principles of musical construction adopted in the 1950s. In Adorno's view, Schoenberg's method was forged from a mimetic need, and his music succeeds despite rather than because of the system. In a rather unspecific critique of the post–Webern generation, Adorno argues that the domination of material has become the main criterion for meaning in new music, to the extent that prefabricated material constitutes a substitute for composition.[5] The internal contradictions of integral serialism are well documented; suffice it here to say that the inability of the system to exclude chance is a manifestation of the non–identical undermining a unifying concept. Boulez has been particularly vociferous in pointing out the shortcomings of integral serialism and has recognised that many of the problems stem from the narrowness of the aesthetic viewpoint. Indeed, Boulez's writings follow a line of development extending from rigorous concern with technical musical matters to wide-ranging aesthetic discussion and interest. As Robert Piencikowski has observed, this tendency is already present in the early essays contained in *Stocktakings from an Apprenticeship*:

Technical problems occupied the front of the stage – and it was the questions raised by the means of giving them concrete realization that led to that of their aesthetic validity. In a word, one passed from the stage at which technique made do with an indefinite aesthetic, to the stage at which it is the aesthetic, made conscious by necessity, that will determine the technical means.[6]

Boulez's continual search for an advanced musical material capable of circumnavigating the aporias of high modernism has in fact amounted to a musical realisation of many of Adorno's ideas.

Répons and its associated theoretical statements have remained consistent with Boulez's frequently stated objective that the organisation of music should be immanent and perceptible in musical terms rather than

---

5 Adorno, 'The Aging of the New Music', trans. R. Hullot-Kentor and F. Will, *Telos*, 77 (1988), pp. 95–116.

6 Robert Piencikowski, 'Introduction', in Pierre Boulez, *Stocktakings from an Apprenticeship*, trans. S. Walsh (Oxford: Clarendon Press, 1991), p. xv.

Example 11.1   Boulez, *Répons*, the five primary chords

imposed externally. This has been a decisive factor in the composer's attempt to integrate the electronic and instrumental aspects of this work under the same scheme. The dramatic entry of the soloists at rehearsal figure **21**, and the spiralling electronic echoes which follow it, are based upon transpositions and transformations of a chord – the fifth chord of Ex. 11.1 – dubbed by Deliège as the '*Répons* chord'.[7] As Boulez and Gerzso have published details of this transposition process,[8] I shall not reiterate them here, but rather comment briefly. Boulez's notion of a three-dimensional arpeggio moving across from the soloists' responses to the electronic echoes, all derived from transformations of the same chord, displays a concern with isomorphism and difference, with obtaining something syntactically related yet distinct, which goes back to the problems he tried to solve with the serial proliferation of the Third Piano Sonata. It should be pointed out, however, that the gap between the abstract pitch derivation and the immediacy of the computer transformations hinders a smooth continuum. The echo is the most salient point of perceptual organisation and aids the less clear sense of pitch derivation. The placing of the soloists on separate rostra to facilitate various trajectories of sound and the diffusion of their computer-transformed playing around the auditorium are the most obvious spatial aspects of *Répons*. It is indicative of Boulez's desire to derive the physical qualities of the music from the properties of the material that the speed at which responses rotate around the performance hall is determined by the loudness of the sounds. Although the technological manipulation of sound dominates the soloists' first entry, this type of response across space is also built into much of the acoustical writing in the work.

Boulez has acknowledged that 'much of the harmonic material in *Répons* can be traced to five chords which are played in the first bar of the

7 Célestin Deliège, 'Moment de Pierre Boulez: sur l'introduction orchestrale de *Répons*', *InHarmoniques*, 4 (1988), p. 183.
8 Pierre Boulez and Andrew Gerszo, 'Computers in Music', *Scientific American*, 258/iv (1988), pp. 26–32.

piece' (see Ex. 11.1).[9] Again, however, this background derivation is an abstraction, since the speed at which the opening statement goes past makes perception of the chords as anything other than timbre – with perhaps the exception of the fifth, the *Répons* chord – well-nigh impossible. Initiated by the entry of the soloists, the real exposition of these chords in fact occurs in the passage between rehearsal figures 21 and 27, which is based on the idea of a tutti sonority followed by episodes for the soloists. This section is based harmonically on a retrograde statement of the five chords. After the episode derived from chord V, chord IV is announced by the orchestra in a block of aggressive counterpoint characteristic of this piece whilst the soloists play transformations of the same material. This process is repeated with varying types of counterpoint through to chord I, and the whole section is rounded off by a statement of chord V from the soloists. These chords provide a constancy against the diversity of the whole section and in addition to providing a harmonic framework constitute a timbral resource. Indeed, it is the sheer excitement of sonority which commands this section.

System and idea

The whole arena of problems and possibilities addressed by Boulez in an article contemporary with *Répons*, 'Le système et l'idée',[10] comes very close to the discourse concerning the claims and potential of art which informs contemporary cultural theory. Boulez's dialectic of system and idea, which reappraises the complex interaction between structure and chance, is redolent of a dialectic which shuttles back and forth between identity and non-identity thinking. Though Boulez's inclination is weighted towards the whole rather than the part, his solution is an Adornian one insofar as it pays homage to both the universal and the particular by loosening the hold of the former over the latter. For Boulez's notion of musical material, this is realised by the system manifesting itself in terms of the structural properties of the music, but relinquishing its grip sufficiently to allow local and contingent configurations thrown up by the material to have an intrinsic role in the musical discourse. The dialectic of system and idea is conceived in terms commensurate with the Adornian dialectic of concept and object. The musical idea is an object whose specificity eludes complete control by the system,

9 Ibid., p. 31.
10 Boulez, 'Le système et l'idée', *InHarmoniques*, 1 (1986), pp. 62–104.

Table 11.1

rehearsal fig.		21	27	32
section	A	B	C	D
	introduction	soloists' entry		'Bali' ostinati
tempo	vif, lent, vif	varié	rapide	vif

rehearsal fig.	42	47	53	69/71	102
section	E	F	G	H	I
	'slow movement'		'scherzo'	'new section' (Répons 3)	'coda'
tempo	lent, mais de plus en plus chargé	lent	rapide	rapide	lent

yet which is in need of manipulation by the system. The system organises the musical object, yet recognises its concreteness and its ability to generate local configurations.

To speak of musical objects, both simple and complex, is by no means novel, but the consistency with which Boulez does so and the enhanced notion of a sound object which he expounds bears comparison with Adorno's and Benjamin's practice of constellation. This tries to explore the immanence of the object, to touch its otherness, by fracturing it and revealing its inner tensions without reducing the object to self-sameness. It conceives of an object being liberated into its own space without being effaced by some higher totality. Constellation is a rethinking of part and whole beyond the idea of organic unity. Boulez outlines in 'Le système et l'idée' and uses in *Répons* a variety of techniques for articulating the interplay of the particular and the general which can usefully be scrutinised through the notion of constellation.

The first of these techniques relates to the use of polar or anchor notes and their associated auras of adjacent phenomena, as Boulez calls them, which gravitate around the central pitch. The sound object constituted by the auxiliary notes is attracted to the stronger sound object constituted by the trilled sonorites. This type of constellation is usually found in the soloists' writing. Constellation is also pertinent to the construction of sound blocks which have an overall envelope but which are made up of an array of interacting sound objects. Finally, and most strikingly, con-

Example 11.2   Principal chord changes (in orchestra)
between rehearsal figures 42 and 47

stellation is relevant to the configurations formed by blocks, to the way in which blocks can interpenetrate, and to the transformation of blocks from within by elements from the outside. An aura of adjacent phenenomena is formed in basically two ways in *Répons*: as an extended anacrusis-type figure or as a chord around a sustained, often trilled, sonority. Boulez argues that these adjacent phenomena graft themselves onto the principal sound object without actually becoming part of it. Whilst they do give the centre a focus it would not normally have, the embellishments possess a life of their own which enables them to form vertical aggregates with one another. Thus there is a certain mimetic immediacy on the surface of the music constituted by these adjacent phenomena, or 'free particulars', which are at liberty to make provisional connections.

The interaction of trills and their associated auras of adjacent notes is most extensively explored in the 'slow movement' which provided the conclusion for *Répons* 1 (section E in Table 11.1).[11] The backbone of this slow section, which lasts just over five minutes, is the chord transformation shown in Ex. 11.2. Although none of these chords are obviously related to the primary chords, they do have the predominant tone/third grouping characteristic of the *Répons* chord, and the fixed E in the top could be related to chord I.[12] D, E♭ and E♮ remain registrally fixed throughout this transformation. It is a different matter in the soloists' parts: here the main pedals, B, C, F, G and B♭, constitute five notes of the *Répons* chord and are rotated in the soloists' parts, amidst the thick

11 The diagram of *Répons* 3 given in Table 11.1 is based on the plan of *Répons* 2 given by Dominique Jameux (*Pierre Boulez*, trans. S. Bradshaw (London: Faber, 1991), p. 368). Jameux also gives details of the instrumentation, sound-processing equipment and seating arrangements for *Répons*.

12 It seems likely that this chord progression, and indeed much more of the music, is based on a transformation of the primary chords, but without information from the composer the derivation is abstract. In technical discussion I have sought to identify features in which there is a clear sense of the basic ideas being constantly present.

Example 11.3 Principal pedals in piano 1 and vibraphone between
rehearsal figures 42 and 43 (texture rhythmically simplified)

ornamentation, throughout the section (see Ex. 11.3). Two notes of the
Répons chord are missing (D and A), but D operates as a pedal in the
orchestra for the duration of this passage.

This chain of pitches becomes the basis for a succession of elaborate
tropes. As a compositional principle this may be traced back to the tropes
and grafts of the Third Piano Sonata, but here there is not the same
emphasis on deriving ornamentation and elaboration from properties of
the underlying material. A second set of pedals, also in the soloists'
ensemble, function as 'dirty' notes, at least initially, as they cloud the line
of the chord V pitches. This secondary succession of pedals can be traced
to a version of chord III. The two chords have B♭, B♮ and C in common.
Initially the lines of pedals are quite clear, but as the ornamentation
becomes more profuse the pedal notes become increasingly buried in
their auxiliaries: the music takes a turn towards non-identity, or – to use
Derridean terminology – metaphor swamps the text. Through its extensive tropes and elaborations, *Répons* exudes what might be considered to
be an awareness of itself as text and of its own metaphorical procedures.
The ornamentation becomes thickest around rehearsal figure 46 (see Ex.
11.4), which is also the climax of the section in general.

It is worth looking at this point in more detail. In the soloists' parts,
the auxiliary notes have become a web of motion perceived more in terms
of contour than of constituent lines. This block (or space), as a whole,
permeates the three complex blocks in the orchestra. Of the orchestral
blocks, the strings and woodwind respond to each other with similar
material whilst the brass interject with their punctuating figures. The
composite woodwind line moves in homophonic flourishes – although the
deviations in the texture create a heterophony – using adjacent phenomena in a manner linked more closely to anacrusis than to the embroidered
lines of the soloists. The responding collective line in the strings utilises
the same features.

Example 11.4   *Répons*, rehearsal figure 46 (from second beat), piano 1

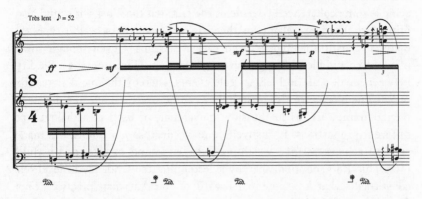

The two composite strands of woodwind and strings are distinguished by timbre but respond and interact with each other across the orchestra to form a continuous texture into which the brass interject with rather more limited flourishes. The staccato marking, the *ff* dynamic and the metallic tone ensure that the brass cut through the texture as temporal markers rather than becoming part of the interwoven fabric; they also play groups of fast repeated notes – the 'morse' patterns which occur throughout the score – often as rhythmic counterpoint within a block. The staccato flourishes have the precision of the repeated note figures but are also readily related to earlier string figurations and the swoops within which they are embedded. Indeed, staccato flourishes are distributed throughout the two/three strands of the orchestral chain of responses, but it is the brass which dominate. Finally, although it is the brass which really distinguish beats, the whole orchestra functions as a single, complex block in the sense that everything is contained within a beat, unlike the lines of the solo ensemble which weave around the beats. The cumulative result is one of heterogeneity within a contained space. It is a swelling and extension of this web formed with the soloists which results in the tropical growth of section G, where adjacent phenomena become the texture itself: melodic material is swamped by its own aura of auxiliaries, non-identity becomes stronger than identity.

One starts to see what Boulez means by a flexible hierarchy of events and an interaction of detail and structure. Individual occurrences – such as a trill, flourish or heterophonic fragment – both constitute an ingredient of a block contributing towards its overall identity and at the same time denote that block, so that a larger texture is prefigured by the local detail. Thus the interplay of figures, as discussed above, triggers larger

203

associations, whilst the dense and potentially chaotic sections of the work achieve some coherence by virtue of the fact that the blocks of sound also initiate connections reliant on the listener's awareness of the types of material constituting blocks from earlier sections – even though these may not be audible in the immense proliferation. Thus there is a fluidity between small-scale and larger-scale events whereby the one denotes the other. The blocks are also elastic: they can be stretched out in a developmental framework, as in the slow movement, or used in a dialogue of different proportions. In his technique of constellation Boulez has managed to achieve relative weighting between sound objects, and a fluid hierarchical organisation, thereby sidestepping the tendency to level out constituents that is a potential hazard of the Adornian practice. This flexible use of blocks is construed in terms of an advanced musical material in which timbre is an essential constituent and an integral part of the syntax.

Not surprisingly, Boulez locates the origins of a technique of block construction in Wagner and especially late Debussy, notably in the Debussian coagulation of complex timbres and slight divergence within a uniform sound block.[13] Célestin Deliège argues that Boulez has realised something which was only on the horizon for Debussy:

We are then – at least if we seek to situate ourselves through some reference to heritage – closer to the clarity Webern maintained in a project of variation. More than that, Debussy's dream finds an expression he could only glimpse, unable to realise it. However, whether it is Webern, Debussy or Stravinsky in his prospective phase, the shackles of an old outline had never been suppressed (even of an indelible ABA). This time the break with the outline is consummate: the form develops through the generation and regeneration of its fundamental moments without having to define a framework agreed in advance.[14]

Debussian intricacy is apparent in the minute gradations within blocks and the delicate coagulation of timbres, yet there is also the presence of Stravinskian blocks and cells – evinced in the cellular counterpoint and heterophony within blocks and in the juxtaposition and superimposition of aggregate sounds. The relationship of Boulez's technique to that of Stravinsky is complex. The cell technique with which Boulez weaves around a pitch, and in which close adjacent notes function more as colourings of the central pitch than as harmonic entities, is clearly

---

13 Boulez, 'Timbre and Composition – Timbre and Language', trans. R. Robertson, *Contemporary Music Review*, 2/i (1987), p. 169.
14 Deliège, 'Moment de Pierre Boulez', pp. 201–2.

Stravinskian; but it is moderated by a Debussian concern with minute deviation within the same sonic block, thus to some extent sacrificing the raw energy of Stravinsky. Given that Boulez conceives of construction within the sound object in terms of organised timbre and the manipulation of sound blocks from the outside as raw timbre, it is to the external organisation of blocks that one should look for the atavism of Stravinsky. Despite the sonic excitement of *Répons* and its emphasis on timbre, its roots in Stravinsky's Russian period are dissipated by Boulez's fascination with language in itself. The modification and incorporation of Stravinsky's technique does, however, allow Boulez a greater degree of flexibility and sophistication in a morphology of blocks than did Stravinsky's juxtapositions and superimpositions.

Clearly the use of block techniques in *Répons*, particularly when seen with respect to Stravinsky, raises the whole issue of what Adorno regards as the regressive qualities of static music. Again, Boulez too seems aware of the pitfalls: his notion of structuring blocks from the inside and the outside creates an environment in which an interaction of different types of temporal organisation is possible. The primarily static forms of construction which exist within blocks are placed in a temporal dynamic by the configurations of blocks utilised by the composer. There is, therefore, what might be termed a narrative or temporal unfolding throughout the piece, evident in the fact that some of the more chaotic sections which occur later in the work would not be comprehensible without the setting out of material earlier. Nevertheless, the temporal organisation amounts to far more than a simple unfolding. In perhaps a more radical conception of developing variation, in which timbre is a significant organisational factor, the basic sound objects of the piece are always there in a form which constantly renews its instants, yet rather than dominate the texture they are thrown into different configurations. *Répons* thus utilises a degree of repetition – albeit with constant divergence – which would have been anathema to Adorno's conception of transformation through time, but does so in a manner which to a large extent avoids generating the passive response from the listener so feared by Adorno. Furthermore, this cross-fertilisation of individual moments with temporal transformation is embedded within Boulez's recognition of and response to the whole issue of identity and non-identity, mimesis and construction. The way in which objects constituting a block retain their identity whilst interacting within the block and within the constellation of blocks is inseparable from their temporal framework; the fact that such objects or moments have a mimetic immediacy whilst contributing to the overall sound owes much to the timbral conception of this work, another integral part of the constructional matrix.

Phantasmagoria

In his article 'Timbre and Composition – Timbre and Language', Boulez comments as follows:

The small ensemble primarily uses the analysis of discourse by means of timbre, creating interest by refinement and division, while the large ensemble primarily uses multiplication, superimposition, accumulation, creating an illusion, what Adorno called (in another context) phantasmagoria.[15]

That *Répons* is the background for these remarks seems likely, but it deals with an interaction of ensemble and orchestra in a manner far more complex than the clear distinctions of Boulez's statement would suggest. Both ensemble and orchestra incorporate aspects of articulation and fusion. The soloists might, at a basic level, be the ensemble of articulation, but their rich elaboration frequently reaches a level of complexity which passes into fusion. Similarly, though the orchestra often does function on a level of fusion, the blocks which it fuses are internally articulated, and the orchestra is at times more articulated than the ensemble.

Boulez's reference to Adorno's musical conception of phantasmagoria is extremely suggestive. The context in which Adorno uses the word – to which Boulez alludes but does not cite – is likely to be the Wagner monograph, in which there is a chapter entitled 'Phantasmagoria'. Adorno's basic premise is encapsulated in his first sentence: 'The occultation of production by means of the outward appearance of the product – that is the formal law governing the works of Richard Wagner.'[16] Those moments in which Wagner has recourse to a magical or mystical realm, as a way of escaping reality or as the image of a superior order, are, by and large, precisely those in which he converges most directly with reality in the shape of a commodity form which effaces its means of production. By concealing the underlying forces or conditions of its production, the art work reproduces those conditions in a transformed manner as an absolute. Thus, although one cannot help feeling that Adorno is fascinated and half-seduced by Wagner's phantasmagoria, his analysis depicts it as insidious deception.

---

15 Boulez, 'Timbre and Composition – Timbre and Language', p. 167.
16 Adorno, *In Search of Wagner*, trans. R. Livingstone (London: New Left Books, 1981), p. 85.

It is surprising, then, that Boulez should use the term in such close proximity to his own ideas, although it does prove to be provocative in relation to *Répons*. This is an instance of Boulez taking an idea or technique and integrating it into his own conception of advanced material, whilst leaving as a residue the original context of the idea. That residue is the aesthetic and ideological field within which the term operates in Adorno's analysis, which cannot be simply divorced from a compositional adoption of the idea. The major difference in the implementation of these terms, however, lies in the fact that Boulez has attempted to make phantasmagoria an integral part of the compositional fabric, whereas Adorno perceives it, in the case of Wagner, as being primarily an instrument for the masking of constructional procedure.

Phantasmagoria as commodity relates to the outward manifestation of the music, its aesthetic appearance (*Schein*), and the extent to which it hides its construction. In a sense, *Répons* does conceal its methods of construction: the sheer sonority and intricate surface texture do take on a life of their own which tantalisingly deflect the ear away from their construction. The Wagnerian illusion of endless melody, in which motivic shapes in fact remain fairly rigid, has a correlate in *Répons* whereby the often seamless flood of sound is frequently constituted by minutely differing sound objects. It seems that Boulez has achieved a dialectic of articulation and fusion, conveyed largely in terms of the inside and outside of blocks rather than in terms of ensemble and orchestra. Nevertheless, this cannot be reduced to purely technical criteria: the ideological force field of phantasmagoria remains in tension with articulation. What Boulez refers to as organisation from the outside does relate to phantasmagoria, but the negative implications are weakened by the articulation as well as fusion between blocks. Picking up the correlation which Boulez draws between articulation/fusion and reality/phantasmagoria, it is almost as if the composer is opening up a dialectic of composition as a distillation of reality and illusion in which the border between the one and the other is blurred.

The dimension of *Répons* that comes closest to the outward appearance of a commodity is obviously the computer sound transformation. Here, again, the criss-crossing of aesthetic currents is complex. The resonance of magic and distance, which in Adorno's analysis of Wagner merely reaffirms the historical conditions of the time, reappears in *Répons*: the vast resonating sound masses of the soloists' entry and coda have a magic dimension, and impressions of distance are intensified by the echoes which spiral around the system so that various areas of the audience hear different aspects of the sound. All of this suggests a 'short circuit', in which the 'other' world of Wagner becomes the super-modernism of information technology: 'phantasmagoria as the point at which aesthetic appearance becomes a function of the character of the commodity'.[17] On this level, and to the extent that these techniques permeate other aspects of the composition, the complexity of the score mirrors the impenetrable web of capital exchange; indeed, the techniques of *Répons* are powerful methods for organising large amounts of information.

Boulez is, however, at great pains to point out that he is not a servant of technology, and that the crossover between the instrumental and computer domains of this work is reflective of a compositional logic rather than of technological supremacy. The music seems to work on two levels: on one level the impact of the soloists' chords (rehearsal figure 21) does seem to hold out the impossible and illusory promise of computer technology; on another it elicits an excitement in sound for its own sake which, as in Stravinsky and Debussy, cannot be contained within a socially constructed moment. The flow of information in *Répons* does not have the rigid identity of much technical information manipulation and capital exchange. It offers ways of opening difference within a flow of repetition: the differing and deferring inscribed in Derrida's notion of *différance* are evident in the interplay of particulars but interact with other processes in the music, thereby not haemorrhaging formations of identity.

In Wagner's phantasmagoria, for Adorno, the 'music pauses and is made spatial'.[18] Certainly, in the fire music which engulfs the end of *Die Walküre* the constituent parts are very much components of the whole, but Adorno is rather insensitive to the degree of internal articulation within this sonority. In further defence against Adorno's critique of static music, it should be noted that his own notion of constellation is itself a spatially derived metaphor. To be sure, in Adorno's writings constellation moves on a temporal axis, but this suggests an interaction of space and time which he is loath to grant to music. In the case of *Répons*, the static construction of the blocks is frequently offset by the constellations in which they are set. Even within those blocks that have an overall identity, one is aware that the particular processes which contribute to them retain a certain individuality of their own. To draw a social analogy: within a defined social space people are able to construct their own

17 Ibid., p. 90 (cf. Jonathan Dunsby on computers and the fantastic, this volume, p. 84 [Ed.]).
18 Adorno, *In Search of Wagner*, p. 86.

spaces, which are not totally identical with the perceived social surface. In other words, reification can be resisted on a more local and provisional basis than Adorno grants. Similarly, spaces within music can resist the dead time of reification. On a slightly larger scale, much of *Répons* evokes the feel of objects reacting to one another in space, but without a sense of emptiness. *Répons*, and Boulez's associated ideas of construction in music, do move beyond an Adornian idea of time as progress, but do not go so far as to transform it into 'the space of simultaneous possibilities' which David Roberts maintains is the other side of Adorno's own paradoxical modern paradigm.[19] Simultaneous possibilites with a degree of contingency do occur within the spaces of *Répons*, but they operate within the latency of an organising material.

What then of the utopian potential in art which informs so much Frankfurt critical theory? Boulez asks a similar question:

So then, what can be done to ensure that variance and coherence, global vision and accident of the instant, the abolition of chance and the preservation of free will, primacy of order and transgression of the law, exist simultaneously?[20]

Though perhaps overstressing the need for control, this comes close not only to a utopian vision of music but also to one of a radical politics. Boulez seeks to combine the best aspirations of both modernism and postmodernism without either one cancelling the other out. The objective remains an ideal, but Boulez has succeeded in creating a musical style with sufficient flexibility to achieve a crossover between the universal and the particular in which the one is not crushed by the other. Momentous as this achievement is, the fact that it has been attained to such a large extent by a conscious advancement of musical material weakens the mediation through the subject which lies at the heart of Adorno's fascination with Schoenberg. Though at times achieving the directness of sonority of Wagner and Stravinsky, *Répons'* blocks lack the rawness of experience which projects through these composers, and which at best cuts through the circle of regression circumscribed by Adorno. This lack of bite is reflected in the homogeneous saccharine tendencies of the choice of instrumentation for the soloists' ensemble. The inner consistency of the music and the absence of hard dissonance dissipate a sense of tension and release, encouraging a certain disinterested contemplation of the music.

And what of the Adornian dream of a second mimesis emerging the

19 Roberts, *Art and Enlightenment*, p. 219.
20 Boulez, 'Le système et l'idée', p. 95.

other side of rigorous construction? The loosening of structural rigour in *Répons* reveals this as a forlorn hope: the solution offered is one in which construction is intrinsically bound up with a primary rather than secondary immediacy; it manifests itself through the sensuousness of individual moments and of the surface aura. That this mimesis fails to permeate all levels of the work, it seems to me, is not indicative of the inadequacy of the material but, again, of the fact that so much has been invested in the efficacy of the material rather than being sustained by subjective experience. Boulez has found a way of working within the language-in-itself sphere of Mallarmé which does not collapse the whole edifice, but this lacks the critical force afforded by mediated expression. As befits a work composed in the era of poststructuralism, *Répons* progresses through an elaborate series of tropes and grafts, with a self-awareness of its own textual strategies, but does not collapse coherence into unbridled difference. Through his dogged attachment to the Adornian precept of historically advanced musical material, Boulez has forged a mode of musical thought which, even if it does not achieve its full expressive and critical potential, is capable of embracing the diversity and contradictions of advanced industrial society on a level as insightful as any cultural-theoretical practice. This late-twentieth-century work does not totally bypass the aporias and difficulties which Adorno detects in modern art, but it offers resources and possibilities which both vindicate and expand the hopes locked in Adorno's convoluted aesthetics.

Bibliography

Abbate, Carolyn. *Unsung Voices: Opera and Musical Narrative in the Nineteenth Century* (Princeton: Princeton University Press, 1991)

Abbate, Carolyn and Roger Parker (eds.) *Analyzing Opera: Verdi and Wagner* (Berkeley: University of California Press, 1989)

Adorno, Theodor W. *Mahler: Ein Musikalische Physiognomik* (Frankfurt, 1960)

Negative Dialectics, trans. E. B. Ashton (London: Routledge and Kegan Paul, 1973)

In Search of Wagner, trans. R. Livingstone (London: New Left Books, 1981)

Aesthetic Theory, trans. C. Lenhardt (London: Routledge, 1984)

'The Aging of the New Music', trans. R. Hullot-Kentor and F. Will, *Telos*, 77 (1988), pp. 95–116

Aristotle. 'On the Art of Poetry', in *Classical Literary Criticism*, trans. T. S. Dorsch (Harmondsworth: Penguin, 1965), pp. 29–75

The Art of Rhetoric, trans. H. Lawson-Tancred (Harmondsworth: Penguin, 1991)

Babbitt, Milton. Review of René Leibowitz, *Schoenberg et son école* and *Qu'est ce que la musique de douze sons?*, in *Journal of the American Musicological Society*, 3/i (1950), pp. 57–60

Review of Felix Salzer, *Structural Hearing* (New York: Charles Boni, 1952), in *Journal of the American Musicological Society*, 5/iii (1952), pp. 260–5

'Past and Present Concepts of the Nature and Limits of Music', *Congress Report of the International Musicological Society* (1961), pp. 398–403, repr. in Benjamin Boretz and Edward T. Cone (eds.), *Perspectives on Contemporary Music Theory* (New York: Norton, 1972), pp. 3–9

'The Structure and Function of Musical Theory', *College Music Symposium*, 5 (1965), pp. 49–60, repr. in Benjamin Boretz and Edward T. Cone (eds.), *Perspectives on Contemporary Music Theory* (New York: Norton, 1972), pp. 10–21

'Contemporary Music Composition and Music Theory as Contemporary Intellectual History', in Barry S. Brook, Edward O. D. Downes, and Sherman Van Solkema (eds.), *Perspectives in Musicology* (New York: Norton, 1971), pp. 151–84

'Responses: A First Approximation', *Perspectives of New Music*, 14/ii–15/i (1976), pp. 3–23

Words About Music (Madison: University of Wisconsin Press, 1987)

Bailey, Walter B. *Programmatic Elements in the Works of Schoenberg* (Ann Arbor: UMI Research Press, 1984)

Baker, Michael. 'A Computational Approach to Modeling Musical Grouping Structure', *Contemporary Music Review*, 4 (1989), pp. 311–25

211

Barthes, Roland. *Elements of Semiology*, trans. A. Lavers and C. Smith (Boston: Beacon Press, 1967)
The Pleasure of the Text, trans. R. Miller (London: Jonathan Cape, 1976)
Camera Lucida: Reflections on Photography, trans. R. Howard (New York: Hill & Wang, 1981)
The Responsibility of Forms, trans. R. Howard (Oxford: Blackwell, 1986)
Beach, David. 'A Schenker Bibliography', *Journal of Music Theory*, 13/i (1969), pp. 2–37
Benjamin, Walter. 'The Storyteller: Reflections on the Work of Nikolai Leskov', in *Illuminations: Essays and Reflections*, ed. H. Arendt, trans. H. Zohn (New York: Schocken, 1969), pp. 83–109
Bent, Ian. 'Analysis', in Stanley Sadie (ed.), *The New Grove Dictionary of Music and Musicians* (London: Macmillan, 1980), vol. 1, pp. 340–88
Analysis [The New Grove Handbooks in Music] (Basingstoke: Macmillan, 1987)
Berger, Arthur. 'Problems of Pitch Organization in Stravinsky', in Benjamin Boretz and Edward T. Cone (eds.), *Perspectives on Schoenberg and Stravinsky* (New York: Norton, rev. 1972), pp. 123–54
Berger, Jonathan. 'A Theory of Musical Ambiguity', *Computers in Music Research*, 2 (1990), pp. 91–119
Bernard, Jonathan. *The Music of Edgard Varèse* (New Haven: Yale University Press, 1987)
'Cracked Octaves, Warped Perspectives: A Response', *Perspectives of New Music*, 30/ii (1992), pp. 274–89
Bernstein, Leonard. 'The Delights and Dangers of Ambiguity', in *The Unanswered Question* (Cambridge, Mass.: Harvard University Press, 1976), pp. 193–259
Berry, Wallace. *Structural Functions in Music* (Englewood Cliffs: Prentice Hall, 1976)
Black, Max. 'Metaphor', *Proceedings of the Aristotelian Society, N. S.*, 55 (1954–5), pp. 273–94
Boretz, Benjamin. 'Meta-Variations: Studies in the Foundations of Musical Thought (I)', *Perspectives of New Music*, 8/i (1969), pp. 1–74
Boulez, Pierre. 'Le système et l'idée', *InHarmoniques*, 1 (1986), pp. 62–104
'Timbre and Composition – Timbre and Language', trans. R. Robertson, *Contemporary Music Review*, 2/i (1987), pp. 161–71
Boulez, Pierre and Andrew Gerzso. 'Computers in Music', *Scientific American*, 258/iv (1988), pp. 26–32
Bowie, Malcolm 'A Message From Kakania: Freud, Music, Criticism', in P. Collier and J. Davies (eds.), *Modernism and the European Unconscious* (Cambridge: Polity Press, 1990), pp. 3–17
Brinkman, Alexander R. *PASCAL Programming for Music Research* (Chicago: University of Chicago Press, 1990)
Brooks, Peter. *Reading for the Plot* (Oxford: Oxford University Press, 1984)
'The Idea of a Psychoanalytic Literary Criticism', *Critical Inquiry*, 13/ii (1987), pp. 334–48
Brown, Andrew. 'Music's Body: Some Notes on Barthes and Schumann', paper delivered at Cambridge University, 1991
Buck, Ross. *The Communication of Emotion* [Guilford Social Psychology Series] (New York: Guilford, 1984)

Bibliography

Burke, Kenneth. 'Four Master Tropes', in *A Grammar of Motives* (Berkeley: University of California Press, 1969), pp. 503–17

Burkhart, Charles. 'Schenker's "Motivic Parallelisms"', *Journal of Music Theory*, 22/ii (1978), pp. 145–75

Cadwallader, Allen. 'Motivic Unity and Integration of Structural Levels in Brahms's B Minor Intermezzo, Op. 119, No. 1', *Theory and Practice*, 8/ii (1983), pp. 5–24

Campbell, Bruce B. Review of Janet M. Levy, *Beethoven's Compositional Choices: The Two Versions of Opus 18, No. 1, First Movement* (Philadelphia: University of Pennsylvania Press, 1982), in *Journal of Music Theory*, 29/i (1985), pp. 183–97

Carner, Mosco. 'Ländler', in Stanley Sadie (ed.), *The New Grove Dictionary of Music and Musicians* (London: Macmillan, 1980), vol. 10, pp. 435–6

Cavell, Stanley. *Must We Mean What We Say?* (Cambridge: Cambridge University Press, 1976)

Citkowitz, Israel. 'The Role of Heinrich Schenker', *Modern Music*, 11/i (1933), pp. 18–23; repr. in *Theory and Practice*, 10/i–ii (1985), pp. 17–22

Clarke, David. 'Structural, Cognitive and Semiotic Aspects of the Musical Present', *Contemporary Music Review*, 3/i (1989), pp. 111–31

Language, Form, and Structure in the Music of Michael Tippett (New York: Garland, 1989)

Clarke, Eric F. 'Mind the Gap: Formal Structures and Psychological Processes in Music', *Contemporary Music Review*, 3/i (1989), pp. 1–13

Clifton, Thomas. 'Types of Ambiguity in Schoenberg's Tonal Compositions' (PhD dissertation, Stanford University, 1966)

Music as Heard: A Study in Applied Phenomenology (New Haven: Yale University Press, 1983)

Cohen, Ted. 'Metaphor and the Cultivation of Intimacy', *Critical Inquiry*, 5/i (1978), pp. 8–12

Cohn, Richard. 'The Autonomy of Motives in Schenkerian Accounts of Tonal Music', *Music Theory Spectrum*, 14/ii (1992), pp. 150–70

Cone, Edward T. 'Beyond Analysis', in Benjamin Boretz and Edward T. Cone (eds.), *Perspectives on Contemporary Music Theory* (New York: Norton, 1972), pp. 72–90

'Schubert's Promissory Note: An Exercise in Musical Hermeneutics', in Walter Frisch (ed.), *Schubert: Critical and Analytical Studies* (Lincoln: University of Nebraska Press, 1986), pp. 11–30

Music: A View from Delft (London: University of Chicago Press, 1989)

Cook, Nicholas. *A Guide to Musical Analysis* (London: Dent, 1987)

'Schenker's Theory of Music as Ethics', *Journal of Musicology*, 7/iv (1989), pp. 415–39

Music, Imagination, and Culture (Oxford: Clarendon Press, 1990)

Cooper, David E. *Metaphor* (Oxford: Blackwell, 1986)

Cooper, Grosvenor and Leonard B. Meyer. *The Rhythmic Structure of Music* (Chicago: University of Chicago Press, 1960)

Culler, Jonathan. *The Pursuit of Signs: Semiotics, Literature, Deconstruction* (London: Routledge, 1981)

Dahlhaus, Carl. *Schoenberg and the New Music*, trans. D. Puffett and A. Clayton (Cambridge: Cambridge University Press, 1987)

Bibliography

The Idea of Absolute Music, trans. R. Lustig (Chicago: University of Chicago Press, 1989)

de Man, Paul. *Allegories of Reading: Figural Language in Rousseau, Nietzsche, Rilke and Proust* (New Haven: Yale University Press, 1979)

The Resistance to Theory (Minneapolis: University of Minnesota Press, 1986)

DeBellis, Mark. 'Conceptions of Musical Structure', *Midwest Studies in Philosophy*, 16 (1991), 378–93

'The Representational Content of Musical Experience', *Philosophy and Phenomenological Research*, 51/ii (1991), 303–24

Deleuze, Gilles and Felix Guattari. *Qu'est-ce que la philosophie?* (Paris: Les éditions du minuit, 1991)

Deliège, Célestin. 'Moment de Pierre Boulez: sur l'introduction orchestrale de *Répons*', *InHarmoniques*, 4 (1988), pp. 181–202

Delong, Kenneth. 'Roads Taken and Retaken: Foreground Ambiguity in Chopin's Prelude in A-flat, Op. 28, No. 17', *Canadian University Music Review*, 11/i (1991), pp. 34–49

Derrida, Jacques. *Of Grammatology*, trans. Gayatri Chakravorty Spivak (Baltimore: The Johns Hopkins University Press, 1976)

'Structure, Sign, and Play in the Discourse of the Human Sciences', in *Writing and Difference*, trans. Alan Bass (London: Routledge and Kegan Paul, 1978), pp. 278–93

'Living on/*Border Lines*', trans. J. Hulbert, in Harold Bloom et al., *Deconstruction and Criticism* (New York: Seabury, 1979), pp. 75–175

Deutsch, Diana and John Feroe. 'The Internal Representation of Pitch Sequences in Tonal Music', *Psychological Review*, 88 (1981), pp. 503–22

Don, Gary W. 'Goethe and Schenker', *In Theory Only*, 10/viii (1988), pp. 1–14

Drabkin, William. 'The New Erläuterungsausgabe', *Perspectives of New Music*, 12 (1973–4), pp. 319–30

Dubiel, Joseph. 'A Schenker Analysis and Some of Schenker's Theories', paper delivered at the Society for Music Theory, Philadelphia, 1984

'"When You are a Beethoven": Kinds of Rules in Schenker's Counterpoint', *Journal of Music Theory*, 34/ii (1990), pp. 291–340

Dunsby, Jonathan. 'Heinrich Schenker and the Free Counterpoint of Strict Composition', *Research Chronicle*, 16 (1980), pp. 140–8

Structural Ambiguity in Brahms: Analytical Approaches to Four Works (Ann Arbor: UMI Press, 1981)

'Music Analysis: Commentaries', in John Paynter et al. (eds.), *Companion to Contemporary Musical Thought* (London: Routledge, 1992), pp. 634–49

'The Poetry of *En blanc et noir*', paper delivered at the Journées Claude Debussy, City University and Institut français, London, 1993

Eagleton, Terry. *The Ideology of the Aesthetic* (Oxford: Blackwell, 1990)

Emmer, Huib. Note to CD recording of Harrison Birtwistle, *Refrains and Choruses* (Amsterdam: Etcetera, 1992) [KTC 1130]

Empson, William. *Seven Types of Ambiguity* (Harmondsworth: Penguin, 1961)

Epstein, David. *Beyond Orpheus* (Cambridge, Mass.: MIT Press, 1979)

Flew, Anthony. *Dictionary of Philosophy* (New York: St Martin's Press, 1979)

214

Bibliography

Fodor, Jerry A. 'Observation Reconsidered', in *A Theory of Content and Other Essays* (Cambridge, Mass.: MIT Press, 1990), pp. 231–51

Forte, Allen. *Contemporary Tone-Structures* (New York: Bureau of Publications, Teachers College, Columbia University, 1955)

'Schenker's Conception of Musical Structure', *Journal of Music Theory*, 3/i (1959), pp. 1–30

The Structure of Atonal Music (New Haven: Yale University Press, 1973)

'Ernst Oster (1908–1977) In Memoriam', *Journal of Music Theory*, 21/ii (1977), pp. 340–4

The Harmonic Organization of 'The Rite of Spring' (New Haven: Yale University Press, 1978)

'Pitch-Class Set Analysis Today', *Music Analysis*, 4 (1985), pp. 29–58

'Pitch-Class Set Genera and the Origin of Modern Harmonic Species', *Journal of Music Theory*, 32 (1988), pp. 187–270

'Debussy and the Octatonic', *Music Analysis*, 10 (1991), pp. 125–69

'Concepts of Linearity in Schoenberg's Atonal Music: A Study of the Opus 15 Song Cycle', *Journal of Music Theory*, 36/ii (1992), pp. 285–382

Forte, Allen and Steven E. Gilbert. *Introduction to Schenkerian Analysis* (New York: Norton, 1982)

Foucault, Michel. *History of Sexuality*, trans. R. Hurley, 3 vols. (New York: Allen Lane, 1979–88)

Franklin, Peter. *The Idea of Music: Schoenberg and Others* (London: Macmillan, 1985)

Freud, Sigmund. 'Mourning and Melancholia', in *On Metapsychology: the Theory of Psychoanalysis* (Harmondsworth: Penguin, 1984), pp. 245–68

Friedheim, Philip. 'Tonality and Structure in the Early Works of Schoenberg' (PhD dissertation, New York University, 1963)

Frisch, Walter. *Brahms and the Principle of Developing Variation* (Berkeley and Los Angeles: University of California Press, 1984)

Frow, John. 'Intertextuality and Ontology', in M. Worton and J. Still (eds.), *Intertextuality: Theories and Practices* (Manchester: Manchester University Press, 1990), pp. 45–55

Gasché, Rodolphe. *The Táin of the Mirror: Derrida and the Philosophy of Reflection* (Cambridge, Mass.: Harvard University Press, 1986)

Genette, Gerard. 'Métonymie chez Proust', in *Figures III* (Paris: Seuil, 1972), pp. 41–63

Gjerdingen, Robert. *A Classic Turn of Phrase: Music and the Psychology of Convention* (Philadelphia: University of Pennsylvania Press, 1988)

Goodman, Nelson. *Languages of Art* (Indianapolis: Bobbs-Merrill, 1968)

Graubart, Michael. Review of H. H. Stuckenschmidt, *Schönberg: Leben, Umwelt, Werk* (Zurich: Atlantis, 1974), in *Tempo*, 111 (1974), pp. 44–9.

Gray, Margaret E. *Postmodern Proust* (Philadelphia: University of Pennsylvania Press, 1992)

Griffiths, David. 'Song Writing: Poetry, Webern, and Musical Modernism' (PhD dissertation, King's College, University of London, 1993)

Grigg, Russell. 'Metaphor and Metonymy', *Newsletter of the Freudian Field*, 3/i–ii (1989), pp. 58–79

215

Bibliography

Guck, Marion A. 'Musical Images as Musical Thoughts: The Contribution of Metaphor to Analysis', *In Theory Only*, 5/v (1981), pp. 29–43
'Analytical Fictions', paper delivered at the Society for Music Theory, Oakland, 1990
'Beethoven as Dramatist', *College Music Symposium*, 29 (1990), pp. 8–18
'Two Types of Metaphoric Transfer', in Jamie C. Kassler (ed.), *Metaphor: A Musical Dimension* (Paddington, NSW: Currency Press, 1991), pp. 1–12
'Varèse Bound', *Perspectives of New Music*, 30/ii (1992), 244–73
'The "Endless Round"', *Perspectives of New Music*, 31/i (1993), pp. 306–14
Hall, Michael. *Harrison Birtwistle* (London: Robson, 1984)
Harvey, David. *The Condition of Postmodernity* (Oxford: Blackwell, 1989)
Hatten, Robert. 'Semiotic Perspectives on Issues in Music Cognition', *In Theory Only*, 11/iii (1989), pp. 1–11
Hegel, G. W. F. *Aesthetics: Lectures on Fine Art*, trans. T. M. Knox, 2 vols. (Oxford: Clarendon Press, 1975)
Hubbs, Nadine M. 'Musical Organicism and Its Alternatives' (PhD dissertation, University of Michigan, 1990)
Huron, David. 'Design Principles in Computer-Based Music Representation', in Alan Marsden and Anthony Pople (eds.), *Computer Representations and Models in Music* (London: Academic Press, 1992), pp. 5–39
Jakobson, Roman. 'Two Aspects of Language and Two Types of Aphasic Disturbances', in Roman Jakobson and Morris Halle, *Fundamentals of Language* (The Hague: Mouton, 1956), pp. 69–96
'Linguistics and Poetics', in Thomas A. Sebeok (ed.), *Style in Language* (New York: MIT Press, 1960), pp. 350–77
Jameux, Dominique. *Pierre Boulez*, trans. S. Bradshaw (London: Faber, 1991)
Johnson, Barbara. *A World of Difference* (Baltimore: The Johns Hopkins University Press, 1987)
Johnson, Mark (ed.) *Philosophical Perspectives on Metaphor* (Minneapolis: University of Minnesota Press, 1981)
Jonas, Oswald. Review of Felix Salzer, *Structural Hearing* (New York: Charles Boni, 1952), in *Notes*, 10/iii (1953), p. 439
Jordan, Roland, and Emma Kafalenos. 'The Double Trajectory: Ambiguity in Brahms and Henry James', *19th-Century Music*, 13/ii (1989), pp. 129–44
Kallir, Jane. *Arnold Schoenberg's Vienna* (New York: Galerie St. Etienne and Rizzoli, 1984)
Kaplansky, Irving. *Set Theory and Metric Spaces* (Boston: Allyn and Bacon, 1972)
Kassler, Jamie C. 'Heinrich Schenker's Epistemology and Philosophy of Music: An Essay on the Relations between Evolutionary Theory and Music Theory', in David Oldroyd and Ian Langham (eds.), *The Wider Domain of Evolutionary Thought* (Dordrecht: Reidel, 1983), pp. 221–60
Katz, Adele T. 'Heinrich Schenker's Method of Analysis', *Musical Quarterly*, 21/iii (1935), pp. 311–29; repr. in *Theory and Practice*, 10/i–ii (1985), pp. 77–95
Challenge to Musical Tradition: A New Concept of Tonality (New York: Knopf, 1945)
Keiler, Allan. 'The Origins of Schenker's Thought: How Man is Musical', *Journal of Music Theory*, 33/ii (1989), pp. 273–98

Bibliography

Kerman, Joseph. 'How We Got into Analysis, and How to Get Out', *Critical Inquiry*, 7 (1980), pp. 311–31

Musicology (London: Fontana, 1985)

Kermode, Frank. 'Secrets and Narrative Sequence', in W. J. T. Mitchell (ed.), *On Narrative* (Chicago: University of Chicago Press, 1981), pp. 79–98

Kinariwala, Neela Delia. 'Debussy and Musical Coherence: A Study of Succession and Continuity in the Preludes' (PhD dissertation, University of Texas at Austin, 1987)

Kingsbury, Henry. 'Sociological Factors in Musicological Poetics', *Ethnomusicology*, 35/ii (1991), pp. 195–219

Kittay, Eva. *Metaphor: Its Cognitive Force and Linguistic Structure* (Oxford: Clarendon Press, 1987)

Kolosick, J. Timothy. 'A Machine-Independent Data Structure for the Representation of Music Pitch Relationships: Computer-Generated Musical Examples for CBI', *Journal of Computer-Based Instruction*, 13/i (1986), pp. 9–13

Korsyn, Kevin. 'Schenker and Kantian Epistemology', *Theoria*, 3 (1988), pp. 1–58

'Towards a New Poetics of Musical Influence', *Music Analysis*, 10 (1991), pp. 3–72

Kramer, Lawrence. *Music and Language* (Berkeley: University of California Press, 1984)

Music as Cultural Practice, 1800–1900 (Berkeley: University of California Press, 1990)

Krumhansl, Carol L. *Cognitive Foundations of Musical Pitch* (Oxford: Oxford University Press, 1990)

Lacan, Jacques. 'The Agency of the Letter in the Unconscious or Reason since Freud', in *Ecrits*, trans. A. Sheridan (London: Tavistock, 1977), pp. 146–78

The Psychoses: The Seminars of Jacques Lacan, Book 3, 1955–1956, ed. Jacques-Alain Miller, trans. R. Grigg (London: Routledge, 1993)

Lakoff, George and Mark Johnson. *Metaphors We Live By* (Chicago: University of Chicago Press, 1980)

Lang, Paul Henry. 'Editorial' [Tovey versus Beethoven], *Musical Quarterly*, 32/ii (1946), pp. 296–302

(ed.) *The Creative World of Mozart* (New York: Norton, 1963)

Laske, Otto. 'KEITH: A Rule-System for Making Music-Analytical Discoveries', in M. Baroni and L. Callegari (eds.), *Musical Grammars and Computer Analysis* (Florence: Olschki, 1984), pp. 165–99

Lerdahl, Fred. 'Analyse de "La terrasse des audiences du clair de lune" de Debussy', *Analyse Musicale*, 16 (1989), pp. 54–60

Lerdahl, Fred and Ray Jackendoff. *A Generative Theory of Tonal Music* (Cambridge, Mass.: MIT Press, 1983)

Lessem, Alan. 'Schoenberg and the Crisis of Expressionism', *Music and Letters*, 55 (1974), pp. 429–36

Music and Text in the Works of Arnold Schoenberg (Ann Arbor: UMI Research Press, 1979)

Lester, Joel. Letter to the editor, *Journal of Music Theory*, 36/ii (1992), pp. 404–7.

Lewin, David. 'Music Theory, Phenomenology, and Modes of Perception', *Music Perception*, 3/iv (1986), pp. 327–92

'*Auf dem Flusse*: Image and Background in a Schubert Song', in Walter Frisch

217

(ed.), *Schubert: Critical and Analytical Studies* (Lincoln: University of Nebraska Press, 1986), pp. 126–52

Generalized Musical Intervals and Transformations (New Haven: Yale University Press, 1987)

Musical Form and Transformation: 4 Analytic Essays (New Haven: Yale University Press, 1993)

Lloyd, Norman. Review of Felix Salzer, *Structural Hearing* (New York: Charles Boni, 1952), in *Notes*, 10/iii (1953), p. 438

Marsden, Alan and Anthony Pople. 'Modelling Musical Cognition as a Community of Experts', *Contemporary Music Review*, 3/i (1989), pp. 29–42

'Towards a Connected Distributed Model of Musical Listening', *Interface*, 18 (1989), pp. 61–72

Maus, Fred Everett. 'Music as Drama', *Music Theory Spectrum*, 10 (1988), pp. 56–73

'Self-Depiction in Writing about Music', paper delivered at the Society for Music Theory, Oakland, 1990

McCreless, Patrick. 'Roland Barthes's *S/Z* from a Musical Point of View', *In Theory Only*, 10/vii (1988), pp. 1–29

'Syntagmatics and Paradigmatics: Some Implications for the Analysis of Chromaticism in Tonal Music', *Music Theory Spectrum*, 13/ii (1991), pp. 167–72

McFarlane, James. 'The Mind of Modernism', in Malcolm Bradbury and James McFarlane (eds.), *Modernism 1890–1930* (Harmondsworth: Penguin, 1976), pp. 71–93

McKilligan, K. M. *Edouard Dujardin: 'Les Lauriers sont coupés' and the Interior Monologue* (Hull: University of Hull Publications, 1977)

Mellers, Wilfred. Review of Felix Salzer, *Structural Hearing* (New York: Charles Boni, 1952), in *Music and Letters*, 34/iv (1953), pp. 329–32

Meltzer, Françoise. 'Eat your *Dasein*: Lacan's Self-Consuming Puns', in Jonathan Culler (ed.), *On Puns: The Foundation of Letters* (Oxford: Blackwell, 1988), pp. 156–63

Meyer, Leonard B. *Emotion and Meaning in Music* (Chicago: University of Chicago Press, 1956)

Music, the Arts, and Ideas (Chicago: University of Chicago Press, 1967)

Explaining Music: Essays and Explorations (Berkeley: University of California Press, 1973)

Mitchell, W. J. T. 'Representation', in F. Lentricchia and T. McLaughlin (eds.), *Critical Terms for Literary Study* (Chicago: University of Chicago Press, 1990), pp. 11–22

Molino, Jean. 'Musical Fact and the Semiology of Music', trans. J. A. Underwood, *Music Analysis*, 9 (1990), pp. 113–56

Monelle Raymond. *Linguistics and Semiotics in Music* (Chur, Switzerland: Harwood, 1992)

Montgomery, David. 'The Myth of Organicism: From Bad Science to Great Art', *Musical Quarterly*, 76/i (1992), pp. 17–66

Narmour, Eugene. *Beyond Schenkerism: The Need for Alternatives in Music Analysis* (Chicago: University of Chicago Press, 1977)

The Analysis and Cognition of Basic Melodic Structures (Chicago: University of Chicago Press, 1990)

Bibliography

Nash, Walter. *Rhetoric: The Wit of Persuasion* (Oxford: Blackwell, 1989)

Nattiez, Jean-Jacques. *Fondements d'une sémiologie de la musique* (Paris: Union générale d'éditions, 1975)

'An Analysis of Debussy's *Syrinx*', in *Toronto Semiotic Circle: Monographs, Working Papers and Pre-publications*, 4 (Toronto: Victoria University, 1982), pp. 1–35

'The Concepts of Plot and Seriation Process in Music Analysis', trans. C. Dale, *Music Analysis*, 4 (1985), pp. 107–18

'Can One Speak of Narrativity in Music?', trans. K. Ellis, *Journal of the Royal Musical Association*, 115/ii (1990), pp. 240–57

Music and Discourse, trans. C. Abbate (Princeton: Princeton University Press, 1990)

'Existe-t-il des relations entre les diverses méthodes d'analyse?', in Rossana Dalmonte and Mario Baroni (eds.), *Secondo convegno europeo di analisi musicale* (Trento: Universita degli studi di Trento, 1992), pp. 537–65

Newcomb, Anthony. 'Once More "Between Absolute and Program Music": Schumann's Second Symphony', *19th-Century Music*, 7/iii (1984), pp. 233–50

Noden-Skinner, Cheryl. 'Tonal Ambiguity in the Opening Measures of Selected Works by Chopin', *College Music Symposium*, 24 (1984), pp. 28–34

Ong, Walter J. *Orality and Literacy* (London: Methuen, 1982)

Parks, Richard E. *The Music of Claude Debussy* (New Haven: Yale University Press, 1989)

Parncutt, Richard. 'Revision of Terhardt's Psychoacoustical Model of the Root(s) of a Musical Chord', *Music Perception*, 6 (1988), pp. 65–93

Pastille, William A. 'Heinrich Schenker, Anti-Organicist', *Nineteenth-Century Music*, 8/i (1984), pp. 29–36

'The Development of the *Ursatz* in Schenker's Published Works', in A. Cadwallader (ed.), *Trends in Schenkerian Research* (New York: Schirmer, 1990), pp. 71–85

Payne, Michael. *Reading Theory: An Introduction to Lacan, Derrida, and Kristeva* (Oxford: Blackwell, 1993)

Peirce, Charles S. 'Logic as Semiotic: The Theory of Signs', in Robert E. Innis (ed.), *Semiotics: An Introductory Reader* (Bloomington: Indiana University Press, 1982), pp. 4–23

Piencikowski, Robert. 'Introduction', in P. Boulez, *Stocktakings from an Apprenticeship*, trans. S. Walsh (Oxford: Clarendon Press, 1991), pp. xiii–xxix

Proctor, Gregory, and Herbert L. Riggins. 'Levels and the Reordering of Chapters in Schenker's *Free Composition*', *Music Theory Spectrum*, 10 (1988), pp. 102–26

Quine, W. V. *Word and Object* (Cambridge, Mass.: MIT Press, 1960)

Quiddities: An Intermittently Philosophical Dictionary (London: Penguin, 1990)

Rahn, John. 'Aspects of Musical Explanation', *Perspectives of New Music*, 17/ii (1979), pp. 204–24

Basic Atonal Theory (New York: Longman, 1980)

Randall, J. K. 'Compose Yourself: A Manual for the Young', *Perspectives of New Music*, 10/ii (1972), pp. 1–12

Read, Herbert. *Art Now* (London: Faber, rev. 1960)

Reisel, R. B. *Elementary Theory of Measure Spaces* (New York: Springer Verlag, 1982)

Richards, I. A. *The Philosophy of Rhetoric* (New York: Oxford University Press, 1965)

Bibliography

Ricoeur, Paul. *Time and Narrative*, vol. 2, trans. K. McLaughlin and D. Pellauer (Chicago: University of Chicago Press, 1985)

Roberts, David. *Art and Enlightenment: Aesthetic Theory after Adorno* (Lincoln, Nebraska: University of Nebraska Press, 1991)

Rothstein, William. 'The Americanization of Heinrich Schenker', *In Theory Only*, 9/i (1986), pp. 5–17; repr. in Hedi Siegel (ed.), *Schenker Studies* (Cambridge: Cambridge University Press, 1990), pp. 193–203

Phrase Rhythm in Tonal Music (New York: Schirmer, 1989)

Ruwet, Nicolas. 'Note sur les duplications dans l'œuvre de Claude Debussy', in *Langage, musique, poésie* (Paris: Seuil, 1972), pp. 70–99

Saluzinsky, Imre. *Criticism in Society* (London: Methuen, 1987)

Salzer, Felix. *Structural Hearing: Tonal Coherence in Music*, 2 vols. (New York: Charles Boni, 1952)

Strukturelles Hören: Der tonale Zusammenhang in der Musik, 2 vols. [Taschenbücher zur Musikwissenschaft, 10] (Wilhelmshaven: Heinrichshofens Verlag, 1977)

Samuels, Robert. 'Derrida and Snarrenberg', *In Theory Only*, 11/i–ii (1989), pp. 45–58

'The Suicide of the Symphony: Musical Narrative and Mahler's Sixth', paper delivered at King's College, London, 1992

Schachter, Carl. 'Either/Or', in Hedi Siegel (ed.), *Schenker Studies* (Cambridge: Cambridge University Press, 1990), pp. 165–79

Scheffler, Israel. *Beyond the Letter: A Philosophical Inquiry into Ambiguity, Vagueness and Metaphor in Language* (London: Routledge and Kegan Paul, 1979)

Schenker, Heinrich. 'Das Hören in der Musik', *Neue Revue*, 5/xxxii (1894), pp. 15–21; repr. in Hellmut Federhofer (ed.), *Heinrich Schenker als Essayist und Kritiker: Gesammelte Aufsätze, Rezensionen und kleinere Berichte aus den Jahren 1891–1901* (Hildesheim: Georg Olms, 1990), pp. 96–103

'Der Geist der musikalischen Technik', *Musikalisches Wochenblatt* (Leipzig), 26/xix (1895), pp. 245–6; 26/xx, pp. 257–9; 26/xxi, pp. 273–4; 26/xxii, pp. 285–6; 26/xxiii, pp. 297–8; 26/xxiv–xxv, pp. 309–10; 26/xxvi, pp. 325–6; repr. in Hellmut Federhofer, *Heinrich Schenker: Nach Tagebüchern und Briefen in der Oswald Jonas Memorial Collection, University of California, Riverside* [Studien zur Musikwissenschaft, 3] (Hildesheim: Georg Olms, 1985), pp. 135–54

Harmonielehre [Neue musikalische Theorien und Phantasien, 1] (Stuttgart: J. G. Cotta, 1906)

Ein Beitrag zur Ornamentik (Vienna: Universal Edition, rev. 1908)

Kontrapunkt: Cantus Firmus und Zweistimmiger Satz [Neue musikalische Theorien und Phantasien, 2/i] (Stuttgart and Berlin: J. G. Cotta, 1910)

'Die Urlinie (Eine Vorbemerkung)', *Der Tonwille*, 1 (1921), pp. 22–6

Kontrapunkt: Drei- und Mehrstimmiger Satz, Übergänge zum freien Satz [Neue musikalische Theorien und Phantasien, 2/ii] (Vienna: Universal Edition, 1922)

'Die Kunst der Improvisation', *Das Meisterwerk in der Musik*, 1 (1925), pp. 9–40

'Fortsetzung der Urlinie-Betrachtungen', *Das Meisterwerk in der Musik*, 2 (1926), pp. 9–42

'Rameau oder Beethoven? Erstarrung oder geistiges Leben in der Musik?', *Das Meisterwerk in der Musik*, 3 (1930), pp. 9–24

Bibliography

Der freie Satz [*Neue musikalische Theorien und Phantasien*, 3] (Vienna: Universal Edition, 1935)

Harmony, ed. O. Jonas, trans. E. M. Borgese (Chicago: University of Chicago Press, 1954)

Free Composition, trans. and ed. E. Oster (New York: Longman, 1979)

Counterpoint, trans. J. Rothgeb and J. Thym, ed. J. Rothgeb (New York: Schirmer, 1987) [1: *Cantus Firmus and Two-Voice Counterpoint*; 2: *Counterpoint in Three and More Voices, Bridges to Free Composition*]

'The Spirit of Musical Technique', trans. W. Pastille, *Theoria*, 3 (1988), pp. 86–104

Schoenberg, Arnold. 'The Relationship to the Text', in *Style and Idea: Selected Writings of Arnold Schoenberg*, ed. L. Stein, trans. L. Black (London: Faber, 1975), pp. 141–5

Theory of Harmony, trans. R. E. Carter (London: Faber, 1978)

Scruton, Roger. *Art and Imagination: A Study in the Philosophy of Mind* (London: Routledge and Kegan Paul, 1974)

The Aesthetic Understanding: Essays in the Philosophy of Art and Culture (London: Methuen, 1983)

'Analytical Philosophy and the Meaning of Music', *Journal of Aesthetics and Art Criticism*, 46 (1987), pp. 169–76

Sessions, Roger. 'Escape by Theory', *Modern Music*, 15/iii (1938), pp. 192–7; repr. in *Roger Sessions on Music: Collected Essays*, ed. Edward T. Cone (Princeton: Princeton University Press, 1979), pp. 256–62

Severini, Gino. 'The Plastic Analogies of Dynamism: Futurist Manifestos', repr. in Umbro Apollonio, *Futurist Manifestos* (London: Thames and Hudson, 1973), pp. 118–25

Shepard, Roger N. 'Structural Representations of Musical Pitch', in Diana Deutsch (ed.), *The Psychology of Music* (London: Academic Press, 1982), pp. 343–90

Smith, Charles J. 'The Functional Extravagance of Chromatic Chords', *Music Theory Spectrum*, 8 (1986), pp. 94–139

Smith, Richard. 'Foreground Rhythmic Structures: A Preliminary Study' (MMus dissertation, King's College, London, 1987)

Snarrenberg, Robert. 'The Play of *Différance*', *In Theory Only*, 10/iii (1987), pp. 1–25

Solie, Ruth A. 'The Living Work: Organicism and Musical Analysis', *Nineteenth-Century Music*, 4 (1980), pp. 147–56

Solomon, Larry. 'The List of Chords, Their Properties and Use in Analysis', *Interface*, 11/ii (1982), pp. 61–107

Street, Alan. 'Superior Myths, Dogmatic Allegories: The Resistance to Musical Unity', *Music Analysis*, 8 (1989), pp. 77–123

Stuckenschmidt, H. H. *Schoenberg: His Life, World and Work*, trans. H. Searle (London: Calder, 1977)

Thomson, William. 'A Functional Ambiguity in Musical Structure', *Music Perception*, 1 (1983), pp. 3–27

'The Harmonic Root: A Fragile Marriage of Concept and Percept', *Music Perception*, 10 (1993), pp. 385–415

Bibliography

Timms, Edward. 'The "Child-Woman": Kraus, Freud, Wittels, and Irma Karczewska', *Austrian Studies*, 1 (1990), pp. 87–107

Todorov, Tzvetan. *Genres in Discourse*, trans. C. Porter (Cambridge: Cambridge University Press, 1990)

Treitler, Leo. 'Mozart and the Idea of Absolute Music', in *Music and the Historical Imagination* (Cambridge, Mass.: Harvard University Press, 1989), pp. 176–214

Violi, Patrizia and Wendy Steiner. 'Ambiguity', in Thomas A. Sebeok (ed.), *Encyclopedic Dictionary of Semiotics* (Berlin: Mouton de Gruyter, 1986), vol. 1, pp. 23–6

Waldeck, Arthur and Nathan Broder. 'Musical Synthesis as Expounded by Heinrich Schenker', *Musical Mercury*, 11/iv (1935), pp. 56–64; repr. in *Theory and Practice*, 10/i–ii (1985), pp. 65–73

Walton, Kendall. *Mimesis as Make-Believe: On the Foundations of the Representational Arts* (Cambridge, Mass.: Harvard University Press, 1990)

Weisse, Hans. 'The Music Teacher's Dilemma', *Proceedings of the Music Teachers National Association* (1935), pp. 122–37; repr. in *Theory and Practice*, 10/i–ii (1985), pp. 29–48

Wellesz, Egon. *Arnold Schoenberg*, trans. W. H. Kerridge (London: Galliard, 1971)

Whittall, Arnold. 'Music Analysis as Human Science?', *Music Analysis*, 1 (1982), pp. 33–53

'Analysis as Performance', in *Atti del XIV Congresso della Società Internazionale di Musicologia* (1987), pp. 654–9

'Webern and Atonality: the Path from the Old Aesthetic', *Musical Times*, 124 (1983), pp. 733–7

Winder, R. 'For Literature, Read Real Life', *The Independent*, 30 March 1991, p. 25.

Winter, Robert. *Beethoven's Ninth Symphony* [multimedia reference work] (Los Angeles: Voyager, 1988) [CD-ROM publication MEC0138]

'The Bifocal Close and the Evolution of the Viennese Classical Style', *Journal of the American Musicological Society*, 42 (1989), pp. 275–337

Wittgenstein, Ludwig. *Philosophical Investigations*, trans. G. E. M. Anscombe (New York: Macmillan, 1953)

Wörner, Karl H. *Stockhausen: Life and Work* (Berkeley: University of California Press, 1973)

Index

223

Index

Index

226